AF324338

Quality higher education remains highly-prized in Asia and Sam Choon-Yin's book makes a compelling case for the role of private education in the development of a more qualified, future-ready workforce for Singapore and beyond. He emphasizes the importance of placing student's learning experiences at the heart of a private school's operations, and when managed correctly, private schools will find an optimal convergence in agendas between educational objectives and commercial goals. To that end, PSB Academy and our university partners have been striving to maintain excellent graduation outcomes among our students, while providing them ample avenues for co-creation and collaboration with the industry, to prepare them for the workplace.

Derrick Chang
Chief Executive Officer
PSB Academy, Singapore

I wish to congratulate Sam Choon-Yin of PSB Academy on the timely release of his book on private education landscape in Singapore. As a whole, the private education institutions provide an alternate pathway to local and international students and in particular, the in-employment adult learners. Sam who has taught and worked over a decade or more in private education is in a good position to provide a deeper understanding of the interplay between public and private education and the role of the Singapore Government. This book is certainly a useful starting point for those wishing to understand private education in Singapore and its transformation via a continuous quality management improvement path and the challenges ahead.

Dr. Steve Lai
Member, Academic Board
PSB Academy, Singapore

This book, 'Private Education in Singapore: Issues and Challenges', is a welcome addition to the literature on private education, which has been growing in importance in Singapore. In particular, it fills a lacuna in the literature by providing a scholarly perspective as well as a practitioner's insight as the author has worked with a private education institute for some time. It is also well-written and easy to read. I do highly recommend both researchers in this area and students in the field to read it.

Dr. Tham Siew Yean
Institute of Malaysian and International Studies (IKMAS)
Universiti Kebangsaan Malaysia, Malaysia

Sam Choon-Yin has written a stimulating book that should be of interest to anyone involved in private education. This book provides strategic insights into the issues and challenges that private education institutions are facing.

Professor Graham Kendall
Provost and CEO, University of Nottingham Malaysia Campus
Pro Vice Chancellor, University of Nottingham, United Kingdom

This is an excellent overview of the situation regarding private education in Singapore. It is an essential resource for all interested in the background to, and current state of, this segment of the education sector in the nation. I recommend it to all interested in education developments in Singapore, including historians, educationists and policy makers, along with the general reader.

Professor Tom O'Donoghue
Graduate School of Education
The University of Western Australia, Australia

Private University Education in South East Asia has the potential to offer students the best of 'both worlds'. Sam Choon-Yin offers a valuable insight into the issues, challenges and best practice for international providers in Singapore's unique higher education environment.

Professor Trevor A. Spedding
School of Management, Operations and Management
University of Wollongong, Australia

In this fascinating book, Sam Choon-Yin provides a wealth of interesting and valuable insights into the current state of the private education sector in Singapore. It should be read by anyone interested in private education, especially educators and students wishing to enter the Singaporean private education market.

Dr. Leong Horn Kee
Chairman, 3dsense Media School and
Austin International Management School, Singapore

Private Education in Singapore

Contemporary Issues and Challenges

Private Education in Singapore

Contemporary Issues and Challenges

Sam Choon-Yin

PSB Academy, Singapore

World Scientific

NEW JERSEY · LONDON · SINGAPORE · BEIJING · SHANGHAI · HONG KONG · TAIPEI · CHENNAI · TOKYO

Published by

WS Education, an imprint of
World Scientific Publishing Co. Pte. Ltd.
5 Toh Tuck Link, Singapore 596224
USA office: 27 Warren Street, Suite 401-402, Hackensack, NJ 07601
UK office: 57 Shelton Street, Covent Garden, London WC2H 9HE

National Library Board, Singapore Cataloguing-in-Publication Data
Name(s): Sam, Choon-Yin, 1974–
Title: Private education in Singapore: contemporary issues and challenges / Sam Choon-Yin.
Description: Singapore : World Scientific Publishing Co. Pte. Ltd., 2017. |
   Includes bibliographical references and index.
Identifier(s): OCN 980331149 | ISBN 978-981-32-2581-7 (hardcover) |
   ISBN 978-981-32-2582-4 (paperback)
Subject(s): LCSH: Private schools—Singapore. | Private universities and colleges—Singapore. |
   Education and state—Singapore.
Classification: DDC 371.02095957--dc23

British Library Cataloguing-in-Publication Data
A catalogue record for this book is available from the British Library.

Desk Editors: Suraj Kumar/Sandhya Venkatesh

Typeset by Stallion Press
Email: enquiries@stallionpress.com

Printed in Singapore by Mainland Press Pte Ltd.

To my wife See Shiau Hong

About the Author

Sam Choon-Yin is currently the Dean at PSB Academy. Concurrently, he serves as the Head, School of Business and Management at PSB Academy. Sam graduated from the National University of Singapore (NUS), University of Technology, Sydney (UTS) and University of South Australia (UNISA) where he obtained his PhD in International Business and Management. Sam's scholarly interests include political economy, underground economy, public governance and corporate governance. His articles have appeared in a wide range of journals, including Asian Studies Review, Asia Pacific Viewpoint, Journal of Asian and African Studies, Journal of the Asia Pacific Economy, New Zealand Journal of Asian Studies, Pacific-Asian Education and South East Asia Research.

Preface

Private education institutions (PEIs) in Singapore are non-government funded education providers that offer:

- education leading to the award of a diploma or degree, or full-time post-secondary education leading to the award of a certificate;
- full-time preparatory courses for entrance/placement tests for joining Ministry of Education (MOE) mainstream schools, or for external examinations.[1]

PEIs also include Foreign System Schools (FSS) offering full-time primary or secondary education wholly or substantially in accordance with a foreign or international curriculum, and privately-funded special education schools.

Improper practices affecting a number of the PEIs in the 1990s and 2000s had some adverse effects on the private education sector, raising concerns among students and parents about PEI courses and qualifications. Criticism were also directed at the system itself for failing to put in place adequate checks and balances on the industry. Businesses, lecturers, students, policy makers, and monitoring bodies were all to blame.

The government reacted by enacting the Private Education Act in 2009 which provided for the establishment of the Council for Private Education (CPE). The CPE tightened the entry requirements to the private education industry by requiring schools to fulfil a set of criteria, including corporate governance and information disclosure as stipulated in the Enhanced Registration Framework.

The changes were followed by the government's commitment to increase the number of places in publicly funded universities. The government set up the Singapore University of Technology & Design (SUTD) in 2010 and Singapore Institute of Technology (SIT) in 2012 as Singapore's fourth and fifth autonomous universities, respectively. In 2014, the Applied Study in Polytechnics and Institute for Technical Education Review (ASPIRE) report was released. It raised concerns that students who had invested time and money to obtain an undergraduate or post-graduate degree might not be able to land on jobs that commensurate with their newly acquired qualifications. The release of the report was soon followed with a series of initiatives by the government that could potentially lower the demand for PEI courses. With more universities being established in home countries, the number of international students enrolling into PEI courses could also shrink, exacerbated by tightening of immigration policies in Singapore and strengthening of the Singapore dollar.

Seven years following the setting up of the CPE, the negative connotation associated with private sector education remains. In September 2016, CPE released the results of the first employment survey of private school graduates. Among the 4,200 students who graduated with a degree from the PEIs in 2014, 58% of them managed to find a full-time job within 6 months of completing their degrees, which compared poorly to 83% of graduates from the National University of Singapore (NUS), Nanyang Technological University (NTU) and Singapore Management University (SMU) in the same period.[2]

This study represents an attempt to describe the key characteristics of the PEIs and detail the changes and developments in the private education sector in Singapore till December 2016. There have been numerous articles and books on the education sector and education system in Singapore but they focus almost exclusively an public education systems and institutions. Scholars have only captured a sliver of the private education sector in Singapore. In S. Gopinathan's recent book on Singapore's education, which serves to review the sector's ups and downs as Singapore celebrates its 50th year of independence, there was no mention of the private education sector at all (Gopinathan, 2015). This is a surprising omission in the education literature in Singapore. The private education sector represents a large segment of Singapore's higher education sector, housing about 300 PEIs and enrolling about 150,000 students both domestically and internationally. Thousands have signed up for PEI courses, paying a good sum of money to acquire and complete their studies at the certificate, diploma, undergraduate and/or postgraduate levels. The present book will, I hope, fill this gap in the literature.

In this book, I do not provide a detailed history of the private education sector, nor do I provide a detailed description of any of the PEIs. The purpose of the book is also not to predict the shape and nature of the private education sector in the years to come. My purpose is more modest. I want to sketch the structure of the sector, and the issues that are confronting the PEIs. The dominant attitude seems to regard the private education sector as low in quality and scandal-prone at least in the Singapore context. I want to write about the contemporary issues and challenges of the PEIs to help readers gain a better understanding of the private education sector.

I started to think about the contents for this book in mid-2014. Since then, there have been numerous changes, constantly shifting the direction that the sector may take. I decided to cease update of events that took place after December 2016. This marked the point at which the manuscript was updated in a substantive way.

The book contains 10 chapters. Chapter 1 gives an overview of Singapore's education sector, with particular reference to state presence, meritocratic principle and growth centricity. Subjecting the private education sector to regulatory regime and frameworks in Singapore is inevitable. What is important is the quality of governance to ensure that the academic standards are enhanced without affecting PEIs' sales and profitability. Meritocracy is widely regarded as the core principle of governance in Singapore and therefore deserves mention. The chapter concludes by highlighting the economy-first mentality that seems to prevail in many aspects of the Singapore economy, including education.

Chapter 2 introduces the private education sector, outlining the size of the industry and key features of the PEIs. The private education sector grew rapidly in the 1990s and 2000s. The market was highly competitive.

Some of the PEIs offered quality education. Others had resorted to making promises that they could not keep. The closure of some of the PEIs left students stranded without obtaining the qualifications and jeopardised the reputation of Singapore as an education hub. The regulatory agency, CPE, was established to regulate the sector.

Chapter 3 discusses the regulatory framework that the government has put in place since 2009 especially the key initiatives of the CPE. CPE has the authority over the registration and regulation of the PEIs, and the legal power to bring errant institutions to court. The statutory board oversees the Enhanced Registration Framework (ERF), which stipulates the mandatory requirements and legislation obligations for the PEIs. The chapter also discusses the EduTrust certification scheme, which is mandatory for PEIs if they intend to recruit international students and offer external degree programmes. Since its formation in 2009, the CPE has closed down institutions that have failed to comply with its minimum standards. The cases are highlighted in the chapter.

Chapter 4 opens up to the demand-side of the equation. Notably, strong aspirations of Singaporeans and other nationals to acquire a degree and the limited places at the public universities to accommodate local and international students' demands for post-secondary education have been the key reasons for the rapid growth in the private education sector. The chapter provides an account of the relationship between education attainment and success in life, and discusses the implications of the ASPIRE report published in August 2014 on private sector education providers.

PEI–University partnership is a common growth model of PEIs. This model is explored in Chapter 5. Education pathways are established for PEI students such that upon completion of the diploma programme awarded by the PEIs, students are able to use the diploma to gain admission to external degree programmes. Both parties are obligated to deliver an agreed service as stipulated in the contractual agreement. Securing such a pathway especially with well-regarded foreign universities offers the PEIs a selling point to attract students to enrol into their programmes. There are various challenges to sustaining effective partnerships. The chapter discusses a fictional partnership to document good practices and illustrate the benefits of particular approaches.

Chapter 6 focuses on the Business School. Despite the criticisms on business schools for ill preparing students to work in the real world, among other things, business programmes remain the most popular courses in the private education sector. The chapter highlights some of the key developments in the sector. Chapter 7 applies Michael Porter's Five Forces Model to assess the competitiveness of the private education sector. It is evident that PEIs are operating in a highly competitive environment. Several implications are drawn from the analysis for the PEIs to overcome the threats and remain competitive.

Chapter 8 raises concerns about the image of the PEIs and recognition of PEI academic qualifications, and suggests that much more needs to be done both at the sectoral and company level to gain greater acceptance and recognition of private education qualifications. Chapter 9 discusses what the private education sector as a whole can and should do to gain greater acceptance from students, parents, and employers. It considers the experience of vocational or technical education in Singapore. Vocational education was once seen as leading youths to nowhere but today, technical education in Singapore has become a means to an end for many students. How did the regulatory agencies manage to reverse the mindset of students and parents? Are there useful lessons for the private education sector to emulate? The chapter provides some answers to these questions. Chapter 10 highlights the key elements for consideration at the company level to sustain the education business in a competitive environment. The chapter reminds us of the nature of the PEI business — an education provider and a service organisation. The issue of balancing the economic and educational goals is an important one as discussed in this chapter, and the main responsibility of PEI leaders really is to avoid the awkward situation where commercial interest overrides everything else.

Acknowledgement

I have been involved in the private education sector for close to two decades. Throughout the years, I have met with and talked to numerous stakeholders in the private education sector — students, parents, employers, business associates, lecturers, administrators, programme consultants, government officials, foreign university partners' representatives, professors of education, and auditors from both local and international regulatory agencies. I have learned so much from them.

I have benefited from the discussions with key players in the industry. I offer profound appreciation to the many colleagues and friends who have helped me understand the private education sector in Singapore. To Derrick Chang, Susie Khoo, Evan Law, Steve Lai, Michael Cope, Tan Boon Leing, Vincent Chong and Dominic Lim, I am grateful to the informative conversations on the private education sector. The usual disclaimer applies. None of these people who have shared with me ideas and insights should be held responsible for anything contained in the book. I should add that the views expressed in this book are those of the author and should not be attributed to PSB Academy.

In writing this book, I have relied on official policy documents, speeches, webpages of the private education institution's (PEI's) in Singapore and data from research houses and various government agencies. There are statements in the book that are a matter of opinion and made with an occasion of privilege as a result of the author's direct involvement in the private education sector. Details about persons, events and others have as far as possible been dutifully checked. Should there be evidence of incorrect misrepresentation of opinions, facts and others, the author would be pleased to make the necessary arrangements at the first opportunity.

I hope that the book will offer some useful information and analysis about the private education sector in Singapore, and contribute to the development of theory and research hypothesis, which is currently lacking. Writing this book has been a truly wonderful experience, and it would not have been possible without the support from my wife, Shiau Hong. This book is dedicated to her.

Sam Choon-Yin
5 February 2017

Contents

List of Tables

Chapter 1

Governance, Meritocracy, and Growth Centricity

1.1 Introduction

Education is about liberating the mind and increasing the capacity of individuals to think critically, cooperate with and care for others, and distinguish right from wrong. Getting it right, education is an enabler of economic growth and sustainable development.

Confucianism, which has served as a moral compass to individuals and philosophical schools of thought for the society and the state in many countries, including Japan, South Korea, China and Singapore, has expounded on the importance of knowledge acquisition. *The Analects* of Confucius noted that: "Those who are born with the passion of knowledge are the highest class of men. Those who learn, and so, readily get possession of knowledge, are the next. Those who are dull and stupid, and yet compass the learning are another class next to these. As to those who are dull and stupid and yet do not learn — they are the lowest of the people".[1]

The importance attached to education is shared by others. In *Development as Freedom*, Nobel Laureate Amartya Sen argues that the provision of education, especially basic education, is an essential element to facilitate economic participation. Too much poverty at the bottom of the pyramid is due to the failure to provide adequate education to children who are growing up poor. Sen reminded us that "Japan had a higher rate of literacy than Europe had even at the time of the Meiji restoration in the mid-19th century …. Japan's economic development was clearly much helped by the human resource development related to the social opportunities that were generated. The so-called East Asian miracle involving other countries in East Asia (such as South Korea, Taiwan, Hong Kong and Singapore) was to a great extent based on similar causal connections" (Sen, 1999: 41). Indeed, "the best way for a nation to survive", writes Kishore Mahbubani in *Can Singapore Survive*, "is to have a well-educated and well-informed citizenry" (Mahbubani, 2015: 12).

This is a book on private education. Worldwide, private education institutions (PEIs) enrolled about a third of the total student enrolment, and accounted for a greater percentage of total higher education institutions.[2] Citing data from Parthenon-EY, *The Economist* reported that the number of students enrolled in private higher education has grown at a faster rate than those in the public sector in Turkey, France, Germany, and Spain (*The Economist*, 2016). Fiscal constraints have imposed a challenge to the government to finance increasing number of students in their pursuit for higher education, permitting the surge of the private education providers to fill the gap and absorb the demand for higher education (Longden and Belanger, 2013; Enders, De Boer, and Weyer, 2013).

However, the profit motive of the education providers has been associated with issues of low quality academic standards (Harman, 2003; Marks, 2007; Ward, 2007). PEIs have been accused of allowing students to ignore strict academic standards in terms of assessment and attendance (Bryman, 2007; Lechuga, 2008). Private education providers have also been accused of recruiting academic staff with marginal qualifications as a means to save costs and of pegging the curricula to the minimal standards (Bernasconi, 2013). Opponents to private school education have pointed to the lack of academic integrity, for example, by maximising class size, thereby creating a non-conducive environment for learning (see Bernasconi, 2013; Kinser, 2013). This concern has been exacerbated by the lack of transparency in both academic and non-academic aspects (Pitcher, 2013; Thian, Alam and Idris, 2016). Others, like De Boer and Goedegebuure (2009) and Montez, Wolverton, and Gmelch (2002), have raised concerns about the role of Academic Deans of for-profit education providers. They are selected by the top management with the approval of the business owners, and they are often held responsible for meeting the financial targets of the education institutions. Lechuga (2008: 304) has warned:

> "Generating profit through education may seem like a novel concept to many in academe, but one cannot deny that revenue generation is of increasing import [sic] to private nonprofit and public colleges and universities. Traditional institutions, however, structure revenue generation activities in a way that maintains faculty autonomy. For-profit colleges and universities function differently. In essence, they have created an education paradigm that readily views revenue generation as the main objective of the institution and have intentionally structured faculty work to meet this objective".

There have been reported cases of improper practices among the PEIs in Singapore. I will discuss the cases in a later part of the book. This chapter looks at a broader picture, and sets the stage for discussion about the private education sector and PEIs in Singapore. It is well known that education and training have contributed significantly to Singapore's socio-economic performance, a country with no natural resources except its people. High standard of education is not a given. It requires hard work and strong commitment from the state and adherence to the principle of meritocracy. This chapter discusses several features of the Singapore economy with particular reference to issues on governance, national identity and economic growth. These are highlighted because of their association with demand for and supply of education in Singapore and the way the education is perceived and conceived in the early days of development.

1.2 Socio-Economic Development in Singapore

Singapore is a city–state of over 5 million people. It does not have any national resources except its people. Singapore has been labelled as a quintessential development state where the state's legitimacy is derived from its ability to develop the country economically.[3] When the People's Action Party (PAP) took over the governance of Singapore in

1959, the economy experienced high unemployment rate, rampant corruption, a high crime rate, a large budget deficit (of US$4.7 million), rapid population growth and public housing problem (50% of the population were living in squatters).[4] Faced with the prospect of infiltration and subversion of communist ideology in the early years, modern social policies and rapid economic development were perceived as the main ingredients to banish the danger of communism. Coupled with a shrunken market following Singapore's separation from the Federation of Malaysia in August 1965, the Singapore government led by PAP switched from the import substitution strategy to export orientation.

Multinational corporations (MNCs), particularly in the manufacturing sector, were attracted to operate in Singapore, a task effectively undertaken by the Economic Development Board (EDB). Electronic giants such as Hewlett-Packard, General Electric, Texas Instrument and National Semiconductor invested in Singapore, creating full employment for Singapore by the early 1970s. Hoon Hian Teck, an economist at the Singapore Management University, attributed Singapore's success to its openness to MNCs. "It was our MNC policy that opened the door to standard off-the-shelf technology that raised our standards of living, created jobs, and caused wages to go up".[5] Industralisation in Singapore began to take shape thanks to the EDB's effort to bring investors into Jurong. The Technical Education Department (TED) and later the Industrial Training Board (ITB) ramped up skills development effort to provide the necessary skilled manpower to support the industralisation strategy. The government supported research and development activities and recruited foreign talents in new growth areas such as biotechnology, life sciences and wireless technology to take Singapore to a higher level of manufacturing-related technological sophistication. Gross domestic product (GDP) per capita of Singapore was 30% of the United States GDP per capita in the 1960s. By the 2000s, Singapore's GDP per capita surpassed that of the United States.

Singapore is a multiracial society with its resident population of about 3.7 million, comprising the Chinese (about 74%), Malays (13%), Indians (9%) and other groups such as Eurasians and Jews (collectively 4%). The government's priority is to maintain social cohesiveness and establish a secular multicultural Singapore. Education is regarded as a crucial element to promote and maintain social harmony by inculcating students with values like filial piety, concern for neighbours, family and nation in the early years through courses such as "Education for Living," "Good Citizen," and "Being and Becoming" at the primary and secondary levels (Gopinathan, 1997). The Singapore pledge as drafted by then Minister for Foreign Affairs S. Rajaratnam in February 1966, and recited by students in all government schools during the assemblies and at National Day ceremonies reminds Singaporeans to be united as one people, *'regardless of race, language or religion, to build a democratic society, based on justice and equality, so as to achieve happiness, prosperity and progress for our nation.'*

Binding the various ethnic groups was constructed through the use of the English language as the main medium of instruction in public institutions and working language for the country. As former Prime Minister Lee Kuan Yew noted, a child learns English and the mother tongue in publicly funded schools to "strengthen his identity and helps him feel connected to his heritage" (Lee, 2012: 172). The decision to use English as the main medium of instruction offers Singaporeans a competitive edge, ensuring 'neutrality' in the sense that the language does not belong to any of the major ethnic groups in Singapore. Lee wrote in his memoir, "We realized English had to be the language of the workplace and the common language. As an international trading community, we would not make a living if we used Malay, Chinese or Tamil. With English, no race would have an advantage" (Lee, 2000: 170).

1.3 Identity and Education

In *Nations and Nationalism*, Ernest Gellner (1983) wrote about the role of mass education in creating a cohesive and nationalistic community. To Gellner, a passport or an identity card merely assigns citizenship of a person from a technical or legal perspective but it does not make the person more or less loyal to the country. The driving principle of nationalism is one state, one culture, through active promotion of education and national language.

In the case of Singapore, social cohesion and development of the national identity through education and language have been the main priority of the government.[6] As Gopinathan (2015: 99–100) points out:

> "… the twin tasks facing education in independent Singapore in 1965 were building social cohesion to ensure order and stability, and knowledge and skill building to ensure economic growth. … Central to these initiatives was a preoccupation with preserving ethnic values and traditions while promoting Western-style modernity. Though a bilingual population has emerged, the dominance of English has in turn made Singapore the most Western, cosmopolitan city in East Asia. Given the PAP's ideological orientation, the focus on values and citizenship education has been on communitarianism rather than individualism, on responsibilities rather than rights".

The role of education in asserting a new nation has not always been smooth sailing. The government's interference in the affairs of the university, for example, has been perceived as an attempt by the government to undermine academic freedom.

Historically, when the University of Malaya was established in Singapore in 1949 with the merger of King Edward VII College of Medicine and Raffles College, the activities of the academics and the university were largely immune from the interference by the government. Maurice Baker noted in his memoir that "the authorities at the University believed in academic freedom as practiced in the United Kingdom and enshrined in the Robbins Report commissioned by the British government and published in 1963," (Baker, 2014: 83). Local academics who succeeded the British professors carried on the tradition, and defended their right to make their own policies.[7]

After gaining self-governance status in 1959, the elected government of Singapore was, as Edwin Lee and Tan Tai Yong put it, dynamic and pro-active, reaching out into every area and "would soon make its impact felt on the University," (Lee and Tan, 1996: 130). In 1960, the government and the university clashed in their viewpoints on the level of academic freedom following a lecture delivered by Professor D.J. Enright.[8] On 17 November 1960, Professor D.J. Enright, an eminent poet and critic and a newly appointed professor, gave a lecture on 'Robert Graves and the Doctrine of Modernism' where a part of it criticised the government for creating a Malayan culture, "a sarong culture," that culminated into the banning of jukeboxes and pornography in print and film. Enright's proposition to leave the people free to make their own choices was seen as an attack on the government's top-down approach. The talk, which was reported in *The Straits Times*, led to two cabinet ministers lambasting Enright verbally and in writing, sending out the message to university lecturers to "keep within the bounds of their work, and not wander into an area which belonged to the politicians" (Lee, 2008: 372). Enright was referred to as a "mendicant and beatnik" professor.[9]

The university's Students' Union criticised the government for trying to strangle free discussion in the university. The government responded by warning committee members of the various university councils, including S. Jayakumar (who later became a Senior Minister and Deputy Prime Minister of Singapore) and Tommy Koh (current Singapore's Ambassador at-large, and former Ambassador to the United Nations), not to enter into the realm of politics. As S. Jayakumar recalled, "the government's Political Secretary Sidney Woodhull wanted a meeting with Student's Union president Ernest Devadason, Tommy Koh (as then president of the Socialist Club) and me (as then Chairman of the Students Council). … From his comments, it was clear that the purpose … was for him to warn us not to step in the realm of politics. He did so in a gentle, non-threatening way, but the message was loud and clear" (Jayakumar, 2015: 34).

The outcome of the Enright's affair, wrote Maurice Baker, was that "the prime minister set the boundaries of academic freedom," and expatriates were expected to "steer clear of local politics and confine themselves to their specialties" (Baker, 2014: 86). Baker defended the government's actions by reminding his readers that the PAP government were then newly elected into power, managing a fragile country and an uncertain relationship with the Communists, and therefore was in "no mood to put up with an English professor, no matter how well meaning, criticising a national cultural policy" (*Ibid*: 86).[10] Koh Tai Ann (1990: 22) argued that the PAP government had to react harshly "to the white man's criticism of an Asian or Malay culture if it was to retain its credibility within the PAP," particularly on matters relating to culture and language.[11]

Several years later, in 1968, Lee Kuan Yew appointed a senior cabinet minister, Dr. Toh Chin Chye as Vice-Chancellor of the University of Singapore to give the university a "national direction" (Lee, 2008: 368). Historian Edwin Lee (2008) devoted a chapter in his book "Singapore: The Unexpected Nation" to Toh's "nation-building thrust" during Toh's eight years (1968–1975) as the University's Vice-Chancellor. Edwin Lee portrayed Toh as one who was concerned about the university's Euro-centric attitudes, and considered "academic decolonization" as "a pre-requisite" for the university to "contribute meaningfully and purposefully to the Singapore nation" (*Ibid*: 389).

Toh recruited more Asian academics as opposed to Caucasian expatri-ates especially in the Arts and Social Sciences, believing that the former would be in the better position to teach Singaporeans because of their familiarity with the Asian social norms, customs and languages. To Lee, Toh had slipped into a "binary mode of reasoning," seeing some subjects such as engineering as value free and the arts and social sciences as not value free so as to justify "his pro-Asian as opposed to Caucasian recruit-ment policy in the Arts and Social Sciences" (*Ibid*: 411).

Interestingly, Edwin Lee concluded the chapter by comparing Toh with Mahathir Mohamad, the former Prime Minister of Malaysia who has famously said that "when the minds are colonised, physical coloni-zation is not necessary" (Mahathir, 2006: 66). To Lee, it seems like Toh has not been consistent in his views about the West. As Lee (2008: 410) noted:

> "Dr Toh lambasted the machinations of expatriate professors, but was silent on the machinations of multinational enterprises. He was on his guard against Eurocentric values in higher education, but did not display the same vigilance towards the American and Eurocentric vision of the World Bank and the International Monetary Fund, as Dr Mahathir had done, so openly and eloquently".

Edwin Lee added: "Though Dr Toh went on about 'intellectual decolonization'; he was concerned, nevertheless, to gear the university to work in tandem with the multinationals, by producing the requisite manpower. He could do this with total confidence, unconscious of irony or discrepancy, because he delinked subjects like engineering, architecture, business, administration, medicine, and science from his polemics about 'intellectual decolonization'" (*Ibid*: 410–411).

The issue of academic freedom and university authority has never really gone away whether the subject contents were written in one's capacity as an academic (like Christopher Lingle[12]) or an intellectual (like Catherine Lim).[13] Chan Heng Chee (2000: 126) noted that such a state was grounded on the belief that "the right of criticism is an alien tradition borne of Western liberal thought; that new states need more power not less, more stability not instability". John Clammer (2001) was especially critical of the community of intellectuals and the universities in Singapore — the latter was labelled as "agents of nationalism," "servants of the national elite" (*Ibid*: 212) and "partners in nation building and state consolidation" to "align themselves with the government's political agenda and to ensure that, to a great extent, the staff do likewise" (*Ibid*: 205).[14]

The delay in the partnership between Yale University and the National University Singapore (NUS) in establishing a liberal arts programme in Singapore, and Warwick University's decision against establishing a local campus in October 2005, both citing the fear of lack of academic freedom as the major concern, suggests that certain factions of the academic committee remain unconvinced that open inquiry and criticism with good intention are permissible in the city–state.

1.4 Governance and Meritocracy

The education sector is vulnerable to improper practices because of the huge amount of resources disbursed through complex administrative procedures that might not have received adequate monitoring from the government.[15] It can be argued that unethical decisions are especially prevalent in the private education sector in the absence of any effective regulatory checks. Families are easy target for manipulation. In this regard, good governance matters.

What is good governance? Former Prime Minister of Singapore Lee Kuan Yew defined good governance as one that is "honest, effective and efficient in producing its people, and allowing opportunities for all to advance themselves in a stable and orderly society, where they can live a good life and raise their children to do better than themselves" (Han, Fernandez, and Tan, 1998: 380). Lee has often credited good governance to Singapore's ability to overcome many challenges after gaining self-governance status from the British in 1959.

The World Bank's *Governance Matters* report has considered various indicators such as the effectiveness of the government, rule of law and political stability in measuring the degree of good governance of a particular country, and it has rated Singapore strongly, putting it among the best governed countries in the world. Covering more than 200 countries, Singapore has obtained a score of close to 100 for five of the six categories of the quality of governance (Table 1.1). An exception was the category measuring political, civil and human rights, which has been on a declining trend.[16] "The tremendous social progress and economic success of Singapore over its four decades since independence," writes N.C. Saxena (2011: 2), "has been strongly driven by a government which was heavily involved in every area of national development, operating through effective and highly competent public institutions which are deemed to be among the least corrupt in the world". And this is what Jonathan Tepperman (2016: 106) has to say about Singapore's ability to curb corruption:

> "Singapore has come close to eradicating corruption altogether than just about any other country. … What makes Singapore's record especially striking is that it didn't start out as a paragon of clean government — anything but. And that makes it a particularly good model for other places trying to clean up their acts (unlike, say, virtuous Sweden, which beats Singapore on Transparency's league tables but which has been a constitutional democracy for more than two hundred years)".

One of the key lessons to be learned from Singapore is that it takes responsible leaders to build and sustain political legitimacy. Getting good people to serve in the public service involves casting the nets wide to identify capable persons from the private sector. Former Minister for Finance Richard Hsu was formally an executive at Shell in the early

Table 1.1:   Governance matters (Singapore).

Year/Indicators	Government effectiveness	Regulatory quality	Control of corruption	Rule of law	Political stability	Voice and accountability
2008	100.0	93.2	98.1	92.3	96.2	37.0
2009	100.0	97.6	98.1	91.9	89.6	40.8
2010	100.0	98.1	98.6	92.9	89.6	40.8
2011	99.5	96.2	96.7	93.4	91.0	47.0
2012	99.5	100.0	97.1	95.7	96.7	53.1
2013	99.5	100.0	96.7	95.3	96.7	52.1
2014	100.0	100.0	97.1	95.2	92.2	45.3

Source: Governance matters, The World Bank, http://info.worldbank.org/governance/wgi/index.asp (Accessed on 28 March 2016).

1960s before he was recruited by the Monetary Authority of Singapore. Former Prime Minister Goh Chok Tong was with Neptune Orient before taking up positions in various ministries. Tony Tan Keng Yam, President of Singapore, who headed the Ministry of Education in 1980–1981 and again in 1985–1991, was the General Manager of OCBC before being approached by Hon Sui Sen to join politics in the late 1970s. Hamilton-Hart (2000) has argued that the clean and efficient Singaporean government was attributed to the "mixed public-private sphere than makes up the governing elite," referring to elite private sector individuals such as S. Dhanabalan, Chandra Das, Ho Kwon Ping, Joseph Pillay and Michael Fam Yue Onn who had close association and a good understanding with the way the public sector works. These individuals moved back and forth between the public and private sectors, and were often found on the boards of the private and privatised state-owned enterprises.

Similarly, the Ministry of Education has been helmed by the who's who in Singapore. They included the first two Ministers for Education, Yong Nyuk Lin from 1959 to 1963 and Ong Pang Boon from 1963 to 1970 whose leadership was characterised as "energetic policy-making with a strong commitment to implementation" (Gopinathan, 2015: 27) — pertinent traits to have during the turbulent years of the 1950s and 1960s; Goh Keng Swee (who was Minister for Education in 1979–1980 and 1981–1984)[17]; Teo Chee Hean (current Deputy Prime Minister, Minister of Home Affairs, and Coordinating Minister for National Security); Tharman Shanmugaratnam (current Deputy Prime Minister, Minister for Finance and Minister for Manpower) and Ng Eng Hen (who has been the Minister for Defence from 2011 till present). Minister for Education, Heng Swee Keat (2011–2015) was formerly Managing Director of the Monetary Authority of Singapore. Heng was the Permanent Secretary of the Ministry of Trade and Industry, Chief Executive Officer of the Trade and Development Board, and the Principal Private Secretary to the late Lee Kuan Yew from 1997 to 2000. To Lee, Heng was "the best Principal Private Secretary I ever had." "He (Heng) has one of the finest minds among the civil servants I have worked with" (Lee, 2013: 209). Since October 2015, the Ministry of Education has been helmed by two individuals. Ng Chee Meng serves as Acting Minister for Education for Schools. He was previously the Chief of Singapore's Defence Force. The Higher Education and Skills portfolio is overseen by Ong Ye Kung who was previously Director at Keppel Corporation, Deputy Secretary of the National Trades Union Congress and Chief Executive Officer at Singapore Workforce Development Agency. Handpicking personalities based on their capabilities to lead ministries, statutory boards and public sector corporations is Singapore's version of *meritocracy*. It does not seem to pose the usual problems of government owned enterprises, but in fact may have contributed to Singapore's success in general and the public sector in particular.

Meritocracy has served as a principle of good governance in Singapore through a highly competitive education system, and system in awarding government scholarships, and appointing persons to top positions in the civil service (Mauzy and Milne, 2002). Meritocracy may be understood broadly as a merit-based system where social position, recognition, career and rewards are associated with the individual merit and differences in gender, age or class differences do not matter. Kishore Mahbubani and Ezra Vogel have credited the meritocracy system in education and recruitment in public service as a key pillar in explaining Singapore's exceptional success in its first 50 years as a nation. Kishore Mahbubani has said that, "The ruthless process of meritocratic selection has meant that Singapore's key institutions, like the civil service and judiciary, are staffed with truly talented individuals. Since independence in 1965, the government has wisely encouraged bright young Singaporeans to join very selective scholarship schemes like the President's and SAF scholarship schemes and other merit-based scholarships. Hence, the cadre of talented Singaporeans who fill key positions in various institutions is among the best in the world" (Mahbubani, 2015: 13). Ezra Vogel makes it clear that the practice of meritocracy is not confined to Singapore. The practice has been adopted in East Asian countries like Japan, Taiwan and Hong Kong. However, a distinguishing feature of Singapore is that the "meritocracy extends upward to include virtually all political leaders," citing Lee Kuan Yew, Goh Keng Swee and Toh Chin Chye who had "distinguished themselves in schools in Singapore or the Peninsular and won competitive scholarships to study in England," and the domination of the PAP Central Executive Committee from the 1970s onward by persons who had "distinguished themselves by meritocratic standards" (Vogel, 1989: 1052–1053).[18]

That said, meritocracy has the effect of creating social classes among people. Meritocracy puts one at the lower spectrum of the economic hierarchy if he or she lacks academic merit. Former Minister Raymond Lim has warned that, "Meritocracy is an eminent fait system to decide who the successful should be, but when taken to its extreme it does mean that those who do not make it get left behind. This is so because meritocracy emphasises the individual "I" rather than the collective "We" … we need to balance our commitment to meritocracy with as great a commitment to community" (Lim, 2014: 49). Indeed, *independent schools* where high-performing students are recruited to "foster creativity and innovation in the citizenry," (Tan, 2008: 21) have been criticised for placing certain students — selected meritocratically — on a track groomed for a life better than many others.[19] Uneven playing field has emerged as some have argued because independent schools have more resources to allocate, greater autonomy to determine how the resources are to be allocated, and the ability to attract high academic achievers.[20]

Moreover, the limited number of places in education institutions of higher standing would create a zero-sum game in a society that values meritocracy, diverting resources and time from non-positional goods like leisure and family time to positional goods, which is wasteful and sub-optimal for the society. As Donald Low has succinctly pointed out, meritocracy "ails out education system where students are graded on a curve, and it explains why parents probably spend much more on private tuition than what is collectively optimal … and those further down the performance curve might feel so discouraged and demoralized that they ultimately opt out of a system in which they feel they will never have a reasonable chance of success" (Low and Vadaketh, 2014: 50–51). The inflow of international students exacerbates the shortage problem in public universities.[21] PEIs have sought to capitalise on the capacity problem by admitting more domestic and international students and developing partnerships with foreign universities. Students set on the path to gain admission to PEI for diploma and degree courses.

1.5 Growth Centricity

While education matters, the thing that matters most is employment. The critical task for the government of the day is to grow the economy and generate good jobs for the people.[22] The PAP government knows this very well. Lee Hsien Loong, as the then Deputy Prime Minister of Singapore, once asserted: "If we ask the people to choose between more freedom, democracy and more economic growth, we have no doubt that they would choose economic growth. But we will never ask them anyway".[23] The remark illustrates that Singapore, at the national level, is preoccupied with economic development, making everything subservient to economic prosperity. The key investment arms of the Singaporean government (Temasek Holdings and Government of Singapore Investment Corporation, GIC) have been conceptualised as strategic institutions to safeguard Singapore's assets, which effectively legitimises economic wealth generation as the primary goal of the institutions.[24] That Singapore is driven by material interests is commonly perceived by Singapore's neighbouring countries. The former Indonesian Ambassador to Singapore alleged that "Singapore tends to be self-centred, lacks empathy and is highly materialistic, is not a warm hearted personality and therefore views Indonesia only in terms of 'profit or no profit'" (Abin, 1991: 99). In the case of private education, growth centricity has culminated into the paradox with regard to whether there should be stricter scrutiny of academic courses in which case PEIs may find the standards too difficult and overwhelming to fulfil and decide to shut down.

The journey toward growth centricity has involved positioning education as a revenue generating sector, to tap on a growing global education market. This is evident in the recommendations from the Committee on Singapore's Competitiveness (CSC), which was set up by the government in May 1997 to "assess Singapore's economic competitiveness over the next decade and propose strategies to strengthen Singapore's competitive position" (Ministry of Trade and Industry, 1998: 1). The committee's view was that Singapore should position herself as the "Boston of the East," offering incentives such as Pioneer Status, Institute of Public Character, and Charitable Status as a means to attract "world-class teaching institutions and private companies committed to offering educational courses to operate in Singapore" (Ministry of Trade and Industry, 1998: 154). The recommendations culminated to the launch of the "Global Schoolhouse" initiative in August 2003.[25] The initiative has three components; to attract good foreign institutions into Singapore, to develop local enterprises and teaching institutions, and to attract international students into Singapore.

The Global Schoolhouse initiative has achieved some successes. The goal set out was to attract 10 top foreign institutions within 10 years. By 2007, the goal was met — there were 15 world-class foreign higher education institutions in Singapore, from China, France, Germany, India, the Netherlands and the United States — offering niche programmes to Singaporeans and foreign students. Well-known colleges/universities, Wharton School of the University of Pennsylvania and Massachusetts Institute of Technology (MIT), established partnerships with SMU and NUS, respectively, to integrate an international dimension into the teaching and research functions of the higher education institutions. Other notable initiatives include the new medical school in NUS Singapore in 2007, a collaborative effort between NUS and Duke University of the United States, the offering of a double master's degree with the partners of NUS' Lee Kuan Yew School of Public Policy, which includes Columbia University's School of International and Public Affairs, the London School of Economics and Political Science, and the Institut d'Etudes Politiques de Paris. The partnerships aim to draw upon the strengths of both institutions rather than duplicate the academic programmes from the source university to the host country. In this regard, they differ quite significantly from the transnational marriage between the PEI and a foreign university partner in the sense that the latter is not based on equal footing in terms of academic orientation and reputation. The lack of academic status of the PEI means that it is in the best interest of both parties to transplant the academic programme of the source university to the private education sector in Singapore.

That said, Singapore faces numerous challenges in its attempt to build an education hub as the following cases show.[26]

* In 2006, United Kingdom's Warwick University turned down the offer to open a campus in Singapore, citing concerns about the level of academic freedom in tightly regulated Singapore.

- Australia's University of New South Wales decided to close its Singapore campus two months after commencement of its first intake of students in 2007 due to low projected student enrolment. The University had a first intake of 148 students, half of its projected target.
- In 2012, New York University decided to close the Tisch School of the Arts Asia in Singapore, citing financial non-sustainability as the key concern. The School, which had received loans and grants from the Singapore government, was established in 2007, offering programs in film, animation, producing, and dramatic writing.
- In January 2013, the University of Nevada and Singapore Institute of Technology (SIT) announced the ending of partnership, following a disagreement on tuition fees increase.
- The closure of the NYU@NUS dual law degree program was announced in May 2013. The program started in 2007 with an initial intake of 39 students but had failed to attract enough students to become self-financing.

The Yale-NUS partnership to establish the Yale-NUS College was mired with issues and challenges before the college admitted its first batch of students in August 2013. The Memorandum of Understanding to establish the liberal arts programme was signed in August 2010. In a series of town meetings that gathered wide interest from Yale College faculty members prior to the finalisation of the programme, faculty members expressed their concerns, including whether Singapore would impose limitations on academic freedom and open inquiry. On 5 April 2012, Yale faculty passed a resolution to urge the Yale-NUS college to "uphold civil liberty and political freedom on campus and in the broader society," and "respect, protect and further principles of non-discrimination for all". About 200 Yale faculty members debated for 90 minutes on the wording of the three-paragraph resolution. In December 2012, the American Association of University Professors issued an open letter to the Yale Community, expressing concern about Yale's collaboration with the "Singapore government". "We are concerned about the implications of the undertaking for academic freedom and the maintenance of educational standards at Yale and elsewhere," the letter noted.[27] Reflecting on the episode, Ng (2013: 286–287) cautioned that there would be "inherent complexities of bringing together two very different cultures into scholarly pursuits … with differing interpretations of the concepts of "liberal education," "democracy" and "freedom". This is a complex issue the new institute (Yale-NUS College) must grapple with, especially in the liberal arts programme".

Growth in the private education sector coincided with the government's plan to position Singapore as a Global Schoolhouse. The number of PEIs in Singapore grew rapidly from 150 schools in 1987 to 305 in 1997 and 1,200 by 2007. The number of full-time international students enrolled in the programmes grew from 9,000 in 1997 to 37,000 in 2007. In his speech delivered at the Global Schoolhouse Conference on 16 August 2003, George Yeo has expressed hope that the private education sector would play a role in raising the contribution of the education sector to GDP from 3.6% to 5%.[28] The growth was also supported by increased international student mobility. Mary Kritz (2016: 345) reported the rise in international student mobility from half a million international students in 1975 to 3.5 million in 2009 with Asian students studying abroad accounting for the largest increase (by 32% between 2003 and 2008 as compared to 2% and 17% in Europe and US/Canada, respectively). Student outflows tend to positively correlate with limited tertiary capacity in the home country and GDP per capita. In 2008, there were 120,000 students enrolled in the PEIs in Singapore of which 45,000 of them were international students.

Because Singapore promotes the meritocratic principle, everyone has an almost equal chance to succeed provided that he or she works hard. Inevitably, the environment raises the demand for education as many regard education qualification as the passport for success and for greater opportunities in the future. Domestic and international students have come to realise that they need to be educated to succeed in Singapore. This does not confine to mere ability to read, write and perform simple calculations, which are important skills to have. They need to be equipped with skills to present ideas clearly and briefly in writing and in person, and strong knowledge and skills relevant to a discipline, whether it is Education, Law, Finance, Engineering or Marketing. The rapidity of change means that teachers, lawyers, finance managers, engineers, and marketers have to refresh their knowledge on a more frequent basis. With infinite knowledge, it has become important (but not necessarily sufficient) for anyone who cares to earn a good salary, improve his/her standards of living and remain employed to obtain relevant education qualifications and refresh their knowledge thereafter. The concern arises when the PEIs make decisions that benefit only themselves and not the interest of those they supposedly serve, thereby requiring some sort of checks and balances to be put in place by the government. How a strong government affects the development and growth tangent of the education sector is a matter of context. In the case of the private education sector, as the following chapters shall illustrate, corporate scandals affecting some of the PEIs have resulted in the imposition of stricter procedures and regulations to protect students interest against deceptive and coercive conduct of the PEIs.

Chapter 2

Private Education Sector in Singapore

2.1 Introduction

It is well known that the Singapore workforce suffered from lower education in the early years of independence. A committee formed in 1976 to review Singapore's technical education noted that only 16% of secondary school leavers furthered their studies at post-secondary education institutions, including the polytechnics. The drop-out rate at Primary 6 was at 40% (Varaprasad, 2016: 30–31).

The well-known Goh Keng Swee report on education published in 1979 found that 65% of the Primary 1 cohort did not manage to obtain at least three 'O' level subjects in secondary school education, and only 19% of primary school cohorts passed both English and the mother tongue language at 'O' level (Goh *et al.*, 1979). In 1980, as Varaprasad (2016: 124) reported, 70% of the working adults had at most primary level education qualification whereas 17% of the professional and technical workers had primary or no qualifications.

There was therefore a large pool of people who have missed out the opportunity to acquire higher education qualification early in their life. Their aspiration to obtain a higher education qualification contributed to the growth in the private education sector in the early 1990s. There was also a large demand for degree courses from polytechnic and Institute for

Technical Education (ITE) graduates, which took in about 45% and 25% of the post-secondary school cohorts, respectively. In the 2000s, growth in the private education sector coincided with the Singapore government initiative to position Singapore as a Global Schoolhouse. This followed the recommendation from the Education Workgroup of the Economic Review Committee. A specific recommendation that was targeted at the subsector of the education industry was to develop private commercial and speciality schools.

As the Education Workgroup of the Economic Review Committee commented: "Singapore has strong publicly funded institutions and an emerging pool of private sector providers. Helping private providers to grow, facilitating partnerships between institutions and attracting new players into the market would create a Global Schoolhouse" (Ministry of Trade and Industry, 2002b). The proposed strategy was "to build a nexus of 40 high-quality schools, each enrolling at least 1,000 international students, so that the schools are of a substantial size and have the experience, credibility and strength to compete overseas" (*Ibid*).

The report by the Education Workgroup identified the lack of a centralised agency along the likes of the British Council, US Education Information Centre and IDP Education Australia to promote Singapore as a learning destination. The committee recommended the setting up of a central agency to spearhead efforts to promote Singapore, leveraging on Singapore's strength such as strong academic reputation, safety, progressive East-meets-West society and the use of English as the language of instruction to attract full fee paying international students.

Accordingly, International Enterprise (IE) Singapore was tasked to attract and encourage international students to come to Singapore to study. It worked closely with the private education institutions (PEIs), with representatives following IE Singapore on its trade missions, to market Singapore as a safe and secure place and develop the education business. Together, they attracted students to study with private education providers in Singapore as well as in higher education institutions such as the National University of Singapore (NUS) and foreign institutions like French business school INSEAD and the University of Chicago Graduate School of Business.

Today, as the local universities move up in international rankings, they attract higher quality of students from around the world. It remains a privilege for Singaporeans to secure a place to study a course of their choice at the local public universities. Looking upon a degree as the ticket to a better future, some of the students have chosen to study overseas but a significant larger number of students decided to take the alternative option of obtaining a foreign university degree through one of the local PEIs. The possibility of completing a degree programme faster — 12 to 18 months for a commerce degree in the PEIs as compared to 36–48 months for a similar degree in one of the local universities — is a pull factor. In 2013, it was reported that 36% of Singapore residents who pursued tertiary studies obtained their degrees through the PEIs, up from 26% in 2008.[1]

2.2 Characteristics of the Private Education Institutions

Who are the private education providers? The regulatory agency, the Council for Private Education (CPE), has classified the private education entities into commercial PEIs, which offer post-secondary certificates, diploma and degree programmes, vocational PEIs that offer courses in specialised/niche areas such as Beauty and Spa, Culinary and Hospitality, Nursing, Healthcare and Social Sciences, Electronics and Mechanics, Art and Design and Performance Arts, preparatory PEIs that prepare students for professional qualifications, particular accountancy, as well as primary and secondary level examinations (e.g. general certificate of education (GCE) 'O' and 'A' levels), and foreign System Schools which offer primary and secondary education that is in accordance with international curricula, primarily to children of expatriates residing in Singapore.[2] When the CPE came into effect, more than 200 private schools were not required to be registered with the CPE because they offered tuition and enrichment services. Private childcare centres, kindergarten and non-academic private entities that offer hands-on learning experiences were also exempted from the Private Education Act.[3] In sum, there were about 500 PEIs when the CPE came on board.

The CPE also excludes the Continuing Education and Training (CET) centres, which are private enterprises and non-private teaching education providers (such as the local polytechnics and the Institute for Adult Learning Singapore) that deliver courses in animation, food and beverage, adult education, hotel and accommodation. The courses are accredited by the Workforce Development Agency (WDA) — a statutory board established in September 2003 to upgrade skills of the Singapore workforce through training and education. There are currently more than 40 CET centres, which are subjected to a "rigorous accreditation and Continuous Improvement Review process by the WDA".[4]

Much of the discussion in this book will focus on the commercial PEIs offering certificates, diplomas and degree courses. Essentially, the primary function of commercial PEIs is to provide post-secondary education to students. They do not have the power to award degrees. They award certificates and diplomas. But they establish partnership with foreign universities largely from the United Kingdom and Australia to offer undergraduate and postgraduate degree courses in Singapore. The partners are not constrained by the traditional calendar. Hence, a degree university course that takes 3 years to complete in the United Kingdom or Australia can be completed in Singapore in 2 years.

As a commercial entity owned by business persons, PEIs aim to maximise profit. Education and profit go hand-in-hand. Recruitment of Academic Deans is by business persons and not by academic members within the faculty as would normally the case in universities. They work closely with business persons to formulate and implement strategic plans and meet targeted goals which include financial goals and education quality improvement. Teaching staff in PEIs focus on teaching. Most of them are not required to perform research nor publish academic papers. As compared to the public funded universities, PEIs are less restrictive and bureaucratic. PEIs respond more quickly and adapt to change, including closure of courses with low demand. PEIs do not have access to certain privileges. For example, the Immigration and Checkpoints Authority (ICA) administers a different policy for PEIs. Unlike international students in the Institutes of Higher Learning (IHL), comprising the local universities, local polytechnics and offshore institutes with local campuses like INSEAD Singapore, international students in PEIs are not allowed to work while holding a student pass.

International students in IHL, on the other hand, are permitted to work during vacation time, and they are exempted from applying for a work permit.

2.3 Pre-CPE Days

Generally speaking, it can be argued that PEIs around the world are largely commercially orientated. The concern arises when the commercial aspect of the business overrides other considerations, including maintaining and enhancing the quality of the academic courses. The means to survive in the competitive environment has led some PEIs to respond to market needs by accepting students who did not meet published entry requirements, offering shorter programmes and diploma courses without requiring class attendance or assessment. This issue arises in many places and well-known higher education institutions. In Australia, 2016 admission figures from the University of Sydney, University of New South Wales, Macquarie University and Western Sydney Australia showed that students with marks up to 40 points below the published Australian Tertiary Admissions Rank (ATAR) cut-off, which represented the minimum academic standard required to complete a course, were admitted in fields such as business and engineering.[5]

The PEIs have a choice which is to be more 'academic' by expanding and improving the infrastructure and facilities, developing and closely complying with the academic framework that details the credit assessment point, learning outcomes and others, appointing external examiners to review the assessment methods and moderate the assessment tasks and academic board to deliberate independently the academic provision. To move into this direction, the PEIs must be willing to demarcate the academic and business functions.

As mentioned, prior to the establishment of the CPE (on 1 December 2009), there were about 500 PEIs in Singapore.[6] They were subject to considerably less stringent regulation. Students were expected to do their own due diligence when enrolling into PEI courses. The PEIs did a one-time registration with the MOE and ensured that requirements on matter related to fire safety and usage of premises were met. They were rudimentary checks by the MOE on school management and teachers. A "light-touch kind of framework where PEIs do a one-time registration with

MOE, and that was essentially it", said Brandon Lee. As Andrew Chua, president of the Association of Private Schools and Colleges Singapore (APSC) put it: "In the past, anyone who could afford to rent two rooms in a commercial building would be able to set up a PEI".[7] The regulatory requirements (to register with MOE) were "fairly basic", for example, every school was required to "appoint a Committee of Management to ensure compliance with existing regulations", the school had to "declare the proposed course offerings and register its teachers, and the school must have at least two classrooms and office/administration space" (MTI, 2002b). The MOE was not an accreditation authority on qualifications, and did not specifically target its effort toward quality assessment of the academic programmes.

The task of promoting and encouraging professionalism in the management of corporations was largely rested on the Singapore Quality Class (SQC) scheme, which was introduced in 1997 and extended to include the PEIs. A new category of SQC was created specifically for the Private Education Organisations (PEOs). Administered by the Standards, Productivity, and Innovation Board of Singapore (SPRING Singapore), the SQC aimed to give public recognition to good PEOs. The award winners could vie for the Singapore Quality Award (SQA) — modelled on US Malcolm Baldrige National Quality Award and the best features of Japan's Edward Deming Prize and the European Quality Award — to be considered as 'world-class schools'.[8]

The SQC assessed the PEOs on seven dimensions — leadership, planning, information, people, processes, customers and results, and gave a score to register the schools' performance. The PEOs reviewed the processes that had been identified for improvement. There were some elements of subjectivity in the awarding of the score as it was dependent on the judgment of the reviewers and assessors who visited each school over a period of a few days. Concerns have been raised with regard to whether an accurate assessment of the schools in student protection (especially international students), lecturer deployment and quality of the academic programmes could be obtained from the audit.[9]

Another initiative, the CaseTrust for Education scheme, was launched in September 2004 to promote best business practices in the private education industry. The Consumers Association of Singapore (CASE), in collaboration with the Economic Development Board (EDB), SPRING Singapore, Singapore Tourism Board and the Infocomm Development Authority (IDA) of Singapore, designed the scheme to instil confidence in students and their parents in the quality of private education providers in Singapore. Of particular concern was the well-being of international students, and the student protection scheme (SPS) was designed to protect international students when private schools failed. The SPS was a compulsory component of the CaseTrust scheme for all private schools recruiting international students. When private schools AIT Academy and UniCampus folded in 2005, tuition fees for the 160 students were protected and compensated. However, mandatory fee protection did not extend to local students although they were affected by closure of the private schools. Other good practices as defined by CASE were clear fees policies, disclosure of the school's commitment to quality, putting in place well-defined systems and procedures to address students' grievances and well-trained support personnel.

Following the news released in January 2009 about a Case-Trusted private school Brookes Business School peddling fake RMIT degrees, questions were raised with regard to the effectiveness of the CaseTrust scheme for education. CASE has relied on what Tan and Teh (2013: 281) referred to as the 'honour system' of assessment whereby compliance by the private schools was assumed, instead of adopting a more thorough system that involved regular audits and checks to ensure actual compliance. Apparently, Brookes Business School did not notify CASE about the 'RMIT' course, and as a result, CASE might not have been aware of the case involving the school until *The Straits Times* broke the story in early 2009. Brookes Business School was expelled from the CaseTrust scheme in July 2009, possibly the heaviest penalty CASE could impose on private education providers as it had limited legal power to prosecute offenders.

With the benefit of hindsight, neither CaseTrust nor the SQC schemes administered by SPRING were equipped with regulatory power to adequately monitor the academic quality of the schools and their courses. CaseTrust was responsible in ensuring that students' interests were protected whereas the SQC scheme covered organisational excellence. The purview of CASE and SPRING did not extend to academic excellence.

The CaseTrust scheme for education was subsequently replaced by the EduTrust scheme in 2009.

2.4 Corporate Scandals

Greed overrides moral actions, paving the way for some of the PEIs to resort to various means to attract students like lowering the entry requirements without putting in place academic support and offering non-accredited degrees with minimal classes to attend and assignments to complete. Cases of schools offering fake degrees made headlines in the local news. On 3 July 2004, for example, it was alleged that the former Chief Executive Officer of Nanyang Institute of Management, had abetted his clerk, in falsifying visa applications of eleven foreign students to speed their approval by the ICA.[10] On 26 February 2008, two other private schools in Singapore, Camford Business School and Boston International, were reported to have employed dubious practice by offering degrees from unaccredited universities. Camford Business School offered degrees from Paramount University of Technology, a well-known degree mill institution based in Wyoming in the United States, whereas Boston International was alleged to have worked with a "West Coast University" which has received accreditation by an agency in the South Pacific Islands of Wallis and Futuna.[11]

Oregon's Office of Degree Authorization (ODA) listed six institutions in Singapore as degree mills as at January 2010, attributed to the government open-door policy to private post-secondary education "without first establishing a strict oversight system" according to as ODA's office administrator Alan Contreras. Contreras was further quoted as saying, "Your government has allowed its name to be used inappropriately. Without enforcement of standards by the government, anything goes. This is why the reputation of degrees issued in Singapore is falling".[12] Several school operators were alleged to have acted improperly thereby adversely affecting the reputation of the private education industry and the ability of the city–state to thrive as a global education hub.[13] The additional worry was that there would be a cascade effect; related businesses such as those in the retail industry and food and beverage industry would suffer and unemployment would soar.

2.5 Private Education Act of 2009

In 2009, the Singapore parliament passed the Private Education Act to tighten up standards and accountability of the private schools in Singapore. The MOE proposed a three-pronged strategy.

First, the Ministry would put in place a robust regulatory framework through the enactment of the Private Education Bill. The regulatory includes the mandatory ERF and the voluntary EduTrust Certification Scheme for PEIs with intent to recruit international students. The regulatory framework encompasses aspects that are related to corporate governance, protection measures to enhance students' interest and welfare, and monitoring of PEIs to ensure that they continue to meet the basic standards and improve their standards. The bill also provides for the establishment of the CPE to look over matters such as registration, quality assurance, investigation, and enforcement action against errant PEIs. The CPE was established on 1 December 2009.

Second, the Private Education Act would provide for the CPE to "cultivate consumer sophistication through the provision of accessible and transparent information on the private education sector for students".[14] The establishment of the Student Services Centre (SSC) within the CPE premise was part of the initiative. At the opening ceremony of the SSC on 22 April 2010, the then Minister for Education and Second Minister for Defence, Ng Eng Hen, emphasised the crucial role of the CPE — to "increase consumer awareness through public education programmes, to help potential students be more discerning about the various educational options available and to make informed choices".[15]

Third, the Private Education Act would provide for the CPE to work closely with the stakeholders to expand and promote the private education sector in Singapore. The CPE would organise talks and workshops with the major players in the industry to enhance the private education providers' systems and manpower capabilities, including the standards of teaching and development of the PEIs' curriculum. The CPE would also work closely with the industry associations such as Singapore Association for Private Education (SAPE) to promote a culture of accountability and responsibility among the PEIs.

2.6 Size, Types, and Key Players

By the end of 2010, 210 PEIs met the basic requirements of the ERF. The month of June in 2011 marked the end of the 18-month transition during which the PEIs were required to move to the more stringent standards and requirements. By the end of 2011, 338 PEIs were registered under the ERF, and the number of PEIs fell marginally to 319 as at 31 December 2013 and 312 as at 31 December 2014 (Table 2.1).

As a 31 December 2015, there were a total of 14,500 teachers and 7,200 non-teaching persons employed in the sector. About 50% of the teaching staff worked full-time in the PEIs whereas the remaining teaching staff were self-employed, retired or working full-time elsewhere. About 90% of the teachers were holding at least a Bachelor's degree.

The types of PEIs in Singapore are presented in Table 2.2. Commercial PEIs such as PSB Academy, Kaplan Singapore, Singapore Institute of Management Global Education (SIMGE) and Management Development Institute of Singapore (MDIS) represent the bulk of the total number of PEIs in Singapore, and they offer a variety of post-secondary certificates, diploma and degree programmes. More than 60% of the students in the private education sector are enrolled in commercial PEIs courses.

Vocational PEIs such as Tourism Management Institute of Singapore, the training arm of National Association of Travel Agents Singapore (NATAS) offer courses in specialised or niche areas such as Beauty and Spa, Culinary and Hospitality, Nursing, Healthcare and Social Sciences, Electronics and Mechanics, Art and Design and Performance Arts. They accounted for 7% of the total student population as at end 2013. About 8% of the student population was enrolled in courses offered by preparatory PEIs, which prepare students for professional qualifications, particular accountancy, as well as primary and secondary level examinations (e.g. GCE 'O' and 'A' levels). Foreign System Schools such as the Australian International School and Canadian International School, offering primary and secondary education that is in accordance with international curricula, primarily to children of expatriates residing in Singapore.

Cumulatively, about 227,000 students enrolled in PEI courses as at end 2013 (Table 2.3). The cumulative figures, as the CPE explains, "represent the number of unique students enrolled with the PEIs for the year..,

Table 2.1:   Number of PEIs, student enrolment and staff strength.

	As on 31 December 2010	As on 31 December 2011	As on 31 December 2012	As on 31 December 2013	As on 31 December 2014	As on 31 December 2015
Number of PEIs	210	338	332	319	312	304
Number of teachers	—	12,000[a]	17,500	21,467	16,079	14,500
Teach on a full-time basis	—	30%	28%	29%	36%	50%
Teachers with Bachelor's degree or higher	—	80%	>80%	86%	90%	90%
Number of non-teaching staff	—	5,500	6,400	6,385	7,409	7,223

Notes: [a]Excluded teachers from PEIs that have been exempted from the need to notify the CPE of teachers deployed.

Source: *CPE Annual Reports* (various years).

Table 2.2:   Types of PEIs (as on 31 December 2013).

		Type of PEIs			
	Total	Commercial[a]	Vocational[b]	Preparatory[c]	Foreign System Schools[d]
Number of PEIs	319	172	65	50	32
Enrolment	227,090	64%	7%	8%	21%

Notes: [a]Commercial PEIs offer a variety of post-secondary certificates, diploma and degree programmes.

[b]Vocational PEIs offer courses in specialised/niche areas such as Beauty and Spa, Culinary and Hospitality, Nursing, Healthcare and Social Sciences, Electronics and Mechanics, Art and Design and Performance Arts.

[c]Preparatory PEIs prepare students for professional qualifications, particularly accountancy, as well as primary and secondary level examinations (e.g. GCE 'O' and 'A' levels). PEIs providing special education courses are also included in this category.

[d]Foreign System Schools offer primary and secondary education that is in accordance with international curricular primarily to children of expatriates residing in Singapore.

Source: *The CPE Annual Report* (2013/2014: 15).

regardless of whether the students were still with the PEIs at the point of data collection" (CPE, 2014: 17). EduTrust certified PEIs captured 61% of the market share with about 140,000 students, not surprising since they were permitted to recruit students from other countries. About 130,000 students (56%) were local and permanent residents of Singapore. The remaining were international students.

In 2014, CPE revised its method of collecting student enrolment. The term "new course commencements" was coined, to count "a new student enrolment in a particular course at a particular PEI" (CPE, 2015: 13). "A student enrolled in two different courses is counted as two enrolments" writes CPE (2016: 13). Essentially, it captures the number of students in the private education sector at the point of course commencement, and shows the flow of students in the private education sector in a given year. In 2014, 151,704 students enrolled in PEIs courses of which 48% were Singapore citizens and permanent residents (Table 2.4). Around 60% of the students were studying in PEIs with EduTrust certifications and 34% of the students were pursuing part-time programmes. In 2015, the number of students enrolled in PEIs courses fell to 148,781. Half of the students

Table 2.3:   Student enrolment in PEIs (2012–2013).

	2012	2013
Total cumulative students	227,000	227,090
% of students who are Singapore citizens and permanent residents	56%	56%
% of part-time students	39%	38%
% of students who are studying in EduTrust-certified PEIs	63%	61%

Source: *The CPE Annual Reports* (2012/2013, 2013/2014).

Table 2.4:   Student enrolment in PEIs (2014–2015).

	2014	2015
Total cumulative students	151,704	148,781
% of students who are Singapore citizens and permanent residents	48%	50%
% of part-time students	34%	35%
% of students who are studying in EduTrust-certified PEIs	60%	62%

Source: *The CPE Annual Reports* (2014/2015, 2015/2016).

were Singapore citizens and permanent residents. Close to 62% of the students were studying in PEIs with EduTrust certifications and 35% of the students were pursuing part-time programmes.

Among the commercial PEIs subsector, it is fair to say that three of them lead the pack at least in terms of student preference (Table 2.5). The top three commercial PEIs in Singapore are SIMGE, Kaplan Singapore and PSB Academy, which were among the first batch of EduTrust certified PEIs.

The Singapore Institute of management (SIM) Group was founded in 1964 as a not-for-profit management institute, a spinoff of the Economic Development Board. It comprises the SIM University (the first private university and soon-to-be sixth autonomous university in Singapore), SIM Professional Development (which offers short training programmes) and SIMGE. SIMGE's vision is "to be the Centre of Leadership and

Table 2.5:   Top 10 most preferred PEIs (2012–2013).

Rank 2012	Rank 2013	PEIs	Votes
1	1	Kaplan Singapore	1,406
2	2	SIMGE	1,265
3	3	PSB Academy	1,066
5	4	Management Development Institute of Singapore	629
6	5	British Council (Singapore)	515
4	6	EASB East Asia Institute of Management	459
8	7	James Cook Australia Institute of Higher Learning	411
9	8	Nanyang Institute of Management	394
11	9	LASALLE College of the Arts	323
13	10	Nanyang Academy of Fine Arts	312

Source: The JobsCentral Learning Rankings and Survey Report (2013: 2).[18]

Management Excellence; and the Embodiment of Lifelong Learning".[16] Like the other PEIs, SIMGE does not have degree granting power. It partners with over 10 international universities and institutions from the United Kingdom, United States, Australia and Switzerland to offer undergraduate and postgraduate programmes to both full-time and part-time students. SIMGE awards the certificate and diploma programmes, and offers the pathways to students with 'O' levels and 'A' levels to enter the degree programmes offered by its university partners upon graduation. SIM launched the Diploma in Management Studies in 1973, its first formal management education programme. Today, SIMGE offers over 70 academic programmes in the fields of Arts and Social Sciences, Business, Information Technology, Computer Sciences and Nursing, and its enrolment stands at 20,000, with full-time international students forming about 17% of the entire cohort.[17]

Established in 1938 by Stanley H. Kaplan, Kaplan has expanded rapidly over the years across the United States and other parts of the world. Kaplan Singapore expanded its offerings in Singapore in 2005 by acquiring the Asia Pacific Management Institute. Kaplan Singapore's mission is to help individuals achieve their educational and career goals.[19] Today, Kaplan awards its own diplomas for full-time and part-time students, and offers bachelor and postgraduate degree programmes in partnership with universities such as Murdoch University, Birmingham City University, Royal Holloway University of London and University College of Dublin. The number of students enrolled in Kaplan numbered 18,000.

PSB Academy was established in 1964 as a productivity unit within the Economic Development Board. Today, PSB Academy is a fully privatised entity, offering programmes in business and communications, engineering and information technology, life sciences and physical sciences. The school aims "to be the premier tertiary education provider nurturing future talents with global orientation",[20] and it has a total of 11,000 local and international students.

The PEIs are not lacking in innovation, drive and ambitions, but many suffered when unethical practices of a few recalcitrant hit the news. Issues relating to weak corporate governance standards are common across all sectors. Agents succumb to short-term gains and make decisions that bring benefits to themselves and the shareholders instead of the interest of stakeholders, especially the students. The private education sector is not an exception, neither is it exclusively prevalent. There are ways to mitigate the problem and raise the standard of corporate governance. Putting in place a regulatory framework in a regime that emphasises good governance is one of the common measures.

Chapter 3

CPE, ERF, and EduTrust Certification Scheme

3.1 Introduction

Rapid expansion of the private education sector in Singapore has led to uneven quality of provisions across the sector. Cases of misrepresentation like those mentioned in Chapter 2 have imposed adverse effect on Singapore's reputation. The private education sector could not be left entirely on its own. The case for more extensive regulation was too strong to be ignored. On 1 December 2009, the Council for Private Education (CPE) was established as a statutory board under the Minister of Education. The rationale for its formation was aptly described in the inaugural issue of the Council's Annual Report.

"In recent years, the private education sector has grown rapidly, driven by the rising demand for lifelong learning and upgrading of knowledge and skills. PEIs play a role in developing human capital, and providing opportunities for Singaporeans who wish to upgrade themselves, including those who aspire to pursue programmes leading to degrees and higher qualifications" (Council for Private Education, 2012: 18).

Indranee Rajah, Senior Minister of State for Education noted at a Private Education Conference that "the lack of a strong regulatory framework to accompany the rapid growth (of the private education sector) had allowed the entry of some fly-by-night operators into the sector. The proliferation of unscrupulous practices and sudden school closures threatened to bring the entire sector into disrepute".[1]

Before CPE, organisational excellence was promoted by Singapore Quality Class (SQC) whereas CaseTrust took care of students' interest and welfare through the fees protection scheme. The academic excellence component was left out. As Seah Seng Choon, Executive Director of the Consumers Association of Singapore (CASE) declared in the wake of comments from the general public after news of Brookes Business School peddling fake degrees broke out in January 2009, CASE's purview did not extend to academic excellence. The academic excellence component "was supposed to be looked after by a council. However, that council did not materialise, to my knowledge".[2] The CPE subsumes the responsibilities of Standards, Productivity, and Innovation Board of Singapore's (SPRING Singapore's) SQC scheme and CaseTrust with the overall aim of building high quality private education providers.

3.2 Council for Private Education

The CPE was set up under the Private Education Act to enforce the rules and regulations that private school operators have to meet. The council's mission is to "strengthen and uplift the private education sector through (1) putting in place a robust regulatory framework, as provided for in the Private Education Act, (2) stepping up efforts in consumer education to promote greater public and consumer awareness; and (3) working with industry associations and private education institutions (PEIs) to develop the private education sector and raise its quality of education and student welfare services".[3]

The CPE consists of a Board led by the Chairman, and 5–17 members. The Board's functions and duties include registering and regulating the PEIs, encouraging and promoting the development of the private education sector and standards of the PEIs in Singapore, advising the government and other public authority on national needs and policies with regards to private education and implementing national policies relating to the sector. From its inception until the end of 2015, the CPE Board Chairman was held by Lin Cheng Ton who was concurrently the Chief Executive Office of Nanyang Polytechnic International. Civil service veteran Khoo Chin Hean took over as the CPE Board Chairman in December 2015. All employees of the CPE, including its inspectors are public servants in accordance to Section 12 of the Private Education Act, and it is mandatory for the CPE to prepare and submit the Annual Report to the Minister for Education, detailing the activities of the CPE during the preceding year.

In October 2016, the SkillsFuture Singapore Agency was established, taking over the formulation of frameworks and regulatory duties of the CPE, which was renamed the Committee for Private Education. The day-to-day management of the CPE functions, duties and affairs would be carried out by the appointed Director-General (Private Education), previously the Chief Executive Officer of the CPE, and the members of the senior management. As the discussion in this book is confined to pre-October 2016 period, the abbreviation CPE shall refer to the Council for Private Education, unless otherwise stated.

PEIs are required to renew their licences with the CPE regularly to ensure that PEIs continue to meet the requirements under the Enhanced Registration Framework (ERF). The requirements are not static in the sense that they are subject to change over time to reflect the dynamism of the industry. PEIs that intend to recruit international students are required to meet additional standards as stipulated in the EduTrust Certification Scheme. Another departure from the previous regime is with regard to the level of enforcement. Unlike CaseTrust, the CPE has the authority over the registration and regulation of the PEIs, and the investigation and enforcement action against errant institutions. PEIs are expected to comply with the direction of the CPE with regard to registration of new programmes and lecturers, suspension or removal of managers and contents of advertisements. Any person who contravenes the direction of the CPE may be found legally guilty of an offence. A PEI that fails to obtain permission from the CPE to offer new programmes, for example, is considered an offence under the Private Education Act [Section, 43(11)].

To date, there have been a number of errant managers in PEIs caught flouting the CPE rules and regulations.

- The pro-tem CPE investigated Brookes Business School and in June 2009, it was revealed that the school issued fake RMIT degrees although the school had no association with the Australian University. The school was shut down by the MOE in July 2009 "on the basis that Yap Chee Mun, the supervisor of Brookes Business School, was not a fit and proper person to continue operate the school".[4] Yap was alleged to have co-opted with students to apply for study loans based on inflated course fees, with the excess sums shared between the school, students and others. In March 2014, Yap was sentenced to 2 years and 10 months in jail after being convicted for charges related to the cash-back scheme scam. In October 2015, Yap pleaded guilty to 30 charges of cheating, and he was further sentenced to 5.5 years in jail.[5] A total of 205 affected students were placed in other schools so that they could complete their studies.

- In October 2010, CPE received an anonymous complaint on the School of Applied Studies (SAS), and began its investigation. Later that month, the CPE was informed of SAS's decision to cease operations, citing financial difficulties as the reason. SAS was granted 1-year registration by the CPE on 20 May 2010, but was not awarded with the EduTrust certificate. At the time of closure, SAS had 300 students. CPE worked with other PEIs to offer placement for the affected students. 108 students were eventually placed in nine EduTrust certified PEIs while the remaining students had either indicated that they did not require placement assistance or were not contactable. In its investigation, CPE found that the former manager of the SAS, Jeremy Low, had failed to keep proper records and ensure that the SAS complied with CPE direction to refund students. Low was also alleged to have made a false statement to the CPE in his application to CPE for EduTrust certification. In January 2013, Low pleaded guilty to the first two charges, and fined a total of S$16,000, or in default faced a combined jail term of sixteen weeks.[6]

- On 16 June 2011, the CPE cancelled the registration of ALG Education Centre on the grounds that the institution had failed to provide the CPE information in compliance with the Requisition Order, and inform CPE about the termination of its partnership with the external degree programme partner, Daemen College. Manager of ALG Education Centre, Ken Yong, was charged by the CPE, and pleaded guilty to the charge in March 2012. He was convicted and fined S$4,000 for contravening the Private Education Act. Thirty students were affected by the closure of the PEI. Twenty four of them were placed with EduTrust certified PEIs to complete their studies. Four opted to look for other institutions of their choice while two were not contactable.[7]

- For failing to obtain written permission from the CPE to offer a course and keeping proper records of students, ex-managers of the Cambridge Business School, Tan Cheng Hoe, Tan Cheng San and Guo Qiaoli, were charged in court in July 2011. The trio admitted to failing to keep proper record of students, and were issued with a stern warning by the CPE on 20 March 2012. The CPE published the warning on its website, and might refuse applications for registration by any of these persons in the near future. The last batch of students of Cambridge Business School completed their studies in June 2011.[8]

- On 20 July 2012, the CPE filed charges against Duclos Hazel Margaret, Manager of Process College, for failing to keep proper records of students, comply with CPE's direction to refund students, and obtain permission from the CPE before making changes to the registered premises. It was reported that Process College had collected fees amounting to about S$190,000 from 30 students between January and April 2010. The students had enrolled in the Confederation of Tourism and Hospitality (CTH) Diploma and Advanced Diploma in Hotel Management programmes, which were not conducted. Complaints from students led CPE to intervene and direct Process College to refund the course fees to students. The College had agreed to refund the course fees in instalments, but the payments failed to materialise. Duclos Hazel Margaret pleaded guilty to two of the charges in November 2012, and was sentenced to four weeks in jail a month later for failing to refund S$190,000 in fees to 30 foreign students and fined S$5,000 for failing to keep proper records of student contract. The case represented the first prosecution by the CPE that led to a jail sentence.[9]

- In April 2014, CPE received feedback that Kings International Business School (KIBS) had offered and awarded students with diplomas in maritime studies without requiring students to attend lessons or submit assessments. CPE completed its investigation, and concluded, among other things, that KIBS continued registration as a PEI in Singapore would not serve the interests of the public, students and prospective students. On 20 April 2015, CPE cancelled the registration of KIBS, the first it did so to a PEI issuing diplomas "without ensuring that students had received proper instruction and assessment." KIBS would not be permitted to offer and conduct private education courses, including the advanced diploma, diploma, certification and preparatory courses which were registered with the CPE. KIBS was instructed to arrange its students to continue their studies with another suitable PEI or refund the students with full course fees.[10] In June 2016, Pek Siew Gek and Tang Yudong, former managers of KIBS were formally charged for "failing to comply with a direction issued by CPE to refund or place out students" and "provision of false information to CPE".[11]

The decisive move by CPE to investigate and act on errant education service providers has restored some confidence in the private education sector. However, the number of cases of improper practices following the establishment of the CPE remains a concern especially in a country known for strong enforcement of regulations.

With public universities' strong emphasis on reputation and worldwide university rankings, safeguarding the integrity of the education sector in Singapore as a whole is a priority.[12] Unlike some emerging countries, Singapore has not seen a proliferation of the number of public universities as it always felt that it was important to keep very high standards in teaching, learning and research. Although PEIs are not in the same category in many aspects as that of National University of Singapore (NUS), Nanyang Technological University (NTU) or Singapore Management University (SMU), any bad news or scandals originating from either the private or public education sector in Singapore would have an adverse effect on the reputation and standing of Singapore's education sector. And in this regard, there is tremendous pressure on the CPE to ensure that the PEIs are well run.

As part of its industry development initiative, the CPE has conducted a series of meetings and focused group discussions with industry stakeholders.

In 2012, for example, the CPE signed Memorandum of Understanding with UK Quality Assurance Agency (QAA), and Memoranda of Co-operation with New Zealand Qualification Authority (NZQA) and the Tertiary Education Quality and Standards Agency (TEQSA) Australia to share best practices and initiatives, and help the private education sector develop its quality standards.

In the same year, the CPE in partnership with Republic Polytechnic launched the Specialist Diploma in Adult Learning and Teaching programme to upgrade and enhance pedagogical knowledge and instructional skills of teachers. The programme aims to support teaching professionals in the private education industry in improving the design and delivery of lessons, improving their assessment of students' performance, and achieving recognition as a qualified private educator. With four intakes a year, the 280-hour programme is conducted over 10 months on a part-time modular basis to accommodate the work schedules of educators ranging from full-time educators to those employed as sessional or adjunct lecturers.

The CPE set up the Student Services Centre (SSC) on 22 April 2010 to reach out to the community and gain wider visibility through the social media. The SSC works closely with agencies such as the Singapore Tourism Board, Economic Development Board (EDB) and Ministry of Foreign Affairs to provide relevant information about the private educator sector to prospective international students. The SSC also serves as a one-stop centre for students and parents to make enquiries and gather information, and provides the platform for students to channel their feedback and complaints.

In May 2016, it was revealed on CPE website that issues surrounding administrative matters (such as time tabling, relocation of school premises and matters relating to examinations) and fees (such as refunds and disputes relating to payment schedule or outstanding fees) were the two main grievances, accounting for 23% and 22% of the total complaints received in 2015, respectively. In that year, the CPE received a total of 769 complaints as compared to 698 and 792 cases in 2014 and 2013, respectively.[13] Of the 3,108 cases handled by the CPE in 2015, 26% of them were complaints whereas the remaining 74% were enquiries.[14] The PEIs are expected to respond to the queries and complaints and keep the CPE informed. In the event that the matter is not resolvable between the PEIs and students, an application will be made with the CPE Mediation and Arbitration Scheme, which was jointly set up by the CPE, Singapore Mediation Centre (SMC) and the Singapore Institute of Arbitrators (SIArb) for the matter to be discussed and resolved via a structured and cost effective dispute resolution mechanism. Just as disagreements between nation states are mediated through representation and rules, disputes between the PEI and its stakeholders can be mediated through the joint institution for the greater good.

3.3 Regulatory Framework

The CPE oversees the two-tier regulatory regime that was put in place in the Private Education Act passed by the Parliament in September 2009. The regime comprises the *ERF* and *EduTrust Certification Scheme.*

Enhanced registration framework

ERF was launched on 21 December 2009. It spells out the mandatory registration requirements and legislation obligations for PEIs. No person(s) or a business entity is allowed to offer private education in Singapore unless the standards spelt out in the ERF are met.

Table 3.1 shows the number of ERF registration status over a period of 5 years. By May 2010, CPE received a total of 308 ERF applications of which 164 applications were completed. As at end 2013, there were 319 private education providers in Singapore, down from over 1,000 in 2007. In 2014, 312 PEIs were registered under the ERF. Of these, 223 PEIs successfully obtained the 4-year registration certificate, and 25 PEIs with 6-year registration period, which is recognised as a mark of quality. In December 2015, the number of ERF registered PEIs fell marginally to 304 with 24 of them holding a 6-year registration period and 223 with 4-year registration. More PEIs have attained a 4-year registration period from 82 PEIs in 2011 to 223 PEIs in 2015, and correspondingly fewer PEIs with 1-year registration period status.

Table 3.1: Number of ERF registration status.

Certification status	As on 31 March 2011	As on 31 December 2011	As on 31 December 2012	As on 31 December 2013	As on 31 December 2014	As on 31 December 2015
Number of PEIs with 6-year registration	2	21	24	25	25	24
Number of PEIs with 4-year registration	82	135	202	220	223	223
Number of PEIs with 1-year registration	178	182	106	74	64	57
Total	262	338	332	319	312	304

Source: *The CPE Annual Report* (various years).

There are four aspects of the ERF — registration, academic governance, academic rigour, and information transparency.

Registration: All private education providers must register with the CPE before commencing operations. The CPE determines the validity period of the registration status (1 year, 4 years or 6 years). The CPE also defines the criteria for registration. For example, the registered name, as stipulated by the CPE, should not contain the word 'university' or any derivative of the term, on the basis that the PEIs are essentially non-degree awarding institutions. Words like 'Singapore' or 'National' are also not allowed to prevent the public from associating the PEIs with the Singapore government. To register as a PEI, the designated manager of the PEI must provide information on usage and safety of the premises, the status of the registered company, the Academic and Examination boards, the courses offered (certificates, diplomas and external degree programmes) and the teaching staff who will be deployed to teach the courses. Private education providers should fulfil a set of prescribed duties and responsibilities, including keeping of proper records and protecting students affected by closure of the schools. The application process consists of two stages — the desktop check and on-site inspection. The latter serves to verify the claims submitted by the PEIs in the registration, and check on the premises, signage and facilities.

The CPE is the monitoring agent appointed by the government to promote PEIs' compliance with the provisions of the Private Education Act. It has the mandate to suspend the registration of a PEI for up to 6 months or cancel the registration of any PEIs that fail to comply with the provisions of the Private Education Act. Of course, not all cases lead to suspension. The CPE may impose a financial penalty, a censure on the errant PEI or administrative penalty in the form of subjecting the PEI to additional terms and conditions.

Academic governance: Academic governance is primarily the responsibility of the PEI Academic Board and Examination Board. It is mandatory for the PEI to establish the Academic Board whose members should develop and review the policies and procedures on all academic matters of the school, develop a set of standards to ensure the academic quality of every course offered by the private schools, and give approval of each person to be deployed to teach course offered by the institution. Each board must consist of at least three members. The Examination Board is established to develop and implement the processes that govern the conduct of formative and summative assessments of the courses offered by the PEIs. It also develops procedures relating to the duties and responsibilities of invigilators and markers, handling of students' appeals with regard to examination or assessment and security of the examination scripts and answer scripts. The Examination Board must consist of at least three members.

Academic rigour: The CPE reviews the courses offered by the PEIs, the minimum entry requirements of the courses, and the track record and profile of the foreign universities issuing the diplomas and/or degrees. To prevent degree mills from establishing a foothold in Singapore, foreign education institutions must be nationally and internationally reputable. The external degree programmes should be subjected to the same academic procedure and assurance process as that offered on campus. CPE forbids the inclusion of the PEI's name on the transcript and degree scroll conferred to the students (unless written permission is obtained from the Singapore Minister for Education) to ensure that students graduating from Singapore receive equivalent qualification, recognition and treatment as those enrolled in home campuses.

The other aspect of academic quality relates to the appointment of lecturers in the PEIs. The CPE imposes strict requirements with regards to the qualifications of the lecturers (in addition to the fact that the lecturer deployed must not be convicted of any offence relating to sexual, child, physical or drug abuse or those associated with the Private Education Act within the period of 5 years preceding the deployment). To engage a lecturer to teach on a course, the person must meet the following qualifications:

- Academic qualifications in the same field of at least one level higher than the level of the course, subject or module appointed to teach if the person has less than 5 years of work experience in the field.
- If the person has at least 5 years of working experience in the same field as the course, module or subject, the person's qualifications in the same field must be at least be equivalent to the level of the course.

- If the person has at least 5 years of working experience in the same field as the course, module or subject, the person is permitted to teach the course if he/she has qualifications in the course in a different field provided that the person has qualifications that are at least one level higher than the level of the course.

Each application for teaching position must be endorsed by a member of the Academic Board. The CPE conducts scheduled checks and sample pre-selected academics from the PEIs list of deployed lecturers to ensure that the PEIs comply with the regulatory requirements. In the event that the PEIs are found contravening the regulatory requirements, a warning or a financial penalty of not exceeding S$5,000 may be imposed.

Information transparency: Private education providers must disclose information about the institutions, including the registration validity period, teachers deployed, fees and facilities and refund policy to the CPE, and publish the information on their respective websites. The purpose is to help students make more informed decision.

PEIs are mandated to ensure that their students have appraised the contents of the student contracts, and adhere to the advertising guidelines to ensure that students are not misrepresented. On course fees, the PEIs must separate the fees that are applicable to full-time and part-time version of the course, and include components of the course fees so that students would not associate the stated course fees as one that covers the course in its entirety. Any operators who fail to comply with the rules and regulations are subject to a fine of up to S$10,000 and a year in jail.

In addition, the PEIs must prepare and submit the Annual Report to the CPE by 31 December every year. The contents of the Annual Report include the financial statements of the PEIs in the last financial year that are prepared in accordance with the requirements of either the Companies Act or the Societies Act. The PEIs are also required to disclose the list of courses offered as well as courses that do not require prior permission of the CPE (courses with duration of less than 30 days or 50 hours), and the number of students enrolled in each of the courses with a breakdown in terms of the number of local students and those who are holding student pass.

EduTrust Certification

EduTrust Certification is voluntary. However, only PEIs that are EduTrust certified are allowed to offer placement for international students who require a Student's Pass from the Immigration and Checkpoints Authority (ICA). In October 2016, the CPE announced that a 4-year EduTrust certification would be mandatory for PEIs offering external degree programmes. An EduTrust certified private institution is awarded with one of the three types of certificates: EduTrust Star, EduTrust and EduTrust Provisional (Table 3.2).

The CPE received a total of 114 applications for EduTrust certification by the end of May 2010. Sixty eight of the applications provided all the relevant documents. On 20 May 2010, CPE released the first batch of results after 18 applications have been accessed. Of the 18 cases, six PEIs were awarded the EduTrust (4 year) — At-Sunrice Academy, East Asia Institute of Management, Parkway College of Nursing and Allied Health, PSB Academy, Singapore Institute of Management and TMC Academy. Seven PEIs were awarded the EduTrust Provisional, and five PEIs failed to receive an award from the regulatory authority.

Table 3.2: EduTrust certificates classification.

Certification	Validity period	Characteristics
EduTrust Star	4 years	This award is given to a PEI that has excelled in key areas of management and the provision of quality education services. This mark is also a recognition of the sustained efforts in organisational improvement.
EduTrust	4 years	This award is given to a PEI that has achieved satisfactory to commendable performance in key areas of management and the provision of educational services.
EduTrust Provisional	1 year	This award is given to a PEI that has attained a minimum level of performance in key areas of management and the provision of educational services. In accepting the award, the organisation acknowledges the need to improve its existing management practices and service provisions, and strives to achieve this.

Source: http://www.cpe.gov.sg/cpe/slot/u54/Press%20Release/Press%20Release.pdf (extracted on 9 September 2010).

As on 31 December 2013, CPE has awarded EduTrust certificates to 49 private institutions and 65 schools have been given the EduTrust Provisional status (Table 3.3). The number of PEIs with four-year registration period increased from 27% as on 31 March 2011 to 43% by the end of 2013 and 58% by end of 2015, which indicates that the PEIs in Singapore are complying more substantially with the regulatory requirements. In April 2015, Australia's James Cook University (JCU) became the first PEI to win the prestigious EduTrust Star award "for having excelled in all key areas of management and the provision of quality education services."[15] Lasalle College of the Arts, which offers undergraduate and postgraduate courses in art, design, animation and film, became the first local institution to be given the EduTrust Star in October 2015.[16]

As on 31 December 2016, CPE assesses the applicants on six criteria (Table 3.4).[17]

Criteria 1: Management commitment and responsibilities (50 points). The criterion consists of four subcriteria, namely vision and mission (1.1), values and culture (1.2), strategic planning (1.3) and defining responsibilities (1.4). The criterion examines the PEIs' management responsibilities in relation to the development of vision and mission statements, and communicating the vision and mission to the stakeholders. It is based on the traditional but still relevant notion that the essential work of the management team entails allocating company's scarce resources, defining SMART goals, coordinating and controlling activities, meeting stakeholders' demands and ensuring that these are documented, presented to the Board of Directors for feedback and approval and communicated to the staff.

Criteria 2: Corporate governance and administration (180 points). There are six subcriteria in the category, namely management of financial resources (2.1), management of resources and facilities (2.2), management of human resources (2.3), management of partnerships (2.4), communication and publicity (2.5), management of information (2.5) and management of feedback and complaints (2.6). The essence of the

Table 3.3:   EduTrust statistics.

Certification status	As on 31 March 2011	As on 31 December 2011	As on 31 December 2012	As on 31 December 2013	As on 31 December 2014	As on 31 December 2015
EduTrust Star (4 years)	0	0	0	0	0	2
EduTrust Award (4 years)	17	34	47	49	49	62
EduTrust Provisional (1 year)	45	60	68	65	60	43
Total	62	94	115	114	109	106

Source: *The CPE Annual Report* (various years).

Table 3.4:   Criteria in the EduTrust certification scheme.

Criteria	Description	Points
1	Management commitment and responsibilities	50
2	Corporate governance and administration	180
3	External recruitment agents	120
4	Student protection and support services	210
5	Academic processes and assessment of students	350
6	Quality assurance, monitoring, and results	90
	Total	1,000

Source: Council for Private Education (http://www.cpe.gov.sg).

criteria is to promote trustworthy relations between the PEIs and their stakeholders, recognising the possibility that the executive managers who look after the day-to-day matters of the PEIs may make decisions that maximise their personal interests instead of the students and shareholders whom they supposedly represent. The criterion prescribes administrative responsibilities of the PEIs and identifies specific evidences that the PEIs are required to furnish for auditing purpose. The criteria does not stipulate the disclosure of committee members, their background and areas of expertise and the number of meetings held in a year nor the requirement to separate the Chairman of the Board and Chief Executive Officer as would normally apply for publicly listed companies. The criterion also does not stipulate nor provide guidelines with regards to the composition of the board in PEIs. The concern is that the board members may share the same interest as the shareholders, and make improper decisions to maximise short-term profits at the expense of the students. Profit motive of education provider has been associated with reduction in quality as some have argued.[18] CPE inspectors are therefore shouldered with the responsibility to uncover improper practices.

Criteria 3: External recruitment agents (120 points). There was a time when PEIs could rely on government agencies such as International

Enterprise, Economic Development Board and Singapore Tourism Board to promote Singapore as a learning destination thereby attracting international students to enrol into the PEI courses. That was part of the Global Schoolhouse strategy driven by economic considerations and the need to attract foreign talents in response to a low birth rate and expected higher demand for skilled labour. Government support in this particular area has weakened. Visitors of CPE website are instead reminded of the 3Rs — What is my *reason* for wanting for pursue further studies? Am I *ready* to do so? Are there possible *risks* involved? — and warned about what they read in PEI promotional materials.[19]

Without a brand name established abroad, relying on external recruitment agents in the host countries to woo potential applicants is a common practice among the PEIs. It is also a practical means to avoid incurring cost of sending staff abroad to conduct their own marketing overseas. The concern arises when PEIs admit students with dubious prior academic qualifications or incomplete supporting documents into their programmes, leading to an influx of international students who may struggle to complete their education. The criterion has three subcriteria — selection of agents (3.1), which requires the PEIs to put in place selection criteria for potential agents so that only reliable and credible agents are engaged; management of agents (3.2), which pertains to ensuring that the recruited agents are properly trained and informed about the programmes and that they are aware of the code of conduct expected from them; monitoring of agents (3.3), which examines the measures in place to monitor the performance of the agents to ensure that the students are not misrepresented in anyway during the process of student recruitment. The PEIs are expected to take timely and appropriate actions on agents, including termination of the contracts, in the event that the agents are found to have violated the contracted agreements and/or code of conduct.

Criteria 4: Student protection and support services (210 points). There are two objectives to the criterion. First, it aims to provide protection to students in the event of sudden closure of the PEIs. Accordingly, all

EduTrust certified PEIs must subscribe to the Fee Protection Scheme (FPS) with CPE approved insurance service providers before they are allowed to collect more than two months of course fees at any one time. Under CPE regulations, the PEIs have up to seven days from the day the course fees are paid to purchase insurance for course fees paid by the students, and they can do so with five appointed insurance companies. PEIs with 4-year EduTrust are required to submit Fee Protection Fee data to the CPE once every six months whereas PEIs with 1-year EduTrust must submit the data once every three months. The student contract, being a legally binding document, must include a detailed breakdown of the fees and agreements that the PEIs and students have mutually agreed on, and it has to be clearly understood by the students prior to enrolment. Policies with regards to transfers, withdrawals and refund of fees must be clearly spelt out by the PEIs and understood by the students.

Second, the criterion examines the level of student support. In a nutshell, PEIs are expected to provide a holistic education to students through the provision of enrichment programmes and enhance student welfare by making sure that their students are medically insured and are able to seek help from course and pastoral counsellors when needed.

Criteria 5: Academic processes and assessment of students (350 points). A total of seven subcriteria exist, and they are as follows. Curriculum design and development (5.1), curriculum planning and delivery (5.2), student selection and admission (5.3), monitoring of learning and student development (5.4), student tracking (5.5), student assessment (5.6) and selection of part-time academic staff (5.7).

PEIs are expected to put in place processes to design and develop their courses, and approve the adoption of external degree programmes. The Academic Board's approval on the design and development outcomes of all the courses is expected. The CPE does not scrutinise the contents of the academic programmes nor specify the academic standards for qualifications. It is the responsibility of the PEIs to ensure that the courses are delivered to achieve the intended learning outcomes of the subjects, and that resources are adequate to support the teaching staff in the delivery of the curriculum.

With regards to student selection, the CPE stipulates the requirement for PEIs to verify the originality of the documents submitted by the applicants. In the event that the applicants do not meet the programme's minimum entry requirements — language requirements and academic requirements — the PEIs are expected to reject the application or administer entry tests to assess the applicant's suitability.

The PEIs are also expected to put in place student support system to monitor students' learning, including student attendance, continuous assessment and class observations. The success of students of each cohort in the PEIs is typically measured by passing rate and graduation rate. The PEIs are expected to compute and analyse progression rate (to show the percentage of students who would progress to the next level of the programme), attrition rate (to track the percentage of students who leave the course prematurely) and employment rate.

With regard to the selection of part-time academic staff, the selection process entails verification of the originality and authenticity of the applicants' academic and professional qualifications and approval of short-listed applicants by the management team and academic board prior to recruitment.

Criteria 6: Quality assurance, monitoring and results (90 points). There are four subcriteria namely measurement and analysis (6.1), which involves the collection and analysis of data for the purpose of measuring the actual performance on indicators against their targets; internal assessment and review (6.2), which examines whether the PEIs have conformed to the EduTrust requirements and identifies opportunities for improvement and enhancement; management review (6.3), which focuses on how the management team utilises data and reviews reports to improve PEIs' operational performance; continual improvement (6.4), which examines the processes, systems and procedures that the PEIs have put in place to promote good governance and provide for good educational experience to their students. Criterion 6 ensures that the PEIs monitor and analyse data and conduct necessary checks and reviews so that they continue to meet the EduTrust requirements.

Changes are underway with the restructuring exercise in October 2016. Notably, the CPE has issued new measures to strengthen student protection (on 21 October 2016) that include the following:

- Compulsory participation of PEIs offering external degree programme in CPE-run annual graduate employment survey. The results of the survey are to be published by the participating PEIs.
- Mandatory EduTrust certification for PEIs offering external degree programme.
- Set appropriate minimum entry requirements for fresh school leavers (without relevant working experiences). As a guide, admission to external degree programmes should require GCE 'A' level, IB diploma or equivalent, polytechnic diploma or its equivalent or a PEI qualification that has obtained articulation arrangement into the degree programme.
- All new PEIs are to have a minimum paid-up capital of S$100,000 to ensure that the PEIs have the financial capabilities to operate.[20]

The CPE has also alluded to enhancing the EduTrust standards, paying particular attention to the quality of the academic programmes and learning outcomes attained by the students, and this implies greater scrutiny on the curriculum, delivery methods, modes of assessments and teaching hours to ensure that students are not deprived of quality education. Greater emphasis on academic excellence may signal further restructuring of the structure of the private education market with the bigger players possibly acquiring or absorbing the smaller ones, a positive change in the context of the private education sector in Singapore to remove weak, small, and fraudulent institutions while increasing legitimacy of those who remained in the industry. The overall structure of the market as alluded many years ago by the Ministry of Trade and Industry should consist of 40 odd good quality and dynamic commercial and specialty schools, each enrolling at least 1,000 international students. As the ministry noted in its report *'Developing Singapore's Education Industry'*: "Surrounding this core of reputable schools would be other smaller niche schools that offer diverse courses, from hotel management to ballet. The key to building this strategy lies in removing the developmental hurdles and market inefficiencies, putting in place a quality assurance framework, and promoting collaboration between the different players. This would then allow the players to flourish and respond to the market's needs, and thus grow the segment organically" (MTI, 2002a: 7).

As this juncture, it may be useful to take a step back to consider the demand side of the equation. The following chapter discusses the aspirations of Singaporeans to pursue higher education to lead a good life. The chapter also discusses a recent development in the higher education sector namely the publication of the (Applied Study in Polytechnics and Institute for Technical Education Review ASPIRE) report, and its impact on the PEIs.

Chapter 4

Aspirations and ASPIRE

4.1 Introduction

There were two universities in Singapore in 1965 — Nanyang University (1956) and University of Singapore (1962). The former was a Chinese-medium university founded by local Chinese community whereas the University of Singapore was one of the two autonomous divisions of the University of Malaya, one of which was located at Bukit Timah in Singapore and the other in Kuala Lumpur. Nanyang University and University of Singapore merged in 1980 to form the National University of Singapore (NUS). An engineering practice-oriented university, Nanyang Technological Institute (NTI) was established in 1981, and became a full-fledged University, Nanyang Technological University (NTU) in 1991.[1]

In August 2000, the third university, Singapore Management University (SMU), was established. It recruited its first class of business students in 2000 — in partnership with the Wharton School of the University of Pennsylvania (established in 1881 through the bequest of businessmen Joseph Wharton).[2] Singapore University of Technology & Design (SUTD) was added to the list of universities in Singapore in 2010. Modelled after the Massachusetts Institute of Technology (MIT) of the United States and Zhejiang University of China, the SUTD offers courses in technology and design in the disciplines of engineering, information systems and architecture.

The number of places in the universities will never be enough to meet the aspirations of Singaporeans. There will always be more applicants than slots available for the public universities. The problem was less worrying in the early years of independence. Low-skilled jobs were plentiful for lowly educated residents. They attended schools to acquire skills, and lifelong learning was not really necessary to earn middle-wage. But as the Singapore economy moved ahead, returns to skilled and educated labour increased whereas those of lowly-skilled and educated decreased. Lifelong learning becomes a necessity for today's workers as a means to reinvent and advance their careers. The influx of foreign talents further caused discomfort among the local students who were grappling with deprivation of local university places and depressed wages at the lower end of the scale.[3] Taken together, as economist Linda Lim (2016: 8) noted, "earned income inequality in Singapore is now greater than in most other developed countries, and overall inequality is even greater if wealth inequality were also taken into account". Singapore students have resorted to paying higher fees for overseas university education and enrolling into programmes on-campus or through the private education institutions (PEIs).

On a wider scale, the influx of migrants to the city–state has led to crowded public places such as eating places and public transport, competition for jobs and the impact on price levels, including housing, appear to be the concerns raised by the majority. The release of the Population White Paper in January 2013, which projected a total population of between 6.5 and 6.9 million by 2020 — of which citizens would constitute only 55% (3.6–3.8 million) — unleashed a torrent of public criticism. Four protests were organised between 2013 and 2015 at Hong Lim Park. The largest anti-immigrant protest of 4,000 people was held on 16 February 2013. Dissatisfaction with the government's open door policy had been identified by the ruling party's supporters as one of the sources of the party's less-than-satisfactory performance at the 2011 General Election where it won 60.1% of the popular votes from 66.6% in 2006. The oppositions won six parliament seats, the highest since independence.[4]

The government responded to the local sentiments by adding 2,000 more places for local students in local universities, and lowering the cap of foreign students in state-funded universities from 18% per cohort as of 2011 to 15% by 2015. In 2012, the Singapore government set the target of reaching the Cohort Participation Rate (CPR) of 40% by 2020, and the establishment of the Singapore Institute of Technology (SIT) and SIM University (UniSIM) as Singapore's fifth and sixth universities and expansion of intakes in universities are key steps in achieving the goal (Ministry of Education, 2012: 23).[5] SIT offers an alternative pathway for polytechnic students to obtain a university degree from reputable universities such as University of Manchester, University of Nevada and DigiPen Institute of Technology. UniSIM issues its own degree, which are to fit the needs of industry and businesses. From July 2013, UniSIM students could apply for tuition fee loan of up to 90% of the subsidised fees payable.[6]

4.2 The End in Mind: To Obtain a Post-Secondary Education Qualification

It can be argued that the aspiration of many Singapore residents is to at least pursue an undergraduate programme and obtain a degree. The *JobsCentral Learning Survey Report* 2014 noted that nearly three quarter of the respondents ($n = 3,078$) had expressed interest to further their education to enhance their career prospects and improve their employability.[7] HSBC's Learning for Life report concluded that 90% of the parents in Singapore believed that an undergraduate degree or higher education was necessary for their children to achieve their life goals. The report also noted that more than 80% of the parents were willing to send their children abroad to obtain a foreign university degree (HSBC, 2015). A year later, HSBC reported that Singapore parents spent on average S$21,000 a year on their child's university education, twice that of the global average. 55% of the Singapore parents surveyed thought that spending money on their children's education was more important than saving for retirement, against the global average of 49% whereas 38% of them (against a global average of 30%) would prefer funding their children's education than paying their mortgage or rent.[8]

Strong aspiration for higher education qualifications can be partly attributed to moderately high intergenerational mobility in Singapore on an absolute term, which offers the participants a good chance to achieve economic success and higher social status regardless of their starting point and background.[9] The association between academic qualification and income levels or what is known as the returns to education has been extensively studied. The benchmark model was derived by Jacob Mincer, an economist from the University of Chicago, who regressed the natural logarithm of earnings against educational attainment and working experience. On an average, the returns to education were about 10% worldwide with higher returns recorded for low and middle income countries (returns to education in Asia was about the world average). Comparatively speaking, women received higher returns than men, and younger persons enjoyed higher returns than older workers.[10]

In the case of Singapore, the rate of return to education in the period from 1980 to 1994 as estimated by Toh and Wong (1999) showed high rate of return to tertiary education (polytechnic and university) as compared to the rate of return to secondary education. Low *et al.* (2004) reported a 13.2% increase in earnings for workers who invested an additional year of education. Sakellariou (2003) and Yeo *et al.* (2007) reported an increase of 13.1% and 13.7% in earnings, respectively, for an additional year of education with a higher rate of return for tertiary education as compared with non-tertiary education. According to the *Report on Labor Force in Singapore* published in 2014, persons with diploma and professional qualifications earned a median gross monthly income of S$4,000 as compared to S$2,814 and S$1,594 for persons with secondary and primary education, respectively. Degree holders earned a median monthly gross income of S$6,800. The data suggests that the level of education is positively correlated with private returns, which explains the obsession among parents and students alike to focus on academic results and acquisition of higher education qualifications.[11]

The relationship between education attainment and economic success in life has been contested. In an influential study, economist Lant Pritchett did not find any association between increases in human capital that have resulted from greater educational attainment of the labour force and the rate of growth of output per worker. Pritchett (2001) conjectured that this could have been due to the reduction in the marginal returns to education as the supply of educated workers increasingly outsizing the demand. The notion that attainment of academic qualification does not automatically lead to higher payoff, especially for qualifications that are not entirely helpful in one's career, has been elevated as the hard truth of today's complex and competitive society, and is supported by the Singapore government.

4.3 Applied Study in Polytechnics and ITE Review (ASPIRE) Report

In January 2014, the government embarked on a study to review the polytechnic and Institute for Technical Education (ITE) systems to better meet the demands of the future and the aspirations of the students. Led by Indranee Rajah, the ASPIRE committee published its findings and recommendations in August 2014 (Ministry of Education, 2014).

The report makes 10 recommendations, covering four themes.

Theme 1 is concerned with helping students in making well-informed education and career choices. The committee aspires to empower youths and working adults to make well-informed decisions about their education and careers by providing them with up-to-date information.

The recommendation under this theme is as follows:

Recommendation 1: to strengthen education and career guidance (ECG) efforts in schools, polytechnics and ITE.

Theme 2 is concerned with strengthening education and training in polytechnics and ITE. The aspiration of the polytechnics and ITE is to continue providing a strong applied education, and equipping graduates with a strong skills foundation to join the workforce.

The recommendations under this theme are as follows:

Recommendation 2: to enhance internships at the polytechnics and ITE.

Recommendation 3: to increase Nitec to Higher Nitec progression opportunities so ITE students can deepen their skills.

Recommendation 4: to establish polytechnic and ITE leads for each key industry sector to strengthen linkages with industry and help enhance programme offerings.

Recommendation 5: to expand online learning opportunities to make it easier for individuals to learn anywhere and anytime.

Recommendation 6: to provide more development and support programmes for polytechnic and ITE students to help every enrolled student succeed.

Theme 3 is about helping polytechnic and ITE students deepen their skills post-graduation. The committee aspires to provide opportunities for graduates to apply the skills they have acquired in schools, and build upon them further in their jobs.

The recommendations for this theme are as follows:

Recommendation 7: to launch new programmes that integrate work and study, such as place-and-train programmes, to provide an additional skills-upgrading option for polytechnic and ITE graduates.

Recommendation 8: to increase post-diploma Continuing Education and Training (CET) opportunities at the polytechnics to refresh and deepen the skills of polytechnic graduates.

Recommendation 9: to support vocation-based deployments during National Service (NS) to help polytechnic and ITE graduates maintain their skills.

Theme 4 is about helping polytechnic and ITE graduates progress in their careers. The committee recognises the aspirations of graduates to obtain further qualifications, and aspires to put in place clearly articulated pathways of progression for the graduates.

The committee recommends the following:

Recommendation 10: to develop sector-specific skills frameworks and career progression pathways in collaboration with industry to support progression based on industry-relevant skills.

Guided by the conviction that "knowledge coupled with deep skills are the key to success", the committee advises students and parents to think through the career options and the various training courses that are available in the market before signing up for a degree. It raises the concern that students who have invested time and money to obtain an undergraduate or postgraduate degree might not be able to land on jobs that commensurate with their newly acquired qualifications. As the economy restructures, as the story goes, some of the capital intensive industries may require specialised skills and knowledge that a general university qualification may not provide.[12] The publication of the report by the ASPIRE committee coincided with rising concerns of over-education and underemployment in South Korea (Cho, 2015), Hong Kong (Cohn and Ng, 2000), the Netherlands (Hensen *et al.*, 2009), Finland (Jauhiainen, 2011), Poland (Kierszlyn, 2013), Spain (Ramos and Sanroma, 2011) and others, where students pursued tertiary education in fields of studies that were lacking in market prospects. They are over-educated in the sense that they have difficulty looking for jobs that match their formal qualifications and many may end up with jobs that actually require lower qualifications.

The ASPIRE report places emphasis on acquisition of deep knowledge and skills relevant to the industry that students really need to advance their careers. The step forward, the report noted, is to create good skills-based progression pathways for polytechnic and ITE graduates, empower the youths to make informed education and career choices, enhance internship opportunities for polytechnic and ITE students, and strengthen the relationship between the industry sector and the educational sector. Singapore Institute of Technology in this respect supports the initiative by providing a platform for polytechnic graduates to deepen their skills and knowledge through an articulated programme with the university and its partner and excel in the chosen field and career.[13]

At this juncture, it may be worth noting that the Singapore government has long recognised the importance of well-trained and skilled manpower. In 1963, Balestier Junior Technical School was established to become the first vocational institute in post-independence Singapore, offering students who had completed at least two years of secondary school (but who were not academically inclined to progress to the 'O' level) courses in plumbing, carpentry, motor mechanics and other craft subjects. In 1968, Technical Education Department (TED) was formed to undertake all vocational and technical training initiatives. In 1973, TED was renamed the Industrial Training Board (ITB) and converted into a statutory board with greater autonomy and decision-making power. One of the initiatives of the ITB was setting up of training centres that would equip school leavers with skills that were relevant to specific companies or industries. Working together with the Economic Development Board, joint training centres were established in collaboration with internationally reputed companies. The first of such training centres was Tata-Government Training Centre set up in 1972, followed by the Rollei-Government Training Centre in 1973 and Philips-Government Training Centre in 1975. As new industries formed, the EDB approached the Japanese, German, and French governments in the late 1970s and early 1980s, which led to the establishment of the Japan-Singapore Training Centre in 1979, German-Singapore Institute in 1982 and French-Singapore Institute in 1983, to raise Singapore workers' competency in advanced manufacturing technology that the EBD had identified as critical for Singapore's growth and development.

Several initiatives have been introduced following the release of the ASPIRE report. The *Earn and Learn Programme* aims to provide opportunities for ITE and polytechnic students to work while they study. A book project, sponsored by the Ministry of Culture, Community and Youth, entitled "A Nation of Skilled Talents" was published in 2015 to profile 50 successful graduates from the ITE and polytechnics (Loh and El Farran, 2015).[14] Essentially, the efforts aim to (i) inform students that there are good jobs and prospects for higher level vocational graduates, (ii) discourage the narrow focus on grades and exams and the paper chase mentality, and (iii) chart a new territory that focuses on matching learning with interest, joy, and mastery of skills.

Government ministers have joined the chorus. Paper qualification, writes Minister Ong Ye Kung, is merely "the means to an end — the end being to achieve mastery — to be really good at what we are doing... So what needs to change is the kind of paper qualifications we want to have".[15] Former Minister for Education, Heng Swee Keat, noted that it is important for us to learn "in every domain, anytime, anywhere for a purposeful, fulfilling life. In other words, we need to live the pioneering spirit, beyond learning for grades, to learning for mastery, beyond in school, to learning throughout life, and beyond learning for work, to learning for life".[16]

Does skill-focused translate to higher returns to education? At least one study appears to suggest so. Sakellariou (2003), in his estimates of the rates of return in formal versus technical/vocational education in Singapore, found higher returns to vocational/technical education (which provided industry/job specific training) as compared to formal education because of better match of skills acquired in school and the industry.

The ASPIRE's recommendations were seen favourably by some commentators as a blueprint in support of industry — focused and practice-oriented curriculum, to develop the persons' capacity to solve unseen problems rather than solve known problems. *The Straits Times* reporter, Sandra Davie writes, "A key new feature is the place-and-train programme, modelled after the Swiss and German apprenticeship schemes. After leaving the ITE and polytechnics, graduates can undergo structured on-the-job training in the workplace which will complement what they learnt in school."[17] The question, as the report notes, is not about whether to acquire a degree to excel, but rather how best to achieve excellence.

4.4 Impact of ASPIRE Report on Private Education Sector

What is the impact of the ASPIRE report and its follow-up actions on the private education sector? Would the recommendations result in slower growth in the private education sector?

The government's initiatives may sway the decision of certain individuals from acquiring a diploma or a degree that is not directly related to their careers. Students are provided with more options to upgrade their skills. Polytechnic and ITE students are offered opportunities to integrate study and work under the *"Earn and Learn"* scheme (launched in March 2015) to strengthen and upgrade students' skills by matching students to suitable employers to provide on-the-job training and mentorship. The

Continuing Education and Training (CET) programme has similarly initiated a number of strategies to refresh and deepen skills of ITE and polytechnic graduates through involvement of the employers, Workforce Skills Qualifications (WSQ) and MOE.

School career counsellors supplement the initiatives by spending hours with ITE and polytechnic students from Year 1 onward to immerse students with industry and occupational knowledge through close links with industrial professionals. The ultimate goal of the *"Education and Career Guidance"* scheme is to help students develop the necessary skills to make their career choices.

The SkillsFuture scheme, an initiative launched in February 2015, aims to shift individuals' focus on paper chase to mastery of skills. Singaporeans aged 25 years old and above are to be given up to S$500 credit to attend courses that focus on skills training and development. A centralised website has been set up to help Singaporeans identify a wide variety of courses in information and technology, communications, accounting, finance, social services and others. Although Singaporeans can utilise the credit to enrol in programmes offered by private education providers, the fact that there are alternatives or substitutes to upgrade skills relevant to the industry serves to remind the PEIs that they are competing with more players in the already intensely competitive education market.

However, an individual's decision to sustain his or her working life in a particular profession or discipline is subject to a host of factors. Good starting pay, job satisfaction, job recognition, room for personal growth, desire for career switch and increments in monetary benefit are some of the considerations. The shift away from Science, Technology, Engineering and Maths (STEM) studies towards business and humanities is reflective of individuals' preference for jobs that come with perceived satisfaction, recognition and higher remuneration at least over the longer term. Prime Minister Lee Hsien Loong, in his visit to California in February 2016, raised a significant concern with regard to the engineering profession in Singapore.

In Silicon Valley where the Prime Minister visited, engineers are valued members of the organisation, and offered challenging and exciting things to do. In the case of Singapore, in the words of Lee, people see engineering "as a support function — my computer is broken, call an engineer and fix it. That's a different conception, and we really need to reposition our conception of what engineering is about, and how important engineering is to us".[18] Engineering related jobs in Singapore were largely confined to behind-the-scene roles. Moreover, despite higher starting salary for engineers as compared to many others, engineers were concerned about the *increments*. "Some with a few years of experience said their annual increase can be as little as S$100". Hence, "people tend to shun the profession for other fields like banking as they perceive it to be dull, not as high paying in the long run and involving work that gets their hands dirty".[19] The Prime Minister has rightly pointed out the need to rethink what engineering means to Singapore at least to try to get some of the Singaporean engineers abroad to return home.[20] Changing the mind-set with regard to what engineers mean to Singapore will take time. Before this happens, engineers will consider switching their careers to the financial, banking and retail sectors that require the individuals to pursue a degree qualification that commensurates with the new career. An article in *The Straits Times* reported the phenomenon. A graduate from NTU with a degree in mechanical engineering was quoted as saying. "The work (first job at a local engineering firm) was monotonous, the pay of my seniors seemed stagnant and they had limited career progression options…. About a third of my friends who studied engineering ended up doing something completely different." He left after five months, and has since become a personal banker.[21] The issue of job availability is another consideration. The difficulty faced by an engineering-trained person to find a job that matches his or her specialised qualification may simply compel the person to work as a business executives or a retail manager. Indeed, when market is tight or as the sector undergoes a downturn in the business cycle, students with specialised qualification may struggle to secure or hold on to the jobs that are relevant to their skills.

It should also be noted that the Singapore education system that emphasises streaming at Primary 4 (up from Primary 3 in 1992) and Primary 6 has the unintended effect of classifying individuals as high achievers and low achievers thereby adversely affecting the status and standing of the individuals. Students are admitted to multiple pathways such as Express, Normal (Academic) and Normal (Technical), depending on their academic results, reflecting the three-tier education model consisting of universities, polytechnics and ITE. Gopinathan (2015: 98), quoting Oakes (1985) study on the 'social properties of tracking' was spot on in that the system has failed miserably in recognising the psychological inclination, particularly the tendency for students to compare with peers, and feel unhappy over the perceived lower status and labelling as slow learners and under achievers.

It is well known that inequity between knowledge workers with intellectual capacity and administrative and production workers is a growing concern, leading many working professionals to associate the acquisition of a formal qualification such as an undergraduate or postgraduate certificate as necessary to fit into the demands of the knowledge-based economy. The private education sector provides educational opportunities to them to further their education and training and to those who might have been previously missed by the educational system for one reason or another. At the same time, the inflow of skilled migrants who command high salaries can potentially widen income and wealth inequality and contribute to social exclusion and discontentment among the locals who feel the power of education in bridging the socio-economic gap. The notion that one can get rich without a degree may fall on deaf ears when their peers with higher educational qualifications are perceived to enjoy a higher standard of living.

The ASPIRE committee acknowledges that changing the mind-set of students and parents "to go beyond qualifications, to go beyond the classroom, to go beyond narrow definition of success" is a tall order, and will take many years, if at all, to make the society change. It is worth quoting the concern at length.

"Some may say that these are lofty goals, high ideals, but how will we actually implement them?.... It is not an easy task. It will not happen overnight. It will take many years, but the journey of a thousand miles begins with a single step. ASPIRE is that step….

This is the beginning, but it is just that — only the beginning…

It is like turning a ship. You turn the ship's wheel, the gears engage. You are fighting against the water resistance. The ship slowly starts to move, and the initial move takes an awful lot of effort. But then it gains momentum and you start to pick up speed, and then you are full steam ahead. This is what the ASPIRE effort is like.

We are contemplating the horizon, trying to figure out what is to come, anticipating as best we can, coming up with solutions and strategies, and then doing it together in a concerted effort….."[22]

At least in the next few years to come, the PEIs will continue to play an important role to provide the upgrading route to a diploma and degree qualification not only to meet the aspiration of domestic students but the aspiration of international students such as those from Mainland China.

4.5 Inflow of Chinese Students to PEIs

The aspirations of Chinese students and the impact on the demand for private education in Singapore merit some discussions. Students from China after all constitute a large proportion of international students in Singapore PEIs.

Like the case of Singapore, limited number of places in universities in China means that not all students who wish to further their academic studies are able to secure a place. Surely, the Chinese government has expanded the higher education institutions, which resulted in an increase in student enrolments from 1.43 million in 1996 to 5.43 million 2002. But the expansion is not enough to meet the demand because of the country's large size in population. The absolute number of students who want to enter higher education remains huge and can be attributed to students' strong aspirations to enhance their academic and economic standings. "To study to become a mandarin," noted Huo (1993: 22) is "the most deeply entrenched and typical educational concept in China".[23]

The aspiration to succeed in education extends to parents and relatives. The one-child policy, which was implemented in 1979 and scrapped in January 2016, exacerbated the situation as many parents wanted the best education for their single children to learn employable skills and gain entrance to higher education institutions. Parents in China pushed their children to work hard, offering a favourable home atmosphere for their children to study at home after school. Parents transmitted high aspirations to their children, expecting their children to excel in life and realise their own unfulfilled dreams. To gain entry to the university, some students chose to repeat the entrance examination to achieve better marks and grades than the previous attempt. Others might simply choose to study abroad.

Advancements in technology have permitted virtual integration of communication with the outside world through drama serials and movies from Hollywood, among others. The relatively low income per capita in China may be misleading as deterrence to securing paper qualifications outside of Mainland China. Wide disparity in income levels exist in China with increasing number of families who are able to afford the fees of external universities. China's one-child policy further allows and encourages families to concentrate their financial resources on single children. Many have gathered information about learning and living in Singapore, Hong Kong, Taiwan, Australia, United Kingdom and the United States from friends and relatives and decided to venture abroad for further studies. From 1978 to 1999, as Li and Bray (2007: 797) quoted from official statistics, the number of students studying abroad was reported at 320,000. By 2006, over 450,000 Chinese students were studying overseas (Ennew and Yang, 2009: 23). Table 4.1 shows that Chinese students represent a significant percentage of international students in key international student destinations — United States, United Kingdom, Canada and Australia. Chinese students represented one-third of the total international student population in Australia and Canada.

According to the Singapore population census of 2010, foreign-born resident population of Singapore numbered 859,787 persons of which

Table 4.1: Chinese higher education students in key destinations.

Destination	Chinese as a % of all international
United States	28.7
United Kingdom	16.7
Australia	34.3
Canada	34.4

Source: OCED (2015).

68.3% were Chinese, 17.6% were Indians and 4.3% per Malays. Among the 587,235 Chinese residents, 57.6% came from Malaysia, 29.7% from China and 7.3% from Indonesia (Nasir and Turner, 2014: 26). More than 400,000 Chinese from Mainland China have settled in Singapore since the 1990s, which coincided with the Singapore government's decision to offer scholarships to students from China to enrol in public universities "on the condition that they worked in Singapore for at least 6 years after graduating" (Liu, 2014: 1227–1228).[24]

The actual number of Mainland Chinese *students* in Singapore is however unknown. Zhao (2016: 181) cited a report published in *The Straits Times*, which put the figure at 36,000. Zhao also mentioned estimates by Chinese scholars who put the figure at 50,000 in 2012, of which over 10,000 were studying in higher education institutions such as the universities and polytechnics, over 10,000 were admitted to Singapore's public primary and secondary schools and the remaining were studying in private schools. One thing for sure is that Chinese students formed the largest cluster of international students in Singapore (Tsang, 2001; Rajaram and Bordia, 2011). In a typical full-time course offered by the PEI, students from China can easily account for more than 50% of the class size.

Cultural similarity is one of the reasons for Singapore's popularity among the Chinese. With ethnic Chinese representing three-quarters of Singapore's population, Singapore is often regarded as having a predominantly Chinese culture. The Speak Mandarin Campaign, which was launched in 1979, and the introduction of Special Assistance Plan (SAP) schools in 1979 where Mandarin was taught at a higher level further enhanced the Chineseness image of Singapore. Mandarin is a commonly spoken language in public places in Singapore, which makes it easier for the Chinese students to blend into the Singapore society. In this respect, Singapore differs from Hong Kong, which is another popular destination among the Chinese students in the sense that Cantonese, and not Mandarin, is the common 'Chinese' language spoken there.

Furthermore, in the late 1980s, the Singapore government initiated the process of formulating the 'Shared Values', culminating in the publication of the White Paper on Shared Values in 1991. The Shared Values — (1) placing the nation before community and society above self,

(2) to treat the family as the basic unit of society, (3) to regard and community support for the individual, (4) to see the importance of consensus instead of contention, and (5) to maintain racial and religious harmony — are strikingly similar with Confucian ethics, which stresses the importance of the group over the individual and emphasises the importance of consensus (Chua, 1995; Lu, 1998). The government's support for the communitarian ideology has reflected in its public policies, including education policies through the national education curriculum (Tan, 2012, 2013). Considering Geert Hofstede (1980, 1984) cultural dimension, one can hypothesise the similarity in culture between China and Singapore. Both countries are categorised as high in power distance (accept inequalities amongst people) and long-term orientation (pragmatic culture) and low in individualism (means high in collectivist culture), uncertainty avoidance (adherence to rules and regulation) and indulgence (strong tendency for pessimism and cynicism). Both countries obtain a close to the middle score for the masculinity dimension.[25]

Similarity in culture helps to lower the stress level for students who studied abroad. Pan *et al.* (2007) considered the stress level of Chinese students in Australia and Hong Kong, and found the stress level to be higher among the Chinese in Australia as compared to Chinese in Hong Kong due to wider cultural distance between China and Australia. However, less stressful does not imply no-stress. Studying in a new environment and adapting to the academic challenges such as the frequent use of English in classes can result in stress regardless of the learning destination.[26]

Zhao (2016: 182) cited two surveys — conducted by MyCOS and China Education Online — which provided some insights into the reasons for Chinese students to further their education in Singapore. The study by MyCOS found that 46.7% of the respondents were attracted by Singapore's quality education, 23.3% by the affordability education, 6.6% by the convenience of immigration, and 6.7% considered open environment and easy application procedure as the main reasons. China Education Online reported 10 competitive advantages that made Singapore the most preferred destination for education among the Chinese, including 'world-class universities with high education quality assurance', 'safe environment', 'western education system', 'bilingual education', 'lower tuition fee and living cost' as compared to studying in the United Kingdom, Australia and the United States, 'IELTS and TOEFL are not necessarily required', 'the best pathway to pursue further study in the West', 'high possibility to get Visa', 'good job prospects in Singapore', and 'Singapore's welcoming immigration policies'.

Gaining entry into a Singapore school requires the applicants to meet both academic and language requirements. For illustration purpose, consider the case of Singapore Institute of Management Global Education (SIMGE). To gain entry into the diploma programmes at SIMGE (in Banking and Finance, Accountancy, Management Studies), Chinese students are required to pass the English Placement Test at Advanced Level administered by SIMGE or obtain IELTS score of 5.5 or equivalent. Students who do not meet the language requirement are recommended to read the Certificate in English Language Upper-Intermediate (Level 5) programme offered by SIMGE (Table 4.2).

Students do not necessarily have to successfully complete the National College Entrance Examination (or *gaokao*) to gain entry into the diploma programmes. This incentivises students from Mainland China to obtain a diploma and degree qualification in Singapore while avoiding the *gaokao*. As can be seen from Table 4.2, students who have completed Year 3 of the Senior Higher School education with an average score of 70% or better are able to gain admission into the Diploma in International Business and Diploma in Management Studies programmes. Alternatively, students who scored an average of 60% in *gaokao* are eligible for entry into the programmes. Students who failed to meet the academic entry requirements are required to sign up for the 6-month Management Foundation Studies programme. Chinese students who have completed Year 2 (or Grade 11) Senior High School education with an average score of 70% or better are eligible to enrol into the foundation programme.

SIMGE's university partners demand a higher level of entry requirements. University of Wollongong's Bachelor of Science programme with major in Psychology requires students to obtain an overall IELTS score of 6.5 with no band less than 6.0 whereas the Computer Science programme offered by the same university requires an overall IELTS score of 6.0 with no band less than 6.0. The university imposes the same requirements to students who are admitted to study the programmes in Australia.

Table 4.2:   Admission criteria for Chinese students at SIMGE (selected diploma and undergraduate programmes).

Programme	Language requirements	Academic requirements
SIM, Singapore		
Diploma in Accounting	• TOEFL 550 with TWE 4.0 (paper based) or 79 (IBT); IELTS 5.5; SAT1 score of at least 550 (critical reading and writing); Pearson Test score of at least 40/100; Pass SIM English Placement Test at Advanced Level	• Senior High School Leaving Certificate (Year 3 Semesters 1 and 2) with average score of 70% or better; credit pass in Mathematics OR • National College Entrance Examination (*gaokao*) of 60% or better; credit pass in Mathematics
Diploma in Banking and Finance		
Diploma in International Business	• Students who do not meet the above requirement may be recommended to take up a Certificate in English Language Upper-Intermediate (Level 5) CEL programme	• Senior High School Leaving Certificate (Year 3 Semesters 1 and 2) with average score of 70% or better OR • National College Entrance Examination (*gaokao*) of 60% or better
Diploma in Management Studies		
Management Foundation Studies		• Senior High School Leaving Certificate (Year 3 Semesters 1 and 2) with average score of 60% or better OR • Senior High School Year 2 (Semesters 1 and 2) with average score of 70% or better OR • National College Entrance Examination (*gaokao*) of 50% or better • Additional requirements for progression to Diploma in Accounting and Diploma in Banking and Finance — credit pass in Mathematics subject at Senior High School Leaving Certificate or *gaokao*

(Continued)

Table 4.2: *(Continued)*

Programme	Language requirements	Academic requirements
RMIT University, Australia		
Bachelor of Business (Accountancy, Economics and Finance, Logistics and Supply Chain Management, Management, Marketing)	TOEFL 580 with TWE 4.5 (paper based) or 92 (IBT) (minimum 20 in all sections); IELTS 6.5 (with no band less than 6.0); Pearson Test of English (Academic) 58 (with no band less than 50); Advanced CAE at Grade B (no band less than Good)	Senior Middle 3: 75% overall average score for all subjects undertaken
Bachelor of Communication (Professional Communication)		Senior Middle 3:80% overall average score for all subjects undertaken
University of Wollongong, Australia		
Bachelor of Computer Science (Digitals Systems Security, Multimedia and Game Development)	Overall IELTS 6.0 (with no band less than 6.0) or its equivalent	Senior High School Leaving Certificate (Year 3 Semesters 1 and 2); Average of 75% in best four academic subjects, excluding Politics and Physical Education
Bachelor of Science (Psychology)	Overall IELTS 6.5 (with no band less than 6.0) or its equivalent	
University of Birmingham, United Kingdom		
Bachelor of Science (Hons) (Business Management, Business Management with Communications, International Business)	• IELTS 6.5 (with no band less than 6.0); Pearson Test of English (Academic) 59 in all four skills OR • Successful completion of a SIM or a polytechnic diploma	Students with international qualifications are expected to do the SIM Diploma in Accounting/SIM Diploma in Banking and Finance/ SIM Diploma in International Business/SIM Diploma in Management Studies first (with average B grades) after which they can progress to do a 2-year BSc programme. All other qualifications will be considered on a case-by-case basis.

(Continued)

Table 4.2: *(Continued)*

Programme	Language requirements	Academic requirements
University of London (LSE and Political Science) United Kingdom		
Bachelor of Science (Hons) (Accounting and Finance, Banking and Finance, Business and Management, Economics, Economics and Finance, Economics and Management, Economics and Politics, Information Systems and Management, International Relations, Mathematics and Economics)	TOEFL 87 (IBT) with at least 21 in both reading and writing skills sub-tests and at least 19 in both speaking and listening subtests; IELTS 6.0 (with no band less than 5.5); Pearson Test of English (Academic) score of at least 54 with at least 54 in both reading and writing elements	National College Entrance Examination (*gaokao*) that meets China university tier-3 institution in the year that it was taken. Mathematics at Senior High School Year 12 must be grade C (minimum 60%).
University of Buffalo, United States		
Bachelor of Arts (Communication, Economics, International Trade, Psychology, Sociology)	TOEFL 550 (paper based) or 79 (IBT); IELTS 6.5 (with no band less than 6.0); PTE Academic 55 (with no subsection score below 50); SAT 1 Critical Reading 500; ACT (English and Reading sections) 20	Most recent 3 years of high school grades with a minimum average of 80%.
Bachelor of Science (Business Administration)		

Source: *2016 International Student Prospectus*, SIMGE, Singapore (http://www.simge.edu.sg; extracted on 19 January 2016).

Comparatively speaking, the National University of Singapore (NUS) requires students to obtain an overall IELTS score of 6.5 with 6.5 in reading and writing components. NTU requires an overall IELTS score of 6.0.

There are variances in the academic requirements for the undergraduate programmes. The University of London admits Chinese students who can gain admission to a tier-3 university in China based on their performance at the National College Entrance Examination. The university imposes an additional requirement on Mathematics due to the nature of its programme (the programme consists of subjects that require strong mathematical knowledge). The University of Buffalo, United States, requires applicants to possess senior high school score, averaging 80% and above whereas RMIT, Australia looks for applications with a senior high school overall average score of 75% and above for its business programmes. NTU welcomes applicants who have *gaokao* score that meets or above the *Tier 1 cut-off score* of the province to apply to the university. At NTU, students who have yet to sit for *gaokao* with good passes in Year 10 and Year 11 are welcomed to apply as well.

Essentially, as far as SIMGE is concerned, students who have completed Year 3 of the Senior High School (or 12 years of formal education) with an average score of 70% or better have the option to enter SIMGE to enrol into one of the diploma programmes. An overall average score of 75% and above permits the students to enrol into one of the undergraduate programmes.

Acquiring higher education goes beyond the objective of satisfying physical needs. As discussed in this chapter, Singaporeans as well as Mainland Chinese sign up for the diplomas and degrees courses through the PEIs to bring them status, honour, and prestige in a materialistic culture that prevails in both countries. The materialistic culture is here to stay which translates to strong demand for higher education. This bodes well for the future prospects and outlook of the education sector, including Singapore's private education sector.

Chapter 5

External Degree Programme

5.1 Introduction

Partnering a foreign university is a common strategy of the private education institutions (PEIs). The partnership provides a pathway for PEI students to further their education after completing the diploma courses. Many students, particularly international students, do not enrol into the PEI course merely to obtain a diploma. They use the diploma to gain admission to an external degree programme offered by a PEI partnered university. PEI–University partnership does not imply co-ownership of either entity. The relationship is contractual or temporary in nature. Teaching may be partially or fully outsourced to the PEI. As part of the agreement, the PEI pays royalty to the degree awarding institution (the university partner).

The university partners are key stakeholders of the PEI and therefore merit some attention in this study. They have helped to increase the supply of degree courses in Singapore, providing local students who have missed out a place at the local university an education pathway to enrol into a variety of academic courses (in business, hospitality, nursing, life sciences, engineering, computer science, and others), stemming the outflow of Singaporeans to other countries to further their education, and establishing Singapore as a major learning destination for international students.[1]

This chapter begins with an overview of the higher education sector in Singapore before discussing the types of external degree programmes in PEIs and some of the challenges of transnational partnerships.

5.2 Governance in Public Universities in Singapore

National University of Singapore (NUS) and Nanyang Technological University (NTU) were traditionally structured as statutory boards. The cabinet members appointed the Vice-Chancellors and the University Councils (with representations from the private and public sectors appointed by the government) to set policies and make key strategic decisions. Faculty/administrative staff members were government employees, with salary structure pegged to the civil service system. Government approval was required for new programmes, and clearance of course contents in which 30% or more of the contents were new. Hiring, firing, and salary decisions were not independent of the Ministry of Education, and it was generally difficult for the management and university leadership to replace unproductive staff and reward productive staff. "On more than one occasion," Kevin Tan (2015: 55) writes, "Tony Tan (former Deputy Prime Minister) had voiced his frustration in being unable to get NUS and NTU to change and adopt new initiatives because of their bureaucratic structures. Both these institutions were constituted as statutory boards but functioned like very large government departments reporting directly to the Ministry of Education".

Decentralisation of public universities was experimented with the Singapore Management University (SMU) in 2000. The idea behind constituting SMU as a privately run university was to take it outside the direct control of the Ministry to "enable the new university to move more quickly and adopt bold initiatives and programmes without a constant need to refer back to the Ministry" (Tan, 2015: 55). The results have been encouraging. Celebrating the 15th Anniversary of SMU in August 2014, its President Arnoud De Meyer proudly highlighted the achievements of SMU, including high quality research contributions from the Schools that effectively placed the University and Singapore on the map of global rankings (the School of Economics, for example, was ranked 1st in Asia and 57th in the World by Tilburg University Top 100 World Economics

School Research Rankings).[2] In 2000, the University Governance and Funding Review recommended granting NUS and NTU greater operational autonomy with regards to staff remuneration. Six years later, the government accepted the recommendations of the Steering Committee of University Autonomy, Governance and Funding Review (UAGF) to corporatize NUS and NTU as non-for-profit corporations, with limited guarantee. Goh Chor Boon and Tan Wee Hin describe the cause and consequence of corporatization this way:

> "...to make Singapore's universities more innovative and entrepreneurial to meet the demands of the knowledge-based economy, the Ministry of Education decided to allow NUS and NTU to be corporatized in 2006...Corporatization would provide the universities with the flexibility to recruit world-class talent; manage their budgets; and build a stronger sense of loyalty and ownership among students, staff, and alumni. NUS and NTU are expected to reach high international standards in both teaching the research and even become models for other regional universities to emulate. An underlying objective is to broad the coverage of various disciplines and to foster the emergence of cross-disciplinary teaching and research" (Goh and Tan, 2008: 158).

Corporatization has enabled the universities to introduce programmes relatively quicker than in the past. Government approval is no longer required for introduction of new programmes and changing the course contents (Mukherjee and Wong, 2011: 140). The extent of government control has also been more relaxed on human resource matters. As Wong Sek Man, then Acting Dean of the Science Faulty, NUS said, with corporatization, ".... we have more discretion in hiring and firing matters. We can make quicker decisions in new appointments with the approval from the Provost instead of seeking the approval from the Ministry of Education (MOE)" (Mok, 2010: 431). This was in contrary to the past where hiring, firing and salary adjustments were not independent of the Ministry of Education, "making it difficult for management and university leadership to replace unproductive staff and reward productive staff" (Mukherjee and Wong, 2011: 140). But Wong added, ".... the NUS senior management still follows the government's rule and regulations and only slow transformation has been experienced. Being deans and associate deans, I have not experienced major changes, let alone the ordinary faculty members" (Mok, 2010: 431).

On matters of national interest, the Singapore government retains the power to allocate scarce resources of the universities in the manner that it sees fit. Tan Thiam Soon, in his capacity as the Provost of the NUS, recounted a remarkable episode that offered a glimpse of the NUS–government relations. As Tan recalled, the Singapore MOE wanted NUS to increase the undergraduate intakes to meet the pressing demands for undergraduate education from Singapore citizens. NUS preferred to expand the postgraduate intakes to make NUS more competitive. Confronted with the tension, NUS finally gave in and followed the admissions plan set out by the MOE. To Tan, "it's NUS obligation to follow the government policy and we are not allowed to move away from the national plan even though we want to move" (Mok, 2010: 431). The episode reminds us that the university has to serve the national interest of Singapore even though the university has been granted the autonomous status.

To accommodate the rising aspiration of and demand from students for higher education qualification, more universities are being setup. As the number of universities increases, students are offered with more choices of courses as well as more places to further their studies. When the Singapore University of Technology & Design (SUTD) opened in 2012, it received more than 4,000 applications and admitted only 340. In May 2015, the university received about 2,500 applications and it admitted 386 students.[3] A year later, it was reported that the university received 3,055 applications and admitted 467 students.[4] The government has planned to raise the number of places at public institutions to 16,000 by 2020, eventually attaining a Cohort Participation Rate (CPR) of 40%. This means that four in 10 students from each Primary One cohort obtains a place in one of Singapore's public universities.

The rise in the number of places in public universities will inevitably make it tougher for the PEIs to recruit students, especially local students from the polytechnics. It seems that the impact has already been felt. In 2014, Singapore Institute of Management Global Education (SIMGE) reported a drop in the number of local students for the first time in a decade — from 20,000 locals out of a total of 23,000 enrolled in 2013 to 18,000 local students out of a total of 21,500 students enrolled in 2014.[5] The recognition of SIM University (UniSIM) by the government as the sixth autonomous university further affects the profitability of the PEIs. Already, UniSIM is a popular pick among working adults (the degree courses are recognised by the industry and 55% of the tuition fees for Singaporeans are subsidised by the MOE).[6] Surely, the recognition would have some influence on students' minds when they are deciding whether to pursue a degree at UniSIM or the PEIs.

5.3 PEI–University Partnership

The higher education landscape in Singapore is *still* characterised by excess demand for post-secondary education in relation to the number of places available at public universities. Admission to the local public universities remains stringent and a privilege that not many are able to enjoy in their lifetime. The PEIs fill the gap by offering alternatives to individuals who have missed out the opportunity to acquire a higher education qualification earlier in their life. International students, who are not able to enrol into programmes offered by one of the autonomous universities in Singapore, are also keen to pursue the external degree programmes with the PEIs (Bhati and Anderson, 2012; Bhati, Lee, and Kairon, 2014).

Table 5.1 shows the list of external degree programmes of university partners of three PEIs in Singapore — Kaplan Singapore, SIMGE and PSB Academy. As can be seen, the partners are established and reputable universities from the United Kingdom (such as Warwick University, Loughborough University, University of College Dublin and Birmingham University), Australia (such as University of Sydney, University of Wollongong and University of Western Australia). Kaplan Singapore has eight partners. Seven of them are from the United Kingdom, and one from Australia. SIMGE has a total of 11 partners, three of which are from Australia, seven from the United Kingdom and one from the United States. PSB Academy has ten university partners of which four are from Australia and the remaining six are from the United Kingdom. There is a long list of courses to choose from but most of them are in

Table 5.1:   Selected PEIs and their university partners.

Name of University Partner	Country	Programmes (number of programmes with the university partner in parentheses)
Kaplan Singapore		
Murdoch University	Australia	Single and double major undergraduate programmes in a wage range of disciplines, including Psychology, Human Resource Management, Communications and Media Studies, Management, Marketing, Business Information System, Cyber Forensics, Information Security (77)
Birmingham University	United Kingdom	Undergraduate programmes in Business Administration, International Business, International Finance and International Marketing (4)
Northumbria University	United Kingdom	Undergraduate programmes in various fields including Mass Communication, Hospitality and Tourism Management and Business with majors in Law, Marketing, Economics, Financial Management, Human Resource Management, International Management and Logistics and Supply Chain Management (14)
Royal Holloway, University of London	United Kingdom	B.Sc (Hons) programmes in Management, Management with Accounting, Management with International Business and Management with Marketing (4)
University of College Dublin	United Kingdom	Bachelor of Business Studies (Hons) programmes in Information Management, Banking and Wealth Management, Business with Law, Finance, Human Resource Management, Logistics and Supply Chain Management, Marketing and Management (8)
University of Essex	United Kingdom	B.Sc (Hons) programmes in Accountancy, Banking and Finance, Financial Management, Accounting and Finance and Marketing and Management (5)
University of Portsmouth	United Kingdom	Bachelor of Arts (Honours) Accountancy and Financial Management
University of Bedfordshire	United Kingdom	Master of Business Administration (1)

(Continued)

Table 5.1: (*Continued*)

Name of University Partner	Country	Programmes (number of programmes with the university partner in parentheses)
SIMGE		
RMIT University	Australia	Undergraduate programmes in Communications, Accounting, Economics, Finance, Logistics and Supply Chain Management, Management, Marketing, Aviation and Construction Management (9)
University of Wollongong	Australia	Undergraduate programmes in Psychology, Information Systems, Information Technology and Computer Sciences with majors in Digital Systems Security and Multimedia and Game Development (5)
University of Sydney	Australia	Undergraduate programmes in Nursing (2)
University of London, International Programmes	United Kingdom	B.Sc (Hons) programmes in various fields, including Economics, Political Sciences, Accounting, Banking, Finance, Computing and Information Systems (14)[a]
University of Sheffield	United Kingdom	B.A. (Hons) in Accounting and Financial Management (1)
University of Birmingham	United Kingdom	Postgraduate programmes in Business Administration and International Business (2) Undergraduate programmes in Business Management and International Business (4)
University of Stirling	United Kingdom	B.A. (Hons) programmes in Retail Marketing and Sports Studies and Marketing (2)
University of Manchester	United Kingdom	B.Sc (Hons) programme in Management (1)
University of Southampton	United Kingdom	B.Sc (Hons) programme in Marketing (1)
University of Warwick	United Kingdom	M.Sc programmes in Engineering Business Management and Supply Chain and Logistics Management (2)[b]
University at Buffalo, the State University of New York	United States	Single and double major B.A and B.Sc programmes in Communications, Economics, Sociology, Psychology, Business Administration and International Trade (14)

(*Continued*)

Table 5.1: (*Continued*)

Name of University Partner	Country	Programmes (number of programmes with the university partner in parentheses)
PSB Academy		
University of Wollongong	Australia	Undergraduate programmes in Management, Marketing, Finance and Supply Chain Management (4)
University of Newcastle	Australia	Undergraduate business and communications programmes with majors in Marketing and Management, Marketing and Tourism, Accounting, Public Relations and Journalism; Undergraduate IT and engineering programmes in Information Technology, Electrical Engineering and Mechanical Engineering; undergraduate programme in Environmental and Occupational Health and Safety (8) Master of Business Administration (1)
University of Western Australia	Australia	B.A. in Communication Studies (1)
La Trobe University	Australia	Undergraduate programmes in Biomedical Science, Molecular Biology and Pharmaceutical Science (3)
Coventry University	United Kingdom	B.Sc (Hons) in Computer Science; double degree undergraduate programmes in business in the fields of Advertising, Marketing, Accounting, Business and Banking and engineering (Electronic and Electrical Engineering) (7)
Edinburgh Napier University	United Kingdom	Double major undergraduate programmes in the fields of Festival and Event Management, Marketing Management, Hospitality Management, Tourism Management, Human Resource Management, as well as Science Sports and Exercise Science (7) Postgraduate programmes in International Business, Entrepreneurship, Human Resource Management, Marketing and Sales (5)
United of London, International Programmes	United Kingdom	B.Sc (Hons) programmes in Accounting and Finance, Banking and Finance, and Business and Management (3)

(*Continued*)

Table 5.1:   (*Continued*)

Name of University Partner	Country	Programmes (number of programmes with the university partner in parentheses)
Loughborough University	United Kingdom	B.Sc (Hons) programmes in Business Studies with majors in Banking and Finance and Human Resource Management (3)
University of Nottingham	United Kingdom	Postgraduate programmes in Business Administration and Finance (2)
University of Hull	United Kingdom	Postgraduate programmes in Business Administration and Economics (2)

Notes: Information is correct as on 13 March 2015. Figures in the parentheses represent the number of courses offered by the university partner through the PEI.

[a]Also offered UOL's Foundation and Diploma programmes.

[b]Also offered University of Warwick's postgraduate awards in Engineering Business Management and Supply Chain and Logistics Management.

Source: Kaplan (http://www.kaplan.edu.sg); SIMGE (http://www.simge.edu.sg); PSB Academy (http://www.psb-academy.edu.sg).

the fields of business. Business Administration, Marketing, Finance, Accounting, Human Resource Management and Supply Chain Management are popular university courses because they open doors to more careers. IT courses in Cyber Forensic, Information System, Computer Sciences and Multimedia are also popular with PEIs and students. Due to higher capital outlay and strict safety and floor capacity requirements, engineering courses are fewer in numbers. They are mainly restricted to land-based PEIs (such as PSB Academy) which have the capacity to house laboratories and physical equipment.

Table 5.2 shows the number of students enrolled in higher education institutions in Singapore. External degree (transnational) programmes attracted 33% of the total student population, exceeding the number of students enrolled in public universities (NUS, NTU, and SMU). The Ministry of Education (2012) reported that 46% of the 25–29 years old possessed degrees, with about half of them graduated from the public universities and the remaining half obtained their degrees from foreign universities in Singapore and abroad.

Table 5.2: Students in higher education institutions in Singapore.

	Number of students	Percentage
Polytechnics	56,048	23
Local universities (NUS, NTU, SMU)	41,628	17
Private institutions' own programmes	26,500	11
Institute of Technical Education	19,207	8
National Institute of Education	2,282	1
All domestic providers	145,665	59
Transnational programmes	80,200	33
Singaporean students enrolled overseas	19,371	8
Total	245,236	100

Source: Ziguras and Gribble (2015: 251, Table 2).

There are several reasons why external degree programmes are popular among students and parents, both locally and abroad.[7]

Shorter programme duration — Generally speaking, an external degree programme can be completed within a shorter time frame as compared to a similar programme in the public universities. A local student with 'O' level qualification may begin his post-secondary education journey by enrolling into a PEI diploma course. Upon graduation — after a year of study — the student is eligible to gain admission into Year 1 of a typical 3-year external undergraduate programme. Because the external degree programme can be completed in two calender years in some of the PEIs, the entire journey will take about 3 years (1 year to complete the diploma and 2 years to obtain the undergraduate degree). On the contrary, one typically has to obtain good 'A' level results (a 2-year programme) to gain entry into the public university in Singapore. With additional 3–4 years of study at the undergraduate level, the student spends at least 5 years of post-secondary education to obtain an undergraduate qualification, as compared to 3 years through the private education route.[8]

Choice of study — Scarcity of places at the public universities in Singapore means that students may fail to secure a place in the universities to study the programme of their choice. For example, a student who had applied to read Business Administration at NUS might have failed to secure a place but instead was offered to read a programme in Real Estate. In the private education sector where more courses especially in business fields are available, the student stands a better chance to gain admission to an external degree programme in Business Administration. The student can do so without travelling abroad for studies. In sum, the student is able to embark on a programme with a PEI that meets his or her interest rather than reading a programme in a public university that does not interest him or her.

Quality — It is fair to say that a majority of the current batch of PEI university partners are committed to academic excellence.

University College Dublin (UCD), which partners Kaplan Singapore in offering the Bachelor of Business Studies (Hons) programmes in Information Management, Banking and Wealth Management, Business with Law, Finance, Human Resource Management, Logistics and Supply Chain Management, Marketing and Management, is Ireland's largest university and has a global reputation for excellence in undergraduate courses, postgraduate master's and PhD studies. "It is ranked among the *Top 1% of universities worldwide* (Times Higher Education World University Ranking 2013–2014), has over two decades of partnership with Kaplan, producing over 6,500 graduates and it's School of Business holds the prestigious *Triple Crown accreditations* from EQUIS, AACSB and AMBA".[9]

SIMGE partners a number of reputable universities. The University of Manchester is part of the prestigious Russell Group of Universities. "The University is highly respected among academic and business communities — a reputation that its graduates also enjoy…. Since 2005, the University has risen from 53rd to 38th in the world and 7th in Europe in the influential Academic Ranking of World Universities Survey conducted by Shanghai Jiao Tong University 2014 — confirming us as a progressive and world-class teaching and research institution".[10] Another SIMGE United Kingdom university partner, the University of Birmingham, offers the undergraduate and postgraduate programmes in business administration and international business. The university, as noted on

SIMGE's website, "has established an international reputation for excellence, with eight Nobel Prize winners among its faculty and alumni…. Birmingham Business School MBA programme is listed within the FT Global MBA top 100 in 2015, with a position of 26th in Europe and 13th in the UK out of all Business and Management institutions in the rankings".[11]

SIMGE lists the following as the unique selling points for the University of Warwick, which offers the MSc programme in Engineering Business Management and Supply Chain and Logistics Management in partnership with SIMGE.

- Warwick has consistently maintained its position in the top 10 of United Kingdom league tables, offering courses with high academic content that are stimulating and challenging.
- University of the Year 2015 in *The Times* and *The Sunday Times* Good University Guide.
- Warwick has been placed 7th in the latest Research Excellence Framework rankings,[12] with 87% of the University's Research activity ranked as 'world leading' or 'internationally excellent'.[13]

PSB Academy selects the university partners based on their academic reputation, accreditations and ranking. Quality university programmes that strengthen the programme offerings and improve student experience are especially attractive to the Academy. Its university partners include Loughborough University, a Triple Crown accredited university from the United Kingdom, and University of Western Australia, which belongs to the Group of Eight Australia. Table 5.3 presents the accolades of a sample of five universities in partnership with PSB Academy.

Lower tuition fees for international students — For the Academic Year 2015/2016, fresh Singaporean students at SMU pay a subsidised fee of S$12,400 a year for a law degree and S$11,200 a year for a business degree (such as Bachelor of Accountancy and Bachelor of Business Management). To apply for the subsidised fees, the Singapore citizens sign a Declaration for Tuition Grant Eligibility form to facilitate the

Table 5.3: Accolades of the universities delivering their programmes at PSB Academy.

Name of University Partner	Country	Accolades
PSB Academy		
University of Newcastle	Australia	• Top 100 Most International Universities (Times Higher Education World University Rankings 2013–2014) • 12 Disciplines ranked in the Top 200 in the world (QS World University Rankings by Subjects 2014) • Australia's Number One University Under 50 (Times Higher Education 'Top 100 Under 50' 2014) • 5 Stars in socio-economic equity and generic skills (Hobsons Good Universities Guide 2015) • Top 3% of Universities in the World (Times Higher Education World University Rankings 2014 and QS World University Rankings 2014) • Australia's Top Performing University Under 50, Australia's Number One University Under 50 (QS "Top 50 Under 50" 2014) • Top 301–400 Universities in the world (Academic Ranking of World Universities 2014) • Over 2,000 University of Newcastle students currently enrolled in PSB Academy
La Trobe University	Australia	• Awarded the best university in Victoria for international student experience (Victorian International Education Awards — student experience, innovation in education — State Government of Victoria, 2013) • Ranked top 100 emerging universities in the world (Times Higher Education, The 100 Under 50 Universities, 2014)

(Continued)

Table 5.3: *(Continued)*

Name of University Partner	Country	Accolades
		• Ranked 38 in the world for our courses in history (including archaeology) and in the top 100 for communication, media studies, linguistics and sociology (QS World University Rankings by Subject 2013) • Australia's best university for research in microbiology and equally good in biochemistry and cell biology, and veterinary science (Excellence in Research for Australia 2012 rankings)
Coventry University	United Kingdom	• Modern University of the Year (*The Times* and *The Sunday Times* Good University Guide 2015) • Ranked 27th United Kingdom University (Guardian University Guide 2015) • In top 10 for number of students studying overseas (Higher Education Statistics Agency (HESA) 2012–2013) • In the world's top 4% of higher education institutions (QS World University Rankings 2013–2014) • 94% employability after graduation (DLHE Survey 2012–2013)
Loughborough University	United Kingdom	• Among the top 1% business schools worldwide to hold AACSB, EQUIS and AMBA accreditation — the highest accolade a business school can achieve. • Consistently rated as a Top 10 United Kingdom business school by national league tables. • Awarded Rating of 5-Stars (QS Stars, 2014).

(Continued)

Table 5.3: (*Continued*)

Name of University Partner	Country	Accolades
		• *The Times* and *Sunday Times* Good University Guide 2015 saw Loughborough ranked 1st for Librarianship and Information Management, 5th for Business Studies and 7th for Finance and Accounting. • The Complete University Guide 2014 saw Loughborough ranked 6th for Business and Management Studies and 7th for Accounting and Finance. • The Guardian University Guide 2015 rated Loughborough 10th in the United Kingdom for Business, Management and Marketing. • The only university to win The Times Higher Education 'Best Student Experience' poll six times from 2006 to 2011. • Winner of 7 Queen's Anniversary Prizes for Higher and Further Education.
University of Nottingham	United Kingdom	• Double crown accreditation — AMBA and EQUIS • Ranked 70th globally and Top 10 United Kingdom universities (The Economist's rankings) • In the top 1 % of all universities worldwide, with a ranking of 77 in the world — QS World University Rankings (2014–2015) • Top 100 MBAs in the Global Employability University Ranking 2014 (Times Higher Education World University Rankings) • Founder member of the Russell Group which represents 24 leading United Kingdom universities committed to maintaining the very best research and an outstanding teaching and learning experience. • A Member of The Association of Commonwealth Universities

(Continued)

Table 5.3: (*Continued*)

Name of University Partner	Country	Accolades
		• Nobel Prize winning academics — University of Nottingham academics have won Nobel Prizes twice since 2003. • Number 1 choice among the United Kingdom's top graduate employers — The Graduate Market in 2014, High Fliers Research • Top 10 United Kingdom universities for global employability — Global Employability University Survey 2013–2014 • Top 25 universities in the United Kingdom — The Complete University Guide 2015, *The Times* Good University Guide 2015 & *The Guardian* University Guide 2015 • More than 43,000 students from 150 countries

Source: PSB Academy (http://www.psb-academy.edu.sg); Information is correct as on 13 March 2015.

university's assessment of their eligibility. Permanent residents pay S\$17,350 for the law degree and S\$15,700 for the business programmes. International students pay a subsidised fee of S\$24,800 and S\$22,400 a year, respectively.[14] To enjoy the subsidised fees, permanent residents of Singapore and international students sign a Tuition Grant Agreement, and commit to work in Singapore-based companies for 3 years following their graduation from SMU.

At NTU, the subsidised fees for Singapore citizens are S\$9,150 for programmes in Accountancy, Business, Accountancy and Business, Business and Computing, and Business and Computing Engineering. Singapore Permanent Residents pay S\$12,800 and international students pay S\$18,300.[15]

The course fees of the foreign universities are higher than the course fees paid by Singapore residents in public universities but lower than the amount paid by the international students. Consider a student who meets the entry requirements to pursue the Accountancy programme at NTU. The total tuition fee (with subsidy) for local students comes out to be S\$9,150 × 3 = S\$27,450 and S\$18,300 × 3 = S\$54,900 for international students. Permanent residents of Singapore pay S\$12,800 × 3 = S\$38,400 for a 3-year course.

In the private education sector, local (Singaporean/PR) and international students typically pay the same fees for external degree programmes. In one of the PEIs, the total tuition cost for both local and foreign students for a six-trimester (2 physical years) Australian business programme is about S\$38,000 (in 2015). Comparatively speaking, Singaporeans pay more for an external degree programme. The international students, on the other hand, pay less.[16] International students also pay less by studying in Singapore for an external degree programme as compared to studying in Australia. A similar course offered over a 2-year period in Australia is priced at S\$54,440.[17] Factoring the possibility of completing the external degree programme within a shorter period of time, foreign universities' degrees obtained through the PEI offer an attractive education pathway to the international students.

Full university experience — PEIs such as PSB Academy, MDIS and SIMGE provide their students with campus or university experience. PSB Academy occupies a 300,000 square feet full-fledged campus in Delta Road, and houses laboratories for engineering, sports, chemistry, and life sciences. Students can take part in a range of activities in sports such as badminton, street soccer and basketball, and others such as photography and dance. MDIS occupies a three-hectare land area in Stirling Road, offering its students life sciences laboratories, a mass communications studio, a hospitality training centre, among others, and sports facilities such as gymnasium and badminton courts. In 2014, SIMGE invested S\$300 million to expand its campus in Clementi, doubling the campus size with new sport and performance arts spaces. SIMGE's Student Development Department engages students to attend specially organised leadership or personal development workshops. Together with 70 students-led organisations, the department organises community events, and cultural, artistic, intellectual, and sporting activities.

5.4 Issues and Challenges

While it is evident that there is a strong demand for transnational education, the sustainability of transnational partnership is dependent on the number of students admitted to the programmes. Typically, the universities consider their partnership with the PEIs as a commercial venture, and an opportunity to internationalise their programmes.

At the same time, the universities are mindful of the institutional conditions as stipulated by national quality and standards agencies such as the Quality Assurance Agency (QAA) for Higher Education in the United Kingdom and the Tertiary Education Quality and Standards Agency (TEQSA) in Australia as well as standards imposed by regional bodies such as the European Association for Quality Assurance in Higher Education and global representatives like UNESCO and OECD.[18]

It is worth noting that higher education institutions in various countries have been subject to greater scrutiny by the respective regulatory agencies for their allegedly lower academic standards. They are under pressure to uphold academic quality standards. In April 2015, the NSW Independent Commission Against Corruption released the report "Learning the hard way: managing corruption risks associated with international students at universities in NSW", criticising some of the Australian universities for lowering their academic standards to accommodate the capabilities of international students who struggled to pass the subjects and complete the programmes of study whether the students are enrolled on-campus or offshore. The Commission has said: "There is pressure on staff within universities in NSW to find ways to pass students in order to preserve budgets, and pressure created by an increasingly competitive market that makes recruitment targets difficult to meet" (Independent Commission Against Corruption, 2015: 4). The Commission reported that the risk of accepting students with false credentials has been especially high, attributed partly to the universities' heavy reliance on agents — who received commissions of between 10% and 15% of the 1st year course fees — to supply international students to the universities. The agents develop the process of vetting student applications, and the university "cannot know how effective their vetting process is and can only examine the later performance of the students to determine whether the students were 'genuine' or not" (*Ibid*: 20). While the report was targeted specifically at the universities in New South Wales of Australia, many of the issues raised are applicable to any of the higher education institutions. Universities with international partnerships are no exception to this phenomenon.

In transnational partnership in particular, the home universities deal with institutions that are geographically far away from the home country. Some of the specific requirements and challenges of the home institutions in their partnership with PEIs are summarised below.[19]

- Ensure that the PEIs in general and the locally appointed teaching faculty in particular have understood the programme and module requirements, and deliver the stipulated requirements in the classrooms accordingly.
- Check the PEIs' recruitment and admission practices to ensure that they do not recruit students who do not meet the stipulated entry requirements.
- Ensure that the PEIs do not market the university programmes that have not been endorsed by the university or use the university's name and reputation to attract students and enrol the students into programmes from other universities.
- Provide detailed subject outlines, induction to locally appointed lecturers, training to key local personals to ensure that they are familiar with the university policies and procedures.
- Monitor the PEIs' behaviour to ensure strict compliance with the contractual agreement, including the university policies, and operational procedures to avoid tarnishing the university's reputation.
- Ensure that the marketing communication is accurate, transparent and unambiguous, and teaching quality is monitored using the same standards as those applied in the home institution.

The reality is that the university could not possibly have access to full information about the PEI (e.g. financial strength), and a decision could be made by the latter to cease operation. Take the example of M2 Academy. A PEI offering in-house diplomas and degrees from the University of South Australia, Edinburgh Napier University and the University of Canberra, M2 Academy folded in October 2015 after a year in operation. M2 Academy Chief Executive and founder Mark Coggins attributed low student enrolment as "one of the considerations that the investors had taken into account" in closing down the PEI.[20] While students interests were largely protected with regard to course fees and continuation of the their studies in Singapore, it certainly would not reflect well on the university to have a partner going out of business because of low enrolment figure. Questions might be raised whether the university was at fault in failing to attract students to enrol into its programmes. Of course, the size of the intakes might just be one of the challenges confronted by the PEI. A host of other factors could have determined the fate of the organisation.

The CPE has imposed stricter processes and procedures that the PEIs must comply with, and it has done a remarkable job to restore confidence in the sector by reassuring the foreign university partners that they are dealing with a PEI that has passed the CPE-imposed registration criteria. But the CPE does not prevent business failure. Hence, the universities are subject to investment risk. That is why transnational higher education efforts are not suitable for all universities. It is important for the home universities to consider their objectives, and conduct country, industry and company risk assessment exercise before taking the plunge.

That being said, credit must be given to some of the PEIs and the university who have worked hard and honestly throughout the years to maintain long and stable partnerships and bring in quality programmes to the Singapore market. The largest PEI in Singapore, SIMGE, has established partnerships that have lasted more than two decades. The partnerships between SIMGE and University of London (United Kingdom) and RMIT (Australia) have existed for more than 25 years. Each partnership enrols more than 8,000 students, a figure that exceeds the total number of Singaporean students studying in either the United Kingdom or Australia (Ziguras and Gribble, 2015: 252). The longevity in partnership provides at least some testaments to reliability and honesty of the PEIs.

From the Singapore regulator's perspective, one of the concerns with external degree programmes is that they may be awarded by illegitimate colleges. Students may get a degree without doing any work or attend any classes; pay a good deal of money to receive a useful certificate. Besides ensuring that the PEIs develop policies and procedures to strengthen the standard of corporate governance, the CPE has taken steps to prevent degree mills from setting foot in Singapore. As part of the Enhanced Registration Framework (ERF), for example, the PEI is mandated to furnish the following information about the external degree programme to the CPE — track record of the foreign education institution in conducting external degree programmes in other countries, the national or international ranking of the foreign education institution, number of students enrolled in the university, graduation rate, student–faculty ratio at home campus and for the external degree programme and teaching faculty's qualifications at home campus and for the external degree programme. In addition, the CPE requires a letter (or other form of official document) from the Vice-Chancellor or President from the foreign education institution to confirm, among other things, that it has conducted relevant checks on the PEI to ensure that the latter has the resources and capability to deliver the university programme, and that the programme offered in Singapore applies the same academic assurance processes as those in the home campus.[21]

Transnational education and transnational partnerships have produced thousands of graduates and contributed significantly to Singapore. Many participants were able to meet their aspirations for higher education qualification without leaving their work, family and home. University partners represent a key stakeholder of the PEIs, offering education pathways for local polytechnics and PEI diploma graduates. The success of the partnership between the PEI and its university partner requires mutual trust and respect for each other. Concerns and conflicts of interest do arise from time-to-time and they must be properly managed.

5.5 Transnational Partnership: A Simple Illustration

It may seem that there is a lack of good understanding of PEI–University cooperation. Understanding of partnership has been taken for granted, leading to an uncritical approach to partnership learning. It is useful in this regard to take a step back and amplify a case study — a partnership between a Singaporean PEI (SPEI) and a foreign university (AUNI) with regard to admission matters, curriculum, teaching and learning, and operational matters. Albeit a fictional case, we hope that the discussion that follows would shed some light on the quality of provision and the issues and challenges encountered in a partnership (based on the author's account of transnational partnerships). Lessons are drawn for existing and future partnerships that may be established in the years to come. The illustration is derived from imagination on what constitutes as an ideal transnational partnership. The narrative can function as an ideological device to help describe, analyse and appreciate the complexity of transnational partnerships.

Admission — The SPEI offers diploma courses, and has an articulation agreement with AUNI so that graduates from the SPEI diplomas are eligible for admission to the university courses. The articulation agreement clearly stipulates the academic and language entry requirements. To achieve a faster turnaround time of reviewing applications, the Course Consultants and Admission Office at the SPEI rely on the agreed entry requirements to pre-assess applicants' suitability to enrol into the external degree programme. Applications who meet the pre-determined entry requirements are sent to the AUNI for confirmation. Offer letters are issued to accepted students by the university. In the event the applicant holds qualifications that differ from the prescribed entry requirements, the applications are forwarded to the university for its assessment. The AUNI makes the final decision whether to accept or reject the application.

The AUNI and SPEI adhere to the agreement that describes aspects of quality management from the design and development of awards through to thematic quality audits. The qualification conferred to the students is equal in academic standing to that conferred on successful completion of the same course in the university. The marketing collaterals are developed collaboratively between SPEI and AUNI. The course brochure contains information about the course and the university, entry requirements, among other things. Care is taken to ensure that marketing practices are in compliance with the regulatory requirements.[22] The SPEI is mandated to ensure that students have appraised the contents of the student contracts. On course fees, PEIs in Singapore separate the fees that are applicable to full-time and part-time version of the course, and include components of the course fees so that students would not associate the stated course fees as one that covers the course in its entirety.[23]

Academic curriculum and policies — SPEI and AUNI students are subject to similar graduating requirements. Because of the significantly smaller number of students enrolled in the AUNI course in Singapore (especially in the early years of partnership), the SPEI preselects the elective modules for its students to undertake (on-campus students are offered more elective modules to choose from). Students are taught the same (but not necessarily identical) core contents, which include international examples, and attempt assignment tasks with similar learning outcomes as on-campus students. Students are provided with detailed Study Guides and they have access to electronic resources of the University. Material and resources directly related to the subjects are posted on the VLE platform hosted by the AUNI. There are no ideological subjects in the course to inculcate a Singaporean or a foreign identity, culture or school of thought.

Students submit their coursework assignments to the *Turnitin*, a web-based academic plagiarism detector, or its equivalent. The SPEI grades selected assessments that are then moderated by the AUNI. After the coursework marks are confirmed, marked scripts are returned to students with comments and feedback. Students may appeal against the results by submitting the academic review and complaint form. After the exam scripts are marked and moderated by the university faculty staff, the results are reviewed by the Examination Board, comprising the Academic Director from the AUNI, the course leader from the SPEI and lecturers, local and foreign, assigned to teach in that particular term. The AUNI conducts a final check on the results before releasing the final grade to students via the university portal. Students are allowed to appeal against the results within a certain number of days of notification of results to the students. On-campus students are subject to the same appeal procedure and policy.

Mode of delivery and teaching staff — The total contact hours for lectures and tutorials are the same for both on-campus and offshore students. The AUNI is obligated to teach part of the course. Locally appointed tutors teach the remaining portion. Co-teaching can be very effective to expose students to different approaches to teaching and learning. However, it may be problematic to establish an effective relationship between the flying faculty and students, and between the flying faculty and local tutors within a short space of time.

The flying-in and flying-out lecturers stay for about a week to deliver the subject contents. One of the challenges of intensive teaching arrangement is that the classes are normally conducted in an intensive mode (on consecutive days), which means that students are exposed to new topics, concepts, and models at a relatively quick pace.[24] To mitigate the adverse impact on students, the SPEI conducts an induction session with flying-in and flying-out faculty before each of the terms commences to share best practices in teaching and learning and identify potential issues and challenges. A cooling day off (with no teaching scheduled on that day) is deliberately allocated during the intensive teaching period so as to allow students to collect their thoughts before continuing with the second half of the subject contents. Students are provided with the learning materials in advance in the online environment to enable students to understand what the university wants them to learn.

Locally appointed lecturers are identified at least two months prior to class commencement, and their curriculum vitae are sent to the AUNI for assessment and approval. Rejected vitae are replaced by others until the modules are fully assigned. Because the university partner is ultimately responsible for the academic standards of the awards made in their name, whether the degree is delivered in Singapore or on campus, the AUNI formally reviews and approves the appointment of local teaching staff through the universities' own programme approval procedures before they are allowed to teach on their respective courses. The university provides support to offshore teaching staff, and holds the lecturer induction programme in each of the term, making sure that they are familiar with the university rules and procedures.

Teaching and learning — The full-time cohort of the AUNI transnational education programme in Singapore consists of mostly international students. One of the concerns is the level of English proficiency of the students in the host institution. The lecturers are concerned as to how to help students who have difficulties in English, whether to modify their teaching pedagogies, allow students to compete with other students who have a stronger command of the language, or make allowances for weaknesses in English.[25]

Language requirements are strictly imposed to measure student's ability to comprehend the texts and make sense of the words they read and hear. Students who do not meet the language entry requirements are enrolled into English language proficiency programmes.[26] Some of the international students who have completed the course excel in their education pursuit, graduating with above average grades.[27] There are others who struggle in their studies, attributing to the inability to develop sufficiently the cognitive aspect of language proficiency, lack of motivation to study and mismatch of course enrolled and their real interest, increased quantity of readings and assessment tasks, relations with classmates, loneliness and homesickness.

Academically weak students are not left on their own. Students are assessed formatively early in the course, allowing lecturers to identify at-risk students and provide academic support before students sit for the final examination. At-risk students are identified in each term — students who failed 50% or more of the subjects taken during the term. The SPEI course leader works closely with the university to identify intervention plans for at-risk students (e.g. undertake reduced load in subsequent terms, and attend skills-based workshops on report writing, time management and interpreting exam questions). AUNI embeds examination and revision techniques into the subjects and programme sessions since these have been identified as areas in which the students have struggled. Regular workshops are conducted with the teaching staff to identify and implement practical and effective solutions to relieve problems faced by international students, and evaluate the efficacy of the practice against academic performance with reference to variables such as task difficulty and effort to ensure that students achieve their learning goals.

Operational matters — Student orientation sessions are scheduled before the commencement of each term. Academic staff from the AUNI travel to Singapore to conduct the session. Students are introduced to the courses, and they are informed about the university's academic policies, ground rules, expectations, academic support programmes, prerequisite knowledge of the disciplines, attendance requirements, and course requirements. The SPEI conducts a separate student orientation session to inform students about the SPEI policies and procedures, immigration department requirements for international students and others. SPEI and AUNI run workshops to familiarise students with the university's online library system, e-learning platform and ways to go about applying for academic consideration through a platform hosted by the university.

The day to day running of the programmes is jointly managed by SPEI and AUNI. At the AUNI, dedicated administrative staff from the International Unit are appointed to oversee the operational matters whereas academic matters are overseen by the Academic Program Director (based in home country). SPEI course administrators and academic course leaders are the initial points of contact. The course administrators are employees of the SPEI dedicated to manage day-to-day operational matters, including attending to students' enquiries and ensuring that documents are duly completed and forwarded to the relevant persons. The SPEI academic course leaders, works closely with the AUNI to maintain overall quality of the courses, manage, and assist in the provision of all on-campus academic guidance and providing support to students, including overseeing academic misconduct investigations, appeals and grievances (including plagiarism, academic misconduct in exams). The academic course leader liaises with and provides academic guidance to lecturers and tutors engaged with the AUNI subjects.

Key administrative staff and academics from both sides meet on a monthly basis through Skype. The Monthly Operations Meetings (MOMs) offer a platform to discuss issues relating to admission, time tabling, orientation and others, find solutions to them, and relationship building. The SPEI and AUNI gather student feedback through the formal Course Evaluation Form at the end of each module. The data supports the evaluation of the delivery and quality of course and provides the opportunity for both parties to review administrative and academic matters in quality improvement measures. Key areas of concern are further discussed in the MOMs to allow for the appropriate monitoring and improvement of the courses.

In summary, while the narrative has not considered all aspects of partnership, two key lessons for future transnational education programmes can be drawn.

- Student-centricity is essential: both SPEI and AUNI are committed to providing quality education. Matters of students' interest are uppermost in their minds. Students are offered courses that are supported by learning materials and resources necessary for them to complete the assessment tasks and acquire the essential skills and knowledge.

The educational institutions are mindful of learning and teaching challenges in relation to intensive mode of teaching by flying-in and flying-out faculty and teaching a class inclusive of international students who are non-native English speakers. AUNI and SPEI work together to enhance students learning experience.

- Develop a cooperative mindset: AUNI and SPEI develop mutual respect and share a stake in administrative, operational, and academic matters. Both institutions work together on all aspects of the collaboration. In addition to e-mail correspondences, monthly meetings are held to plan, discuss, and make decisions. Communication channels are established for on-going review of measures to address issues and challenges that the institutions encountered from time to time, and the roles of the AUNI and SPEI are clearly specified.

Chapter 6

Business Schools

6.1 Introduction

Business schools have existed since the late 19th century in Europe and the United States. Ecole Superieure de Commerce of Paris (now ESCP-EAP), the world's first business school, was established in 1819. In the United States, business education began with the gift by Philadelphia businessman Joseph Wharton to the University of Philadelphia to establish the first American business school in 1881. This was soon followed with the establishment of business schools in Tuck (1900), Harvard (1910) and Chicago (1920), among others.

The number of business schools in the United States grew rapidly after World War II in tandem with rising demand for education and economic progress. By 1955, business had become the most popular undergraduate programme in the United States. This period saw a proliferation of the Master in Business Administration (MBA) programme. Earl Cheit (1985: 46) reported that in the academic year ending in 1965 "American business schools conferred only 7,585 MBA degrees. The size of the graduating class grew more than six-fold to 46,650 by 1977". By 1997–1998, the number of MBA degrees awarded in the United States had grown to over 100,000 (Zimmerman, 2001: 3).

Business courses are very popular with the private education institutions (PEIs). One reason is that they require lower capital outlay to establish as compared to courses in the engineering and life sciences faculties. And because business forms the backbone of the economy, demand for business courses is generally higher than in other fields. While these may sound promising for the PEIs, they actually translate to very intense competition in the business education market as students have the option to shop around for the right course before making a decision. The level of competition in the private education sector is discussed in detail in the next chapter. An overview of the business schools and courses in the private education sector is the main focus point of this chapter.

6.2 Critics of Business Education

Let's open the discussion on some negativity about business education. The rise of business education across many parts of the world has not been smooth sailing.[1] Joseph-Christopher Spender (2014: 430) noted that "business schools have attracted a steady drumbeat of criticism over recent decades; that they promote greed in their students, prioritize academics' concerns over managers; shy away from the tough ethical and sustainability issues around doing business; overlook the student's professional needs for soft skills, are little more than a recruiting pipeline and finishing school for the privileged, and so on". This is a pretty long list of criticisms, renewed certainly with much cited corporate scandals affecting some large private corporations such as Enron and WorldCom and the 2008–2009 economic crises. Some of the commentators put the blame on questionable managerial decisions and poor corporate governance standards. Business Schools were accused of propagating profit-first mentality. Questions were raised as to whether business schools had paid adequate attention to social responsibility, ethics and governance. Finance courses, for example, were said to have encouraged the development and use of financial instruments to maximise personal gains. Share options — designed to align the interest of the professional managers and shareholders — incentivise the professional managers to resort to short-term profit maximisation motive through unethical practices such as manipulation of financial statements.

The attack on business education has been focusing on improper practices of a few organisations, Enron and WorldCom especially and massively advertised cases like the 2008 Madoff investment scandal in the United States and the 2008 *Sanlu* tainted milk scandal in China. Most business graduates in reality have nothing to do with companies such as Enron or WorldCom. And many were not involved in the creation and application of sophisticated financial products that had led to the 2008–2009 economic crises.[2] Even putting the blame on Business Schools for Enron's and WorldCom's mishaps is questionable for at least two reasons. First, Enron's Andrew Fastow and Kenneth Lay obtained undergraduate degrees in Economics outside the College of Business whereas, WorldCom's Bernie Ebbers gained his first degree in physical education. Second, as Neubaum *et al.* (2009: 10) pointed out, they "were years past their university training and worked in an organizational context far removed from the classroom". Business education does not programme students as robots to do evil things. Humans are imperfect creatures in the sense that business students do not become on the whole more greedy and self-centred just because they have received education in business. Like other clinical professions such as doctors and lawyers, it seems unfair to put the blame on business programmes for having trained students who ended up doing things dishonestly.

Neubaum *et al.* (2009: 10) conducted a massive survey, involving 1,080 undergraduate students from a research university in the United States, to empirically test the claim that business education has produced and developed amoral profit-first managers. They concluded that business education has played no role in shaping the personal moral philosophies (defined as a set of beliefs, attitudes, and values that could shape ethical decision) of business students. The study found no significant difference in students' attitude towards profit whether the students were enrolled in business or non-business courses. The study also examined the personal moral philosophies of business freshmen and business seniors. If the critics were correct, one would expect the business school seniors to possess stronger profit attitude than the freshmen. On the contrary, the study found that the business school seniors were actually more concerned with environmental and social factors and that they would take a firm's environmental and social performance into account when seeking jobs. The results prompted the authors to conclude that "blaming business theories for the amorality of managers might be misplaced" and that it might "misdirect the attention of educators truly wishing to improve the consciousness of corporate America" (*Ibid*: 20).

Business education has also been frequently criticised for lacking scientific rigour and paying much attention to collection of facts and best practices. "Critics question the proliferation of narrow, excessively specialized courses and the heavy emphasis on detailed descriptions of current practice and rigid rules of management" (Schlossman, 1987: 10). The 1959 Gordon–Howell report (named after economists Robert Aaron Gordon and James Edwin Howell) described American business education as a "collection of trade schools lacking a strong scientific foundation". The subsequent recasting of business schools with financial support from the Ford Foundation emphasised abstract and basic research and doctoral education to develop problem-solving abilities and differentiate between 'what is hearsay' in management and 'what is fundamental'. Business schools started to educate future managers from "describing how firms differs in their debt/equity ratio, to thinking about capital markets, setting prices of debts and equity, adjusting for risk, and determine appropriate debt/equity ratio", and from "giving students the rules of thumb based on past observation to teaching students how to arrive at solutions to problems they would likely to encounter" (Zimmerman, 2001: 7).

Have business research, theories and management tools constructively changed companies and the way people work? In the context of the Management discipline, as Santiago Iniquez de Onzonol (2010: 22) puts it, "good Management is one of the best antidotes to most of the world's illnesses as it promotes convergence and understanding among civilizations. We need true leaders, good managers, and good management is synonymous to ethical management, nothing more but nothing less". Zimmerman (2001) cited the Agency Theory, Capital Asset Pricing Model, Decision Theory, Game Theory, Linear Programming models with constrained resource allocation, risk management and Queuing Theory, among others as insights from research in business with practical applications in the real world.

In a series of articles, Nick Bloom and his associates have argued that the quality of management and good management practices have contributed significantly to organisational excellence in terms of productivity gains, sales growth and returns on capital.[3] In *The Art of Strategy*, Avinash Dixit and Barry Nalebuff (2008: X) show how game theory can provide a system of thought about issues such as negotiation, bargaining, contracting, financing, and investing in "outdoing adversary, knowing that the adversary is thinking to do the same to you". Behavioural social scientists have also made significant contribution in our understanding of how humans make choices. Consider the anchoring effect which illustrates the human tendency to rely exclusively on certain information when making decisions. In *Thinking, Fast and Slow*, Nobel Laureate Daniel Kahneman highlights the example of a supermarket offering a sales promotion of Campbell's soup at about 10% off the original price. On some days, the supermarket put up a sign on the shelf that said LIMIT to 12 PER PERSON. On other days, the sign said NO LIMIT PER PERSON. The limit imposed by the supermarket has become an anchor against which other deals are measured. The idea of buying more was superior to buying less. Indeed, shoppers purchased on average twice as many cans when the limit was in force as they bought when the limit was removed. Anchoring effect, concludes Kahneman (2011: 126), explains why arbitrary rationing is such an "effective marketing ploy".

Abstract economic concepts such as equilibrium price and quantity in demand and supply model can also be usefully applied in the real world. The implication of the model is not about determining the equilibrium price and quantity. In reality, it is not possible to know whether the current price is the equilibrium price or otherwise. The usefulness of the concept in particular and the demand–supply model in general rests on the analysis of the change in the price and quantity resulting from changes in factors affecting demand and supply (such as the impact of the imposition of production tax on price and quantity). An extension of the model using the elasticity concepts can further inform us about the burden of the tax, whether the consumers bear more of the tax or the sellers. The assertion that the theories and concepts are irrelevant to business and business decision-making is unfounded. The wealth of knowledge generated through business education if performed effectively and in an ethical manner can achieve organisational excellence, create jobs and wealth to the society and improve the living standards of the people.

6.3 Business Schools in Singapore

In Singapore, business courses did not take off until 1957 when the Bachelor of Commerce (Accountancy) was offered in Nanyang University, 2 years after the Chinese-language University was set up. At the University of Singapore, the Department of Economics began to offer Business Administration as one of the subjects taught in 1961. The subject was recommended by Professor Leslie JG Wong, a Canadian born Chinese who was Professor of Finance at the University of British Columbia in Canada, and a friend of Professor Thomas Silcock who was the Head of the Economics Department at the University of Singapore.[4] Four years later, in 1965, the Department of Business Administration under the Faculty of Social Sciences was set up. The first cohort of 32 students graduated in 1968 with the Bachelor of Business Administration degree. In 1969, the School of Accountancy was moved out of the Singapore Polytechnic and merged with the Department of Business Administration at the University of Singapore to form the School of Accountancy and Business Administration, an initiative of Dr. Toh Chin Chye who was then the University's Vice-Chancellor.[5]

With the merger of University of Singapore and Nanyang University in 1980, the School of Accountancy and Business Administration became the Faculty of Accountancy and Business Administration, which resided in the National University of Singapore (NUS). The faculty consisted of the Department of Accountancy and Department of Business Administration. The School of Accountancy was moved to the then Nanyang Technological Institute (NTI) in 1987, and the School of Management at the NUS was renamed Faculty of Business Administration not long after.

At NTI, graduates from the Bachelor of Accountancy programme continued to receive their degrees conferred by NUS until 1991. In 1990, the School of Accountancy was renamed the School of Accountancy and Business (SAB).[6] SAB launched the Bachelor of Commerce programme with specialisations in Actuarial Science, Banking, Marketing and Human Resource Management. The programme was renamed the Bachelor of Business degree in 1991. In the same year, NTI became the Nanyang Technological University (NTU), and the Nanyang MBA

Table 6.1: Enrolment in university first degree courses in Singapore (2014) — male students.

Course	Number of students	% of total male students
Engineering Sciences	12,895	41
Humanities and Social Sciences	3,756	12
Natural, Physical and Mathematical Sciences	3,223	10
Business and Administration	3,092	9

Source: *Yearbook of Statistics*, Singapore 2015.

programme was established. NUS launched its part-time MBA programme in 1980. Today, MBA programmes offered by NUS and NTU are among the top 100 globally. Both business schools are accredited by the Association to Advance Collegiate School of Business (AACSB) (NUS business school in 2003 and Nanyang business school in 2005) and the European Quality Improvement System (EQUIS) (NTU in 2004 and NUS in 2009).

Table 6.1 shows the enrolment in university first degree courses in Singapore in 2014. Among the male students, Business and Administration was the fourth most popular choice, accounting for 9% of the total male population. Engineering Sciences was the top choice with 41% of the total male students opting for engineering related courses in the universities. Among the females, Business and Administration was the second most popular choice with 19% of the total female population opting to read business related courses (Table 6.2). Humanities and Social Sciences, which consisted of courses in Economics, Sociology, History, Geography, Psychology, Political Science and others was the top choice, accounting for 24% of the total enrolment. With regard to enrolment in higher degree courses — full-time and part-time postgraduate diploma and higher degree courses in public universities, including the National Institute of Education — Business and Administration was a popular choice among students, with 17% of the total enrolment. It ranked second, behind Engineering Sciences (Table 6.3).[7]

Table 6.2: Enrolment in university first degree courses in Singapore (2014) — female students.

Course	Number of students	% of total female students
Humanities and Social Sciences	7,534	24
Business and Administration	6,052	19
Engineering Sciences	5,543	17

Source: *Yearbook of Statistics*, Singapore 2015.

Table 6.3: Enrolment in higher degree courses in Singapore (2014).

Course	Number of students	% of total students
Engineering Sciences	6,059	32
Business and Administration	3,014	17
Natural, Physical and Mathematical Sciences	2,317	12

Source: *Yearbook of Statistics*, Singapore 2015.

6.4 Business Courses in the Private Education Sector

In the case of the private education sector, about 50% of the PEI courses are in the fields of Business and Administration with Humanities and Social Sciences and Services taking second and third spots, respectively (Table 6.4). JobsCentral Learning Ranking and Survey Report 2013, which reported the survey results of 8,367 individuals, ranked Business Studies/Management as the most popular course with 2,548 votes (or 30% of the voters) (Table 6.5). Hospitality/Tourism/Food and Beverages (F & B) rose in the ranking from 4th place in 2012 to 2nd place. Finance/ Investment and Accounting were ranked 3rd and 4th, respectively. Sales/ Marketing course makes the list of top five courses. JobsCentral Learning Ranking and Survey Report 2015 reported that 34% of the voters preferred Business Studies/Management courses (Table 6.6). Second place

Table 6.4:   Distribution of post-secondary courses (diploma, bachelor, and postgraduate) offered by PEIs.

Courses	As on 31 December 2014 (in %)	As on 31 December 2015 (in %)
Business and Administration	49	48
Education	4	4
Engineering Sciences	4	5
Fine and Applied Arts	6	7
Information Technology	8	7
Humanities and Social Sciences	10	9
Services	10	10
Others[a]	9	10

Note: [a]Include fields in Mass Communication, Information Services, Health Sciences, Architecture and Building, Law, Natural, Physical, Chemical and Mathematical Sciences.
Source: *CPE Annual Report* (2014–2015), *CPE Annual Report* (2015–2016).

Table 6.5:   Top 5 most preferred courses of study in private education sector (2013).

Rank 2012	Rank 2013	Courses of study	Count
1	1	Business Studies/Management	2,548
4	2	Hospitality/Tourism/F&B	1,930
2	3	Finance/Investment	1,049
3	4	Accounting	1,043
5	5	Sales/Marketing	805

Source: *JobsCentral Learning Rankings and Survey Report* (2013: 5).

went to Accounting with 15% votes followed by Finance/Investment (13%), Arts and Social Sciences/Psychology (11%) and Human Resources (10%). Taken together, it can be concluded that business courses are well received in Singapore.

Broadly speaking, two levels of business courses — certificate and diploma — are offered in the PEIs. The certificate course (Table 6.7) equips students with the fundamental concepts and terminologies

Table 6.6: Top 5 most preferred courses of study in private education sector (2015).

Rank 2015	Courses of study	Percentage of voters
1	Business Studies/Management	34
2	Accounting	15
3	Finance/Investment	13
4	Arts and Social Sciences/Psychology	11
5	Human Resources	10
	Others	17

Source: *JobsCentral Learning Rankings and Survey Report* (2015: 5).

associated with the business discipline.[8] The course has specific subjects that students must take. Accounting is a common subject at this level, to familiarise students with the rules of debit and credit. Introductory to Business is another common module, to give students a broad overview of the various disciplines in business management such as Marketing, Management, Finance, and Economics. Study skills-type subjects are introduced at the certificate level to improve students' reading, writing and presentation skills, their ability to interpret charts, decipher case studies, paraphrase reading materials and produce academically accepted papers. Course fees range from approximately S$1,800 to S$3,500, and the certificate programmes can be completed in two to six months. It is worth noting that students with PSLE (Primary Six) qualification can gain entry to the certificate programme, as in the case of the Certificate in Sales and Marketing programme in Marketing Institute of Singapore (MIS) Training Centre, provided that the applicants are able to demonstrate that they have at least 4 years of working experience.

A sample of PEI diploma courses in business is listed in Table 6.8. The average duration for diploma is 12 months for part-time, and 8 months for full-time.[9] Management Development Institute of Singapore (MDIS) offers the lowest course fees tuition for part-time (local) and full-time (international), whereas Kaplan Singapore offers lowest course fees for full-time (local). In some PEIs, the diploma courses allow graduates

Table 6.7: Certificate courses in business at selected PEIs in Singapore.

Institute	PSB Academy	Kaplan Singapore	Management Development Institute of Singapore (MDIS)	SMF Institute of Higher Learning	Marketing Institute of Singapore (MIS) Training Centre	SIM GE
Programme Title	Certificate in Business Management	Certificate in Foundation Studies	Professional Certificate in Business Management	Certificate in Foundation Studies	Certificate in Sales and Marketing	Management Foundation Studies
Modules	Business Communication	English for Academic Purposes	Communication Skills	Introduction to Accounting	Business Communication	Study Skills for Effective Learning
	Fundamentals of Accounting	Mathematics	Principles of Accounting and Finance	Fundamentals of Economics	Mathematics for Marketing	Introduction to Management
	Fundamentals of Economics	Critical Thinking	Fundamentals of Marketing	Introduction to Management	Fundamentals of Marketing	Elements of Economics
	Fundamentals of Marketing		Principles of Business Management	Ideas and Critical Analysis	Understanding Customers	Principles of Accounting and Business Finance
					Introduction to Selling	Sales of Marketing Management
Duration (number of months) (full time)	3	2	4	4	6	6

(Continued)

Table 6.7: *(Continued)*

Institute	PSB Academy	Kaplan Singapore	Management Development Institute of Singapore (MDIS)	SMF Institute of Higher Learning	Marketing Institute of Singapore (MIS) Training Centre	SIM GE
Entry Requirement	Local: 2 GCE 'O' level (grade 1 to 6) 3 GCE 'N' level (grade 1 to 6) NITEC qualification	Local: GCE 'N', 'O' Levels or NITEC or equivalent qualifications	Local: Full GCE 'N' Levels or 3 GCE 'O' Level or ITE NITEC, COS or NTC qualification	Local: Age 16 years and above; Minimum GCE 'O' Level with 3 credit passes (including English) or Nitec	Local/International: Completed Secondary 4; Completed Secondary 3 with at least 1 year of working experience or Completed Secondary 2 with at least 2 years of working experience or Completed Secondary 1 with at least 3 years of working experience or PSLE/Completed Primary School Education with at least 4 years of working experience Equivalent qualifications for regional countries	Local: 3 GCE 'O' Level credits
	International: Year 10 Year 11	International: Year 9–11	International: NA	International: Qualification equivalent to Year 11		International: Students will be assessed on qualifications equivalent to the GCE 'O' level examinations

English Requirement	IELTS 4.5 or Pass GCE 'N' level English or Pass PSB Academy Certificate in the English Proficiency at Level 3	Minimum IELTS score of 5.5 or Pass the Kaplan English program at Level 5	C6 pass in English as First Language (EL1) or IELTS 6	GCE 'O' Level English Language C6 or IELTS 5.0 (no individual band less than 5.0) or Pass SMF Institute English Test	GCE 'N' level or IELTS 5.0 or Pass MIS English Test	GCE 'O' Level English Language C6 or IELTS 5.5 or TOEFL score of at least 550 (paper-based) plus four in the Test of Written English or SAT1 score of at least 550 or Pearson test score of at least 49/100 or Pass SIMGE Certificate in English Language at Level 5.
Course Fees (full time)[a]	S$1,776	S$1,552	S$2,247	S$2,525	S$3,403	S$3,585

Note: [a]Inclusive of 7% GST; may or may not include administrative fees, exam fees and miscellaneous charges.

Source: websites of the respective PEIs (PSB Academy: http://www.psb-academy.edu.sg; EASB Institute of Management: http://www.easb.edu.sg; Kaplan Singapore: http://www.kaplan.com.sg; Management Development Institute of Singapore: http://www.mdis.edu.sg; Marketing Institute of Singapore: http://www.mis.edu.sg; SIMGE: http://www.simge.edu.sg. Accessed on 15 June 2015.

Table 6.8:   Diploma courses in business at selected PEIs in Singapore.

Institute	PSB Academy	Kaplan Singapore[a]	Management Development Institute of Singapore (MDIS)	SMF Institute of Higher Learning[b]	Marketing Institute of Singapore (MIS) Training Centre	SIM GE[c]
Programme title	Diploma in: Business Administration (General) Business Administration (Human Resource Management) Business Administration (Marketing Management) Business Administration (Accounting and Finance) Business Administration (Banking and Finance) Business Administration (Supply Chain Management)	Diploma in: Accountancy; Business and Information Management; Business and Law Advanced Diploma in: Finance; Management Marketing	Diploma in: Business Administration; Business Management; Marketing; Accounting Advanced Diploma in: Business Administration; Business Management Graduate Diploma in: Human Resource Management; Banking and Finance	Diploma in: Business Management	Diploma in: Business; Marketing Management; Digital Marketing Advanced Diploma in: Marketing Management; Business Management; Digital Marketing; International Events Management and MICE; Tourism and Hospitality Management	Diploma in: Accounting; Banking and Finance; International Business; Management Studies

Number of modules	Diploma: 8	Diploma: 8 Advanced Diploma: 6	Diploma: 8 Advanced Diploma: 8	Diploma: 9	Diploma: 8 Advanced Diploma: 6	Diploma: 15
Duration (number of months)[d]	Diploma: 9	Diploma: 8 Advanced Diploma: 7	Diploma: 7 Advanced Diploma: 9	Diploma: 10	Diploma: 9 Advanced Diploma: 6	Diploma: 18
Entry requirement[d]	GCE A Level or Higher NITEC or GCE 'N', O Level, NITEC holders or equivalent qualifications (bridging modules required)	GCE 'A' levels or Higher NITEC or GCE 'N' or GCE 'O' levels (to complete the Certificate in Foundation Studies programme)	Age 16 years and above and Partial GCE 'A' levels or Minimum of GCE 5 'O' levels or ITE, CBS, ITC or Higher Nitec holders or Professional Certificate in Business Management	Full GCE 'A' levels or ITE Higher Nitec or SMF Certificate in Foundation Studies	2 GCE 'A' levels credits or 5 GCE 'O' levels credits with at least 1 year of working experience or 4 GCE 'O' levels credits with at least 2 year of working experience or 3 GCE 'O' levels credits with at least 3 year of working experience or 2 GCE 'O' levels credits with at least 4 year of working experience or	5 GCE 'O' levels passes, including English as First Language (EL1) or SIMGE Management Foundation Studies

Table 6.8:   *(Continued)*

Institute	PSB Academy	Kaplan Singapore[a]	Management Development Institute of Singapore (MDIS)	SMF Institute of Higher Learning[b]	Marketing Institute of Singapore (MIS) Training Centre	SIM GE[c]
					1 GCE 'O' levels credits with at least 5 year of working experience or 5 CGE 'N' levels credits with at least 2 year of working experience or Higher NITEC or NITEC with at least 3 years of working experience or MIS Certificate in Sales and Marketing or Certificate in Retailing	

English requirement		IELTS 5.5 Applicants who do not meet the English language requirement are required to complete Foundation Studies subjects	C6 pass in English as First Language (EL1) or IELTS 6	C6 pass in English as First Language (EL1) or IELTS 5.5 (Reading and Listening 5.5; Writing and Speaking 5.0) Pass SMF English placement test	C6 pass in English as First Language (EL1) or IELTS 5.5	C6 pass in English as First Language (EL1) or IELTS 5.5
Course Fees[e]	Diploma: S$6,078	Diploma: S$5,029 Advanced Diploma: S$4,708	Diploma: S$5,048 Advanced Diploma: S$5,586	Diploma: S$4,879	Diploma: S$8,588 Advanced Diploma: S$7,148	Diploma: S$11,770

Notes: [a]Kaplan Singapore also offers the Professional Diploma in Banking and Investment Management and a range of Global Diplomas.

[b]SMF Institute of Higher Learning offers a range of other diplomas which are in the teach-out mode.

[c]SIMGE offers the Diploma in Economics, awarded by the University of London.

[d]for Diploma programmes and full-time local students; students with extensive work experience may be considered by the PEIs on a case-by-case basis (entry requirements for Advanced Diplomas, Graduate Diplomas and international students are not included in the table; see the PEIs' respective website for information); additional entry qualifications may be required to certain diplomas.

[e]for full time students only; inclusive of 7% GST but may or may not include miscellaneous charges.

Source: Websites of the respective PEIs (PSB Academy: http://www.psb-academy.edu.sg; EASB Institute of Management: http://www.easb.edu.sg; Kaplan Singapore: http://www.kaplan.com.sg; Management Development Institute of Singapore: http://www.mdis.edu.sg; Marketing Institute of Singapore: http://www.mis.edu.sg; SIMGE: http://www.simge.edu.sg, accessed on 15 June 2015.

to gain one-third module exemptions in a 3-year undergraduate pro-gramme. As such, the academic entry requirement of GCE 'A' levels qualification or equivalent is stipulated. Students with GCE 'O' or NITEC qualification can gain entry into the diploma courses. However, they need to read additional modules (bridging modules) typically in Accounting, Marketing, and Management or show evidence of a number of years of working experience before they are permitted to read modules that demand higher level thinking skills.

Table 6.9 highlights the undergraduate business courses in selected PEIs. The university signs the articulation agreement with the PEI to admit students who have successfully completed the PEI diploma course, and to agree on other qualifications (such as local polytechnics) that can gain direct entry to Year 2. The average duration of Bachelor programmes is 16 months for full-time and 24 months for part-time for a 2-year pro-gramme. The courses are co-taught by flying-in and flying-out faculty from the universities and locally appointed lecturers and tutors. Kaplan Singapore offers the lowest tuition fee at approximately S$19,000 for a degree course with the University of Essex whereas the most expensive business courses in the sample are conferred by the University of Manchester which partners SIMGE. A BSc course in General Manage-ment, International Studies or Human Resource Management is priced at S$31,000.

With globalisation and technology advancements, business schools can no longer be driven solely by the supply side — to recruit good lectur-ers in delivering the courses. To achieve sustainable growth, the school has to be demand-driven — to gain a good understanding of industry needs, incorporate them into the existing curriculum, look for new mar-kets in the home country and elsewhere and introduce new courses that are high in demand. The major disciplines in the undergraduate business courses in a sample of four PEIs are listed in Table 6.10.[10] Broad based business courses (i.e. Business Studies, Management, International Business/Finance/Management/Marketing) are popular with PEIs and students. The courses identify and solve a wide range of business issues, giving them a strong practical focus and the opportunity for graduates to gain employment. Interestingly, courses that allow students to gain advanced technical knowledge in fields like Accounting, Marketing,

Table 6.9: Undergraduate courses in business at selected PEIs in Singapore.

University	University of Manchester	University College Dublin	Royal Holloway, University of London	University of Essex	University of Wollongong	University of Newcastle
Country	United Kingdom	United Kingdom	United Kingdom	United Kingdom	Australia	Australia
Partner PEI	SIMGE	Kaplan Singapore	Kaplan Singapore	Kaplan Singapore	PSB Academy	PSB Academy
Does the University allow direct entry to Year 2 of the undergraduate programme?	Yes	Yes	Yes	Yes	Yes	Yes
Programme Duration						
— Entry to Year 2	24 months	18 months	18 months	18 months	24 months	16 months
Teaching	Fly-in, fly-out & local tutors	Fly-in, fly-out & local tutors	Fly-in, fly-out & local tutors	Fly-in, fly-out & local tutors	Fly-in, fly-out & local tutors	Fly-in, fly-out & local tutors
Intakes	Mar | Sep	April	May | Nov	June	Jan | May | Aug	Jan | May | Aug
Course Fee 2016 (Approximate)						
— Entry to Year 2	S$31,000	S$22,000	S$21,000	S$19,000	S$24,000	S$26,000

Source: websites of the respective PEIs (PSB Academy: http://www.psb-academy.edu.sg; Kaplan Singapore: http://www.kaplan.com.sg; Management Development Institute of Singapore: http://www.mdis.edu.sg; SIMGE: http://www.simge.edu.sg, accessed on 13 November 2016.

Table 6.10:   Undergraduate courses in business (by disciplines).

	PSB Academy		SIMGE		MDIS		Kaplan Singapore	
	University of Newcastle	Others (University of Wollongong, etc)	RMIT	Others (University of Birmingham, etc)	University of Sunderland	Others (Bangor University, etc)	Murdoch University	Others (Swinburne University of Technology, etc)
Management	*✓	*✓	✓	*✓			*✓	*✓
Marketing	*✓	*✓	✓	✓	*✓		*✓	*✓
Finance		*✓			*✓			*✓
Logistics and Supply Chain Management		✓	✓					✓
Accounting	✓	*✓	✓		*✓			*✓
Human Resource Management		✓		*✓			*✓	✓
Business Studies		✓				*✓		*✓
Media, culture, communication			✓	✓	✓		*✓	*✓
International Business/Finance/ Management/Marketing				*✓			*✓	✓
International Trade				*✓			✓	✓
Economics				✓			*✓	✓
Business Information Systems				*✓			*✓	
Business Administration				*✓				✓
Banking						*✓	*✓	*✓
Business Law							*✓	*✓

Note: *✓ : Indicates programmes with double major.

Source: Extracted from http://www.psb-academy.edu.sg, http://www.mdis.edu.sg, http://www.simge.edu.sg, http://www.kaplan.edu.sg on 13 November 2016.

Human Resource Management, Supply Chain Management, and Media Communications are also popular with the PEIs, reflecting the current market reality; increasingly, more students know what they want with regard to their interest and career plans. There seems to be room for PEIs to offer courses in specific skills. Expanding fields of business in Entrepreneurship, Innovation, Project Management, Retail Marketing, Digital Marketing, Business Analytics, and Corporate Social Responsibility are yet to catch-up in the private education sector based on the under-graduate courses currently on offer in the sample PEIs.

There seems to be a growing consensus among the hiring companies that degree courses and PEI diploma courses do not produce graduates with the skills they need. The focus on research in the fields of business has led managers to allege that academics were focusing too exclusively on their areas of interest, imparting knowledge to students that are irrel-evant to the real world. In the universities, academics have been said to write articles and produce theories that are not practical, understood only by their peers rather than the practitioners. The practitioners read *The Economist, Business Week* and *Harvard Business Review* to gain practical insights rather than high impact-rated scholarly journals. The corporate world likes to see, as part of the business education, more realistic, practi-cal, hands-on education and greater emphasis on the development of the 'people' (leadership, interpersonal skills). Students also believe that if the courses they read offer them a platform to learn skills that are recognised in the labour market, the course itself would have value.

Getting the business schools in the universities to change may be more challenging. They may want to be isolated from the real world, pur-sue pure research to develop breakthrough ideas and discoveries. PEIs on the other hand are more flexible. It is easier for PEIs to integrate with the business community to expose their students to practical ideas that will make their students more valuable to the labour marker. I believe that business schools in the private education sector have an edge over the universities to produce students who are industry ready. PSB Academy, for example, recruits lecturers with relevant academic qualifications combined with a number of years of relevant working experience. In the course of my work, I have seen teaching staff carrying out their duties with commitment, supporting students in their studies and imparting knowledge, skills, and real world experience. They may not have published articles in Tier 1 journals or obtained advanced degrees in Ivy League Universities but they are certainly excellent mentors and teachers (this is of course not true in all cases).

Business schools in the private education sector have to do more by reaching out to leaders and senior managers in business, science, and industrial fields and setting up of business advisory panels to advice on current academic practices. They should work in collaboration with the industry to offer internship opportunities to students (local residents for a start) as a tool to expose students to the real working environment. PEIs should establish network with the industry players and be the first to enter the new market with new or improved products. This would allow the PEI to gain advantage over its actual and potential rivals and have the time to improve its product. While it may not take too long for others to copy ideas and compete with the incumbent to capture some parts of the share through innovative advertising and effective marketing planning, establishing a foothold in the market early by being the best PEI in that particular field offers a chance for the PEI to stem off potential entries. And there is room for PEIs to shift their focus towards improving soft skills; teach courses that aim towards enhancing students' communication abilities, understanding of ethical issues, analytical and critical thinking skills and ability to use information technology in addition to discipline specific concepts and tools in topics such as Accounting, Economics, Marketing, and Statistics.

While business education is about imparting students with business concepts, tools, and know-how so that graduates become effective members of the business community, this is easier said than done. For one thing, business courses attract diverse group of students. Students enrolled into the PEI courses can have vastly different prior qualifications. There are students with science or engineering background, while there are others with a foreign qualification in commerce, tourism or mass communication. Broadly speaking, the former group of students has a stronger capacity in Mathematics, and therefore encounters fewer problems with quantitative subjects like Business Statistics and Finance. Commerce students, on the other hand, are generally speaking more comfortable with arts and humanities or equivalent, and can possibly do well in Marketing and Organisational Behaviour. Besides the qualitative–quantitative dichotomy, there are certain disciplines that require different, possibly even unique cognitive skills. Subjects like Econometrics, Business Law, and Accounting belong to this category.

A business course is therefore challenging for both students and lecturers. This is true in all teaching institutions, and not just the PEIs. More worrying are the full time classes which are typically made up of international students who are schooled outside of Singapore during their formative years, and heavy reliance on part time or sessional staff to conduct the classes. Some of the international students may have a weaker command of the English language. There are others who were compelled by their parents to study abroad. They are less motivated to study. They find ways to absent themselves from classes without flaunting ICA rules. Even if they are in class, they may not pay attention, preferring to sit at the back of the class and engage with electronic devices. They free-ride on group assignments. The lucky ones manage to obtain a marginal pass. With less committed teachers and poor teaching methods, the problem gets compounded. Sessional or part time teaching staff, in particular, may treat a teaching assignment as merely a contractual agreement, devoting their time and energy only during the contracted hours. The teachers may go from one topic to another without ascertaining whether students have understood the concepts. They care more about completing the syllabus, and were unconcerned about connectivity between concepts. Without a strong sense of ownership, teachers simply brush through concepts after concepts. We often hear of students blaming everyone and everything except themselves after failing a subject. Teachers are no exception. When the class achieves a low passing rate, teachers blame the students for lack of motivation in their studies, poor attitude (playing with cellphones in class) etc. The same comments came from flying-in and flying-out faculty from PEI university partners about their teaching experience in the PEIs. While there is some truth in their claims, they are certainly not helpful.

Of course, this does not apply to all the sessional staff. I have benefited from extensive discussion with teachers in the business and commerce faculty. I have spoken to teachers who have a strong sense of ownership and commitment to the class and who are genuinely concerned about students' learning by constantly finding ways to improve their teaching to fit the learning abilities of students are respected by students. They are mindful that students especially in the private education sector learn at different rates. Some are able to catch on relatively quicker while others need more time to reach the same level of understanding. Good teachers inject activities in class before a next topic is taught, and utilise the web to further engage with students, especially the weaker ones. They receive outstanding evaluation results, and students generally do better in the coursework and examinations.

Teachers are so overwhelmed these days by the pace of living and working due largely to advancements in technology and information over-loading that they spend less time really thinking about the art of teaching. They should take a pause and start questioning their assumptions. The assumption that the same teaching style can be applied to every class and cohort is especially problematic for flying-in and flying-out faculty in transnational partnerships. Teaching a group of British or Australians students in their home countries is certainly not the same as teaching a group of Asian students of various nationalities. Salman Khan (2012: 20), founder of the Khan Academy, has correctly observed that "the pace of learning is a question of style, not relative intelligence. The tortoise may very well end up with more knowledge — more useful, lasting knowledge — than the hare". Instead of trying to win business by lowering the entry requirements or academic standards, the PEI should build a strategy around effective teaching and learning that would differentiate the PEI from the pack. A differentiation strategy is particularly appropriate for the PEI that operates in a dynamic and competitive environment.

Chapter 7
Competitive Analysis

7.1 Introduction

This chapter applies the Porter's Five Forces Model on the private education industry. We show that business schools in general and those in the private education sector in particular are operating in a highly competitive environment. While the barriers to entry are high, the availability of substitutes, strong bargaining power of the buyers and sellers and intense rivalry among the incumbents are jeopardising the profitability of the industry. Implications are discussed in the concluding section. For example, high fixed cost to total cost ratio that is typical of a financial structure of business schools suggests the strategy to offer business courses in overlapping fields to allow the private education institutions (PEIs) to spread the fixed cost over a larger volume of students. Economies of scale can be achieved by introducing modules such as Critical Thinking Skills and English for Academic Purposes that provide common intellectual experience for students regardless of their major.

7.2 Porter's Five Forces Model and its Application to the Private Education Sector

Economic theory tells us that in a competitive environment, firms' profit is driven to the normal level with less competitive firms leaving the industry. Understanding the competitive forces in the private education sector and their underlying causes serve to inform the industry structure and the necessary measures that PEIs can put in place to at least remain in business.

Harvard Business School Professor Michael Porter developed the Five Forces Model in his book "Competitive Strategy" in 1980. The model is used to identify the key factors that shape competition and affect industry's profitability (Porter, 1980). To Porter, competition is not about demolishing the rivals. It is about winning sales and earning profits through the creation and improvement of value for customers. Building a strategy around teaching and learning to enhance student learning experience in the PEI is an example.

The model is applied to determine the profitability of the PEIs and the forces that shape the conduct of the PEIs with particular reference to the business schools. The model consists of the following forces — threat of entrants, threat of substitutes, bargaining power of buyers, bargaining power of suppliers and the intensity of rivalry. Table 7.1 shows the major and sub-themes of the model as it applies to the private education sector.

Table 7.1:   Five forces model and the private education sector.

Themes	Sub-themes
Threat of entrants	Size of capital outlay; resource requirements; impact of information technology; the role of regulatory agency such as Council for Private Education (CPE)
Threat of substitutes	Availability of other courses; suitability of courses offered by the PEIs; gap in course fees
Bargaining power of buyers	Ease of identifying alternative courses; propensity to switch among the students; the power of parents; the power of employers
Bargaining power of suppliers	Potential for PEIs to merge and form an alliance; access to talent, including academics; the power of (potential) partners, including foreign universities, employers, industry associations, accreditation boards
Competitive rivalry	Number of PEIs; size of the market; nature of the product; intensity of competition among the PEIs

Source: Author.

Threat of entrants

Michael Porter (2008: 8) writes: "New entrants to an industry bring new capacity and a desire to gain market share that puts pressure on prices, costs, and the rate of investment necessary to compete… The threat of entry, therefore, puts a cap on the profit potential of an industry. When the threat is high, incumbents must hold down their prices or boost investment to deter new competitors". The threat of entry is low in the private education landscape for the following reasons.

First, establishing a PEI is an expensive undertaking, including setting up a business school. Imagine building a campus and acquiring the resources and facilities required of a school, tables, chairs, computers, books, and many others. While business schools are able to operate in high rise buildings, which means lower rental as compared to a land site, the importance of securing a premise that is accessible by students translates back to higher rental for space. Education is a high fixed cost to total cost ratio business (developing the curriculum and materials for a course, for example, is a high fixed cost exercise although replicating the course incurs a low marginal cost), suggesting the importance for the PEIs to operate at high or near full capacity.

Second, to start a business in the private education sector, a potential entrant has to register with the CPE and comply with the Enhanced Registration Framework (ERF) and/or EduTrust requirements — stricter and more comprehensive than the past. Compliance activities are not cost free. For a start, all PEIs are required to meet the minimum financial standards — a paid-up capital of at least S$100,000 — to reflect their financial capabilities to operate.[1] Compliance is also labour intensive and involves opportunity cost when staff from the organisation are diverted to support compliance activities. A study published in October 2015 found that 3–11% of the operating expenses are incurred by higher learning institutions in the United States in complying with the United State federal regulations, and a further 4–15% of faculty members' time has been spent for the same purpose.[2] While there is no similar study to measure the cost of complying with the CPE regulations, the general sentiment is that Singapore companies are increasingly worried about rising cost of compliance with government regulations. In its survey of more than

1,000 companies between 10 October 2016 and 23 November 2016, Singapore Business Federation found that 31% of the respondents cited complying with government regulations as a key challenge, ahead of access to financial capital, technology disruption and venture to overseas markets.[3]

Taken together, high capital outlay and the high cost of compliance with the regulatory requirements act as a high barrier to entry, which is good piece of news for the incumbent PEIs to protect their current market share.

Threat of substitutes

A substitute performs a similar function and serves a similar purpose thereby threatening the profitability of the product or service offered by the incumbent. The significance of threat of substitutes is that it can potentially erode the profitability of the firm. "When the threat of substitutes is high", explained Porter (2008: 17), "industry profitability suffers....If an industry does not distance itself from substitutes through product performance, marketing, or other means, it will suffer in terms of profitability — and often growth potential".

Notably, a formal academic education is not the only path to succeed in one's career. In-house courses can equip participants with specialised skills and knowledge in fields such as sales management and digital marketing and help them to scale the career ladder. The duration of in-house training is typically shorter. The programme is less demanding in terms of the effort put in to complete assessment tasks, if any at all, and number of articles or books to read.

In-house training and short courses run by non-PEIs (e.g. consulting agencies) however are not perfect substitutes of PEI diploma courses. The latter for one thing offers the graduates the option to advance to a degree-awarding programme upon completion. The former does not. It is a perception on the value of the programme that counts. There are a host of factors impacting the decision, and the weights assigned to the factors are unique to the individual. Managing threat of substitutes in this regard requires the PEIs to influence the perception of students with regard to the value of obtaining a PEI qualification.

Online courses represent another substitute to PEI courses. Massive Open Online Course (MOOC) offer free online courses in Economics, Finance, Banking, Investment, Statistics, and others to wide audiences. Coursera maintains a MOOC-like business and operational structure, offering short courses in various disciplines from top universities, including Yale, Stanford and Duke. Students are supported by massive amount of information online in completing the courses, which they can do so at the comfort of their home.

Taken together, it can be argued that the threat of substitutes is a worrying phenomenon in the PEI industry.

Bargaining power of buyers

Powerful customers, noted Porter (2008: 14) "can capture more value by forcing down prices, demanding better quality or more service (thereby driving up costs), and generally playing industry participants off against one another, all at the expense of industry profitability". Customers, in the education sector, refer to potential and existing students. To some extent, parents play a role as well, especially in the case of fresh school leavers.

Advancements of technology have allowed working professionals to opt for alternative modes of learning; online studies through Coursera, Khan Academy, distance learning and flexible learning mode. E-learning platforms allow professors to share their course materials online for free or a low fee. Online learning allows learners to pause, reflect, go back to the concept and attempt problems or exercises as necessary at their own pace without fear and embarrassment.

The government's emphasis on skills building has incentivised Singaporeans to opt for skills-based courses to accommodate student's performance learning needs, budget and time. More choices of courses and ease of access to information have led to greater power to the buyers. The SkillsFuture scheme in particular offers Singaporeans a platform to identify and eventually enrol in short courses that are more relevant to the individuals. A dedicated website by the administering agency, the Workforce Development Agency, gives easy access to visitors to the various skill-based courses such as auditing, word processing, project management and payroll administration. Completing two or three such courses in a shorter period of time may be perceived as a more worthwhile investment than enrolling in a 3-year undergraduate programme.

The power of students is also derived from the ease of switching courses. Is it possible, for example, for students who are currently enrolled in the Diploma in Business Administration with School ABC to switch to read the Diploma in Business Management with School XYZ? Possibly yes since PEI business courses are quite standardised in terms of programme duration, entry requirements and modules offering. Kaplan Singapore offers the Diploma in Accounting. The same is offered in Management Development Institute of Singapore (MDIS) and Singapore Institute of Management Global Education (SIMGE). PSB Academy offers a Diploma in Business Administration, a programme very similar in module offering courses offered by other PEIs (the core modules are typically Management, Marketing, Economics, Business Statistics, and Accounting). Similarity in the courses implies that a business student can successfully apply for credit module exemptions when he/she transfers from School ABC to School XYZ. In essence, the allowance of credit transfers across schools and homogeneity of courses in programme structure and duration lower the switching cost and raise the power of the buyers.

Students are inclined to demand for better services from the PEIs. They form expectations with regard to the quality of the programmes, mode of assessment, the ability to appeal against coursework and examination results, all lead to the willingness to switch to alternative education providers when their needs are not met. Employers that sponsor their workers to the course and parents are increasingly more vocal, demanding more value in the programme and capturing more of the value for themselves. Notably, the establishment of the CPE has tilted the balance of power between the buyers and the PEIs, in favour of the former. Students and parents have greater access to information about the private education sector and the PEIs in particular. The PEIs have to succumb to the pressure to be more student-centric in dealing with students to avoid dealing with the CPE on complaints raised by their students who can do so easily through various channels.

Taken together, there is a strong buyers' bargaining power and it does not bode well with the future profitability and growth potential of the PEIs in Singapore.

Bargaining power of suppliers

The vitality of the industry is inversely related to the bargaining power of suppliers. As Porter (2008: 13) points out, "powerful suppliers, including suppliers of labor, can squeeze profitability out of an industry that is unable to pass on cost increases in its own prices". In the context of the private education sector, the discussion below shall confine to two key suppliers — university partners and academics as a source of labor.

Transnational partnerships provide a progression pathway for students enrolled into PEI courses. The universities have a large pool of PEIs to consider partnering with. Quality of PEI courses (syllabi, level of difficulty of the examinations, etc.) and resources in the PEI (library facilities, computer labs, classroom facilities, and space for learning) are important considerations. Often, the university sees the partnership as a commercial venture, which means the reputation of the PEI and its ability to bring in a certain number of students per intake are important considerations. A foreign university is more willing to partner with larger and more reputable PEIs, which form the minority. That is why more established PEIs such as SIMGE and Kaplan Singapore are able to secure partnership with a relatively larger number of foreign higher education institutions. These PEIs do not depend heavily on adding more partners, and possibly do not mind ceasing one or two partners with lower student intake and profit thereby raising their bargaining power in negotiation. This is not the case for smaller PEIs which form the majority. Their dependence on existing partners and the difficulty in securing new partners limit their willingness and ability to extract maximum profit and gain for themselves; weakening their bargaining power.[4]

With rising middle class population in Vietnam, Myanmar, China, and India, foreign universities have a wider option to establish partnership with host institutions elsewhere. Some of the emerging countries have limited tertiary capacity, young age population structures and growing employment opportunities for tertiary educated persons. They welcome universities from abroad to teach their young and give students more study options. There is a risk that some good universities may bypass Singapore and form transnational partnership with other countries. In this regard, the private education sector in Singapore can be characterised as one with strong supplier power.

With regard to the academics, PEIs rely extensively on the supply of part-time teaching staff to teach on their courses. They are working adults who hold a full-time job elsewhere and make themselves available to teach in the evenings and weekends. There are others, such as consultants or semi-retired professionals, who are available to teach both day and evening classes. Those who are able to teach day classes are fewer in numbers, especially in certain disciplines such as Business Law and Auditing. Those who are able to teach common modules like General Management and Principles of Marketing stand a good chance of securing teaching assignments with at least one of the PEIs.

Being casual employees implies that many may treat the job as merely a contractual agreement to teach during the stated hours in exchange for monetary reward, and nothing else. To raise the probability of securing teaching assignments, it is not unusual for part-time lecturers to establish their contacts with more than one PEI, and teach in courses offered by various PEIs at any one time. The demand for their service is particularly high if they possess certain qualifications (PhD and active in research) or expertise (auditing, taxation, business law). University courses are typically delivered by academically qualified (AQ) staff for accreditation-seeking universities. Apart from meeting the academic requirements (PhD qualification and research publications of at least three in the past 5 years), academic staff are required at least from the Association to Advance Collegiate Schools of Business (AACSB) per-spective to actively participate in the universities' activities in order to be classified as "participating". This poses a challenge to PEIs as not many sessional staff in the PEI market are able to fit into the category. Being remarkably good at what they do and the fact that they are not obligated to teach for a particular PEI raise the bargaining power of sessional staff, especially those who are able to teach in day classes and possess advanced qualifications.

Competitive rivalry

A major factor determining the extent of rivalry in an industry is the num-ber of sellers. An industry with many sellers is associated with intense competition. The private education sector in Singapore is predictably competitive. It consists of 312 PEIs as at the end of 2014. While the establishment of the CPE has resulted in a significant reduction in the number of players, with 300 odd players, the industry remains competitive perhaps not surprisingly in view of the large base to start with.

There are many buyers in the private education market. High demand for education in the recent past has been attributed to the growing middle class population in the emerging economies in the Asia Pacific region, the perception of higher education attainment as the passport to good life, and attraction of Singapore as the place to send children for further education. Students from emerging economies such as China, India, Vietnam and Myanmar are especially interested in business programmes, viewing a business qualification as a worthy investment to get a job and get rich quickly. Employers continue to demand for academically qualified workforce both locally and within the Asia Pacific region.

The private education sector has experienced slower growth in terms of student numbers, causing the incumbents to compete more aggressively for market share. The availability of substitutes such as online courses and distance learning programmes has contributed to higher levels of rivalry among the PEIs. More opportunities to enrol in local universities have the effect of lowering the number of potential students both locally and internationally enrolled PEI courses. Low cost in switching from one PEI to another especially for students enrolled in business programmes is another contributing factor. The inflow of international students has been adversely affected by a stronger Singapore dollar. Countries such as the United States and Australia are wooing students directly from China, India, and elsewhere whereas emerging economies like India are building more universities to increase enrolment ratio. Rivalry is intensive in the education sector because of high fixed cost to total cost ratio. PEIs incur high capital outlay, investing in the campus, including classroom and library facilities. It makes economic sense for the PEIs to grow the volume of student population to reap economies of scale which translate to increased competitive intensity.

Competition in the market for diploma and undergraduate studies is especially intensive. In 2014, there were 2,872 active PEI courses. Diplomas accounted for 25% of the total active courses whereas bachelor programmes accounted for 21% (Table 7.2). To compete, PEIs engage in

Table 7.2: Types of courses offered by PEIs (2011–2015).

Courses/As on 31 December (in %)	2011	2012	2013	2014	2015
Postgraduate	5	7	7	9	8
Bachelor	15	17	17	21	21
Diploma	39	32	32	27	25
Certificate	24	20	13	6	6
Preparatory	17	11	13	10	9
Foreign System Schools[a]		8	8	14	16
Others[b]		5	10	13	15[c]

Notes: [a]Provide primary and secondary education in accordance with international curricula primarily to children of expatriates in Singapore.
[b]Include English proficiency and special education courses.
[c]Include Workforce Skills Qualifications (WSQ) courses.
Source: *CPE Annual Reports* (various years).

intensive advertising campaigns both through the traditional platform and social media, highlighting the accolades, university partners, particularly their rankings and awards earned. PEIs create the wants the students seek to satisfy; multiple pathways allow students who would not qualify for a programme in mainstream education to a short-duration bridging programme, and subsequently enrol into a higher level academic programme at the PEIs, including an undergraduate programme, never mind that the university is relatively less well known. To stand out in the competition, PEIs strive to achieve top rankings in competitions organised by agencies such as Asia One People's Choice and JobsCentral.

Taken together, PEIs operate in a competitive market. Below, I suggest some broad measures for PEI consideration to unlock value and remain competitive:

- Strengthen the brand position of the PEIs. This is especially important because the actual worth of the investment in education is felt only after the purchases or students have bought and used the 'product'.

- Develop a student-centric culture in the PEIs; pro-actively taking care of students' academic and non-academic needs.
- Cultivate relationship with industry players, for example, through setting up of the business advisory panel.
- Emphasise holistic development of students via innovative teaching pedagogy and methods of assessment. At UniSIM, students are required to take charge of their pre-class learning by accessing materials on the e-learning platform, engage in in-class activity to exchange views and decisions, and post-class reflection by consolidating what students have learned via e-portfolio and online group discussion. As Tsui Kai Chong, Provost of the university, explains, "by so re-configuring learning responsibilities and sharpening higher order thinking, formative habits can develop into lifelong practices" (Tsui, 2015: 257).
- Inculcate a competitive mindset; winning awards and obtaining certificates of excellence to protect the PEI's market share and serve as barriers to entry.
- Diversify the portfolio of products. Students have varied expectations. Some may prefer to acquire a qualification from a university of high ranking and one that is accredited by bodies such as AACSB and European Quality Improvement System (EQUIS), others do not. Product diversity offers choices to students, and therefore stands a better chance to attract and admit more students.

In addition to operating in a highly competitive environment, PEIs face the challenge of getting their courses more recognised by the hiring companies, a topic we will turn to in the next chapter.

Chapter 8

Academic Quality, Course Recognition

8.1 Introduction

In the previous chapter, we have shown that the private education institutions (PEIs) in Singapore operate in a very competitive environment. A PEI competes with about 300 players. The buyers and sellers have strong bargaining power relative to the PEIs and intense rivalry among the incumbents potentially caps the profitability of the market players. The establishment of new public universities such as the Singapore Institute of Technology, offering programmes in Engineering, Infocomm Technology and Businesses (e.g. in Accountancy and Hospitality Management) that are catered specifically to graduates from the local polytechnics, further dampens the growth prospects of PEIs.[1] One in five polytechnic graduates would have secured a place with the public university in 2016 as compared to less than 15% 4 years ago thereby lowering the number of potential students enrolling into PEI courses.[2]

PEIs have relied on international students to fill up the classrooms. But that market is highly unpredictable and externally driven. Universities around the world are eyeing to capture a share of the global education market. Exchange rates matter. Instead of migrating to Singapore to further their education, weaknesses in the United States, European and Australian currencies relative to the Singapore dollar encourage students

145

from China or India and elsewhere in the region to study on-campus. International students who are pursuing a PEI course and holding a student pass are not permitted work during vacation. This compares unfavourably with international students in local polytechnics and universities who are allowed to work during vacation and are exempted from applying for work permit. The world economy is also undergoing much slower growth due to slow recovery in the western countries, continued stagnation in Japan and decelerated growth in China.

Advances in cloud and virtual technology are allowing universities to offer on-line education. Students are able to complete courses and earn a certificate of accomplishment from reputable universities at the comfort of their home. International students themselves are seeing greater opportunity at home with plans to build more universities to increase the enrolment ratio.

In a speech delivered at the Singapore Association for Private Education Conference in October 2015, Council for Private Education (CPE) Chief Executive Officer, Brandon Lee, reported a drop in student enrolment in the private education sector in 2014 as compared to the previous year, especially in the degree segment. "Nearly every PEI in this (degree) segment, bar a couple of exceptions saw declines in the range of 10–30% … We have had more closures since the beginning of this year — 10 in total including two regulatory closures. Another eight have indicated to us that they wish to deregister in the coming months". Lee cited rising costs in rent and wages as a contributing factor and "certainly the strong Singapore dollar makes it less attractive for international students to study in Singapore and makes it easier for more Singaporeans to study overseas".[3]

The days where some of the larger PEIs were able to be selective and reject applications into their courses are possibly gone. Whether Singapore continues to be an attractive place to study is contestable in view of the rising cost of living and restrictive policy for immigrants. Competition will force the less efficient PEIs to merge with others or cease operations altogether. The consolidation of the industry will eventually lead to shrinking in the number of players in the industry.

Many of the problems are external in nature. They are more difficult to predict and control. Because they can directly affect the profitability of PEIs, it is useful to identify the problems and take actions to mitigate the impact. The most important action or decision to make, in my opinion, is finding ways to improve the quality of student learning experience. Before taking this further, it is necessary to begin by discussing a very specific challenge that confronts the private education sector, the issue of course recognition and academic standards.

8.2 Current Situation

Thousands of students from Singapore and abroad have graduated with a diploma or a degree with the PEIs. Many have gained employment or advanced their career. Alas, the PEIs' contribution to Singapore's progress is rarely noted in the mainstream media. Instead, scandals affecting some of the PEIs often hit the headlines. Critics of private education hark on the courses' (short) duration, qualification of the teaching staff and quality of the courses.

In recent years, much has been done to raise the quality and corporate governance standards of the PEIs. The establishment of CPE has provided the overall direction for developing, reviewing and implementing policies and procedures related to corporate governance and work environment. Has the sector's image and reputation improved?

Table 8.1 shows the Customer Satisfaction Index of Singapore (CSIS), which gathers the respondents' experience with an entity (the National University of Singapore (NUS), for example). Modelled after the American Customer Satisfaction Index, the CSIS is maintained by the Institute of Service Excellence at the Singapore Management University (SMU) to give the satisfaction score ranging between 0 and 100 with a higher score representing greater customer satisfaction.

Unlike public education institutions where an index is presented for each of the institutions, the PEIs are lumped together with an index score.[4] The 2-year data for 2014 and 2015 revealed a significant 1.7 point (or 2.5%) year-on-year decline in satisfaction for private education due to lower satisfaction from students in vocational programmes (satisfaction for non-vocational courses actually registered a small increment in satisfaction) and those who study on a part-time mode. In 2016 Quarter 2, the private education sector obtained a score of 65, which was significantly lower than the score obtained by the public education sector (77.1 points for the universities sub-sector and 74 points for the polytechnics sub-sector). Customer satisfaction for public education was higher in 2014

Table 8.1:   Customer Satisfaction Index, Singapore.

Year	Private education	Public education	Universities	Polytechnics	National score
2007	69.5	—	70.9	69.2	68.7
2008	71	—	68.7	69.9	67.8
2009	66	—	70.7	68.7	68
2010	65	—	69.3	68.5	67.2
2011	74.5	70.3	72.5	69.8	69.1
2012	69	67.5	66.7	69.6	69.9
2013	72.2	72.8	73.1	72.2	70.7
2014	65.8	73	73.5	71.1	71.1
2015	64.1	74.1	75.6	69.8	70.2
2016Q2	65.0	75.7	77.1	71.5	—

Source: Customer Satisfaction Index of Singapore (various years).

and the gap widened in 2015. It is interesting to note that in 2011 and 2012 the satisfaction score for private education was higher than the score for public institutions. Overall, there is no clear evidence to suggest any improvement in the reputation of private education sector after the establishment of the CPE.

Even some of the PEIs are not defending the values of 'Singapore private education', and doubt their association with the sector. Take the case of Australia's James Cook University (JCU). In April 2015, JCU Singapore became the first PEI to win the prestigious EduTrust Star award "for having excelled in all key areas of management and the provision of quality education services. This mark is also a symbol of recognition for sustained efforts in organisational improvement". Quite remarkably, in the same newspaper article that reported the significant milestone in the private education industry in Singapore, the award was seen by JCU Singapore as a means to boost its chance of securing the recognition in Singapore "as a foreign university branch campus, *rather than being classified as a Private Education Institution* as it is currently labelled" (emphasis added).[5] Slightly more than a year later, the university was offered the branch campus status by the Singapore government. By calling itself "an Australian university with a campus in Singapore" instead of a

PEI, JCU Singapore has gained "legitimacy and clarity" to its "position" and "ambition" to be "one of the great universities of the tropics," said the university's Vice-Chancellor.[6]

There is clearly a need to shift the mind-set of stakeholders with regard to 'PEI qualifications', and much more needs to be done.

8.3 Course Recognition

In the minds of students and their parents, ultimately the question is whether the diploma and degree courses are recognised by hiring companies. The JobsCentral Learning Rankings and Survey 2013 identified "Recognition of Certificate" as the most important factor affecting a person's decision to enrol in PEI courses with 92.2% of the total respondents of 8,367 people indicating it as a very important factor.[7] "Recognition of Certificate" remained a deciding factor in the survey conducted in 2015. Around 93% of the 2,932 voters indicated course recognition as a very important factor.[8]

In their study on international students' reasons to study in a PEI in Singapore, Min, Khoon, and Tan (2012) found that students held four motives; (i) to acquire quality education in Singapore (academic and education), (ii) to have the opportunity to work while studying (work), (iii) to migrate to Singapore and get a good job upon graduation (career and migration) and (iv) to live in a foreign country (pleasure and experience). Career and migration appeared to have the highest level of motives among the 263 students surveyed with academic and education, career and migration and pleasure and experience occupying second, third, and fourth spots, respectively.[9] Clearly, programme recognition is associated with these factors, and has strong implications in terms of meeting the aspirations of the students and PEI revenue objective.

8.4 How Do We Assess the Value of PEI Courses?

Starting salary of graduates provides an indication of whether the qualification is industry recognised. How do graduates from the private education sector in Singapore perform in this regard? Hiring companies' recognition of the PEI courses is especially important in the Singapore context where no agency, including the CPE, endorses PEI courses.[10] It is no secret that hiring companies distinguish between degrees obtained from a foreign university and those acquired from the local universities by offering fresh graduates from local universities a salary of 10–15% more than their counterparts from the private institutions.

Some of the hiring managers may have a higher regard for graduates from the PEIs probably because they were the product of the industry themselves. Therefore, they have a better understanding of the demands of the programme and the amount of hard work that one has to put in to earn the diploma and degree. Others continue to view a foreign degree obtained through the private education sector and the PEI diploma negatively. For example, government agencies such as the Monetary Authority of Singapore (MAS) have effectively closed the doors on graduates from the private education sector. MAS set the minimum qualification requirements for financial advisors on 1 February 2014, requiring applicants to have (i) a full certificate in GCE 'A' Level; (ii) an International Baccalaureate Diploma qualification; (iii) a diploma awarded by a polytechnic in Singapore; or (iv) any other academic qualification which is equivalent to the qualifications set out in sub-paragraph (i), (ii) or (iii) above. On what is deemed as equivalent to the qualifications set out in (i), (ii) and (iii) above, MAS provides the following response:

"As there are many possible equivalent qualifications, especially from foreign institutions, it is not MAS' intention, nor is it practicable, to provide an exhaustive list of such qualifications. In this regard, individual financial advisers should conduct their own due diligence assessment on whether a particular qualification may be deemed equivalent to the minimum academic qualification requirement. Financial advisers may use the following guiding principles to determine whether a qualification could be considered as being equivalent to a full GCE 'A' Level certificate, International Baccalaureate Diploma qualification or diploma awarded by a polytechnic in Singapore:

1. The total number of training hours of the course is at least 900 hours, or the course duration is at least 2.5 years on a part-time basis;
2. The assessment method is minimally 50% examination-based; and
3. The qualification allows for admission into a university."[11]

Most, if not all the PEI will not be able to meet criterion 1. Typically, PEI diplomas can be completed within a year on full-time basis, and 15 to 18 months on a part time basis.

I am of course not suggesting that the MAS should not revise the qualified minimum requirements. Hiring companies have every right to determine the terms of employment. My purpose, rather, is to highlight a contradiction that career seeking students and hiring companies have to resolve. On the one hand, the government, through the CPE, has for 7 years now put in place a set of strict guidelines and regulations for PEIs to comply with, essentially to raise the standards of private education in Singapore. On the other hand, some of the hiring companies, including those in the public sector, continue to maintain a bias against PEI qualification.

Another way to assess hiring companies' recognition of PEI courses is to conduct resume audit studies. The approach examines how employers perceive and respond to characteristics of job seekers, including race, gender, qualifications, nationality, and others. In recent years, at least two studies have applied the approach, one in the United States (Deming *et al.*, 2016) and the other in Malaysia (Lee and Muhammad Abdul Khalid, 2016). Deming *et al.* (2016) sent fictitious resumes to apply for business and health jobs as a means to measure hiring companies' perception of the value of post-secondary qualification acquired through private and public higher education institutions in the United States. The results showed that applicants with BA in Business from for-profit colleges were 22% less likely to receive a callback as compared to applicants with similar academic qualification from public schools. In the health sector, applicants who had acquired qualifications from for-profit colleges were 57% less likely to receive callbacks for interviews. The results suggested that employers viewed for-profit post-secondary credentials "as a negative signal of applicant quality" (*Ibid*: 780). In another study, Lee and Muhammad Abdul Khalid (2016) examined whether racial discrimination exists in Malaysia when it came to hiring of fresh graduates. Fictitious Malay and Chinese resumes were sent to hiring companies in the private sector. The study found that Chinese resumes were far more likely to receive a call for interview than Malay resumes, and the probability of callback was higher if the applicant was proficient in the Chinese language. In assuring the value of PEI courses in Singapore, a similar approach can be applied to ascertain if stereotyping exists in the mind of the hiring agents and if there is adverse pre-judgment of applicants' capability, presumably using the type of institutions awarding the qualification as a proxy for unobserved variables.

8.5 Sources of Low Recognition of PEI Courses: Myth or Reality?

Broadly speaking, there are at least five sources for lower recognition of PEI Courses.

Issue 1: PEIs are Not Government-Linked Companies (GLCs)

In August 1991, Singaporeans received with enthusiasm the news from the government about the establishment of the Singapore Open University (SOU), modelled after the Open University system in the United Kingdom. The government-linked SOU was to offer working adults a second chance to obtain a degree through a more flexible mode of teaching and learning after missing out on a degree earlier in their life. Six months following the announcement, the government changed its mind. Instead of establishing SOU as a *public institution*, the government announced that it would assist a PEI to offer similar courses. As Kevin Tan (2015: 44) wrote: "This sudden change of mind confused and upset many potential students who thought that the SOU would be *their ticket to better job prospects*" (emphasis added), suggesting a strong negative connotation attached to PEI qualifications.

The perception seems to be unfounded. For one, the Public Service Division (PSD) of Singapore does not close its doors to potential applicants who have graduated with a foreign university. As noted in the FAQ on its website, there is "no central government authority that assesses or accords recognition to degrees for employment purposes. In general, degrees from universities accredited by the home government of the country where the university originates will be considered for appointment into the Public Service…. This applies to all degrees, regardless whether they were obtained full time or part time, through distance learning or twinning programmes".[12] There seems to be a tendency to associate private education qualification with lower job prospects. Reversing the mindset remains a challenge to both the CPE and PEIs.

Human Resource practitioners have also pointed out that they paid attention to applicant's cognitive and soft skills as well in assessing the person's suitability for the job. The fact that the applicant has graduated from National University of Singapore (NUS) or Nanyang Technological University (NTU) does not automatically establish the person as more qualified than others. Siddharth Jain, Chief Creative Director of gaming company Playware Studios, considers other aspects, such as working experience and the projects the applicants have done in schools: "When we look at a candidate, we've looking at his cover letter, the number of projects he has done, the kind of resume he has…. Just the fact that you're from NUS or NTU doesn't give me any comfort because we've had experiences where students have a lot of bookish knowledge but not enough hands-on exercise".[13]

But there is no proof to support these claims. On the contrary, the results of the first graduate employment survey of PEIs suggest that the negative connotation associated with private sector education has remained. In January 2016, the Council for Private Education, with the support from the Ministry of Manpower and Ministry of Education, announced the move to gauge the worth of private degrees. The government appointed Forbes Research in October 2015 to conduct an 18-week long study on graduates from nine PEIs.[14] In September 2016, CPE released the results of the employment survey. Among the 4,200 students who graduated with a degree from the PEIs in 2014, 58% of them managed to find a full time job within six months of completing their degrees, which compared poorly to 83% of graduates from *public* institutions like the NUS, NTU and SMU in the same period.[15]

Issue 2: Improper Practices

The intensity of competition and ever rising costs of operations have resulted in some private schools making false promises about the school facilities and academic programmes. A combination of greed and stiff competition has driven the PEIs to take on more risks. When more cautious PEIs see their rivals moving ahead of the sales curve, they want to leap ahead even if this means lowering the entry requirements for their programmes and shortening the programme duration. They do so just to make the programme appear more attractive and appealing to potential students; a myopic view in decision-making without due regard to how people may think about programme quality, corporate governance and integrity of the operators.

Corporate scandals and corporate failures are of course not uncommon, and they do not normally adversely affect the whole industry. The closure of a food stall selling chicken rice due to unhygienic food preparation practices does not deter consumers from patronising other chicken rice food stalls. Similarly, closure of a PEI due to economic and business conditions should not be seen as any different from any other company that has decided to call it quits. Closure of the PEIs due to improper practices like offering unaccredited or fake degrees to unsuspecting students is treated somewhat differently. The cases are widely reported in the local media, framing the problem as systemic in nature and relating to PEIs' overwhelming focus on the commercial aspect of the business which overrode everything else. Images of students from countries like Vietnam, Indonesia, and Myanmar failing to recoup the thousands of dollars that they had paid to the PEIs, and the adverse impact of the scandals on Singapore's reputation further heightened the negative image of the entire private education sector.

The reality is that the industry is made up of PEIs with varying standards and quality. There are robust PEIs with quality and relevant courses. The CPE has classified the PEIs into various categories to depict the standard of compliance with its rules and regulations. Students can do their part by selecting a reputable PEI and university, graduating with good results and demonstrating their non-academic credentials on their resumes and in interviews. Qualifications from a good standing institute for higher learning deserve recognition. Inderjit Singh, Ang Mo Kio GRC MP and CEO of Solstar International, advised students to pay particular attention to the university offering the degree "because the standards are different… So, don't just go for paper, you should go for quality paper".[16] The comments mirrored Prime Minister Lee Hsien Loong's view about private degrees. In a forum organised by MediaCorp on 4 September 2014, Lee cautioned "You have to do your homework and make sure that you study for a degree which is rigorous, which is valuable, and where you can, which has jobs available".[17]

Issue 3: Equating Short Duration Courses with Low Quality

Some of the PEI have positioned their courses as ideal for students who wish to complete the programmes within a short period of time. Several Members of Parliament (MPs) have cautioned against choosing a PEI programme on the basis that it allows faster graduation. Mountbatten MP Lim Biow Chuan noted that "getting a degree is very much a training of the mind. If you are chasing a degree because of speed, I think you'll short-change yourself…. It's very difficult to say that getting a degree in super-fast time amounts to quality teaching".[18]

The danger arises when critics lament on a 3-year degree programme that could be completed within 24 months without fully understanding how the PEIs operate. Shorter programme duration at PEIs (24 months for a typical 3-year undergraduate programme) is attributed to innovative scheduling and time-tabling, compressing a typical 3-year programme to 2 calendar years. This is possible because of shortened study breaks in between semesters and faster turnaround time in marking and moderating of coursework and final exams. For example, PEIs may offer the undergraduate programmes on a trimester mode of 17 weeks of teaching with each student reading four modules per trimester on a full time basis, allowing the student to read 24 modules in 2 calendar years. Moreover, the programme duration as stated on the website or programme brochure indicates the minimum time required to complete the course. Students have the option to do less and learn more by taking fewer modules per term.

In the case of PEI *Diploma* courses, claims that PEI students are short changed or embark on a non-rigorous programme are unfounded on the basis of comparison between a PEI Diploma and a polytechnic Diploma. PEI Diplomas are not similar to a polytechnic which takes an average of 3 years to complete. They are not meant to be similar. PEI Diplomas are in most cases mapped to Year 1 of an undergraduate programme thereby allowing the graduates to proceed to Year 2 upon completion. No PEI has claimed that its Diploma course is equivalent to a polytechnic diploma. That is the perception of some of the employers, and the perception is incorrect.

Issue 4: Equating Research Active Doctorate Holders as Qualified Lecturers

Some of the employers have voiced their concern about the qualifications of PEIs' lecturers. Unlike public universities, a majority of the lecturers in PEIs do not possess a PhD nor are they active in research. Does the quality of teaching measured by students' understanding of the subject contents equate to possession of a PhD of the number of papers the lecturer has published in journals? The correlation is contestable.

Universities participate in ranking games. The 'publish or perish' mentality exerts great pressure on academic staff, especially newer staff to publish in reputable journals. Universities emphasise research outcome in staff promotion, hiring, tenure, and compensation. Research active PhD holders spend more time on research, and correspondingly less time devoted to teaching-related activities such as class preparation and student consultation.

The essential idea of education is to produce students who are industry ready, and infuse various perspectives in classes to enable students to think straight, morally and critically. The trouble in most university education is that much of what goes on in classes is almost exclusively focused on models, theories and frameworks without some serious empirical analysis. The most helpful lecturers are not those with doctorate degrees. Salman Khan, founder of the Khan Academy, observed that "professors who knew their subject.. simply weren't very good at sharing what they know". Teaching, to Khan, "is a separate skills — in fact, an art that is creative, intuitive, and highly personal" (Khan, 2012: 17). Asit Biswas and Julian Kirchherr have called for universities to consider previous working experience for hiring and promotion "to boost the practical value of higher education for university students".[19] Their observation is spot on.

In the years that I have been involved in the private education industry, I have seen many non-doctorates and non-research active doctorate teaching staff with many years of working experiences in the relevant industries who have received excellent evaluation results from students. There is no direct correlation between the academic qualifications of the lecturers and the end of course evaluation results. The CPE has stipulated the academic qualifications required of a teaching staff, and the PEIs have complied with the requirement. PEIs' teaching staff conduct their duties with much commitment, supporting the students before, during, and after the scheduled classes to ensure that their students are equipped with the knowledge and skills to succeed in their courses and these are what matter most to students and students' success. The value add in class derives from the passion for teaching and the type of knowledge, skills and real world experiences the lecturers can bring into the class.

Issue 5: PEI Courses are Not Recognised by Stakeholders

This is a myth. Critics of private education have overlooked the fact that there are organisations and institutions based in Singapore and elsewhere that offer recognition for PEI courses. Employers have sponsored their staff to sign up for academic and training courses with the PEIs. For-profit organisations are rationale, and they invest in education when the perceived private returns exceed private cost. There are also self-help groups such as Mendaki, Singapore Indian Development Association (SINDA) and Chinese Development Assistance Council (CDAC) that provide strong encouragement and financial assistance of up to 95% of the course fees to low income self-funding individuals in their quest to upgrade their knowledge and skills. Individuals apply for PEI certificate and diploma courses are eligible to seek for financial support.

Similarly, the Workforce Development Agency (WDA) provides funding for students to embark on PEI courses. WDA provides Singaporeans and Permanent Residents of Singapore aged 21 years old and above funding of up to 95% of fees for certifiable courses approved by WDA, which consisted of courses accredited under the Singapore Workforce Skills Qualifications (WSQ) system and courses that are non-WSQ but funded by the Singapore WDA. The latter includes courses offered through private education such as Advanced Diploma courses in Management, Marketing and Finance awarded by Kaplan Singapore and other short courses offered by PEIs like SIMGE and MDIS.[20]

The foreign university partners represent another crucial source of support for the PEIs, peer reviewing, quality-checking and endorsing the PEI courses. Participating foreign universities have to protect their reputation and good standing. PEI courses are carefully reviewed and scrutinised by the home institution to ensure that the curriculum and mode of assessment are rigorous before graduates from PEI courses are allowed entry to the degree programme. The articulation agreement that is eventually agreed upon and signed by both parties allows graduates from PEI courses to gain entry into the degree programmes offered in collaboration with their universities' partners. Upon entry, students studying in the degree programmes must meet the respective university academic standards, some of which are accredited by international accreditation agencies such as the Association to Advance Collegiate Schools of Business (AACSB). Students must also comply with the university academic policies, rules and expectations. After all, the degree awarded by the university is the same as the degree awarded to students on campus.

As can be seen, while there are valid concerns about PEI courses and they have to be properly managed, some of the concerns are hearsay and ought to be taken with a pinch of salt. But that does not mean that the latter is unimportant. PEIs also have to deal with myths and reduce the communication and perception gap. The sustainability of the PEIs requires a two-pronged approach. The following chapter considers the industry as a whole whilst the strategies at the company level will be discussed in Chapter 10.

Chapter 9

Transforming the Private Education Sector: What Needs to be Done?

9.1 Introduction

The basic premise is that there is much more to do and learn. Two considerations are put forward. First, it may be useful to consider the experience of vocational or technical education in Singapore. Today, technical education qualification in Singapore is widely accepted by the industry and is gaining popularity with students and parents. A case can be made to emulate some of the initiatives aimed to change the mindset of vocational education, and study their implications to the private education sector. Second, I argue that it is timely for the regulatory agency to pay more attention to the teaching standards and academic frameworks and put greater emphasis on academic quality. The current framework as exemplified in the Enhanced Registration Framework (ERF) and EduTrust certification scheme is largely procedural based where the private education institutions (PEIs) are expected to develop procedures and provide paper work evidences to demonstrate compliance. I argue that a procedure focused approach, while serving its objective to impose some accountability mechanisms, is inadequate. For the overall betterment of the private education sector in Singapore, the next stage of development would require the relevant regulatory agency to shift its focus from procedure to product to give greater assurance to students that the qualifications attained with the PEIs are valued by the hiring companies.

9.2 The Case of Technical Education

Effort to change the image of vocational education in Singapore had an early start. Under the Technical Education Department (TED) in 1968, public campaigns were introduced in Singapore to change public's perception towards vocational education. Top of the trade television and Apprenticeship of the Year awards were established to promote vocational education. When TED was replaced by the Industrial Training Board (ITB) in 1973 and later Vocational and Industrial Training Board (VITB) in 1979, further efforts were put in place to improve the image of vocational education. Greater autonomy was given to the institution to initiate changes to upgrade the quality of training and curriculum as a means to respond to the changing skilled manpower needs in Singapore. However, despite the greater efforts to improve the quality of training, writes Law Song Seng (2015: 167), "the poor image of vocational training remained a challenge for many more years".[1]

A significant turning point came in the early 1990s following the release of the government report entitled "The Report on Upgrading Vocational Training" (VITB, 1991). The report proposed replacing the term 'vocational' and renaming VITB as the Institute of Technical Education (ITE). The rationale for the change as noted in the report was that "pupils and parents have a poor image of vocational training. The term 'vocational' as in 'vocational training' is often assorted with a low image. … This is mainly due the perception that vocational institutes are for school failures …. similarly, in view of the negative perception that VITB is a place for school failure, it is proposed that VITB be renamed. … Removing the term 'vocational' would help to break the negative associations, long entrenched in the local context".[2]

More targeted measures were introduced by the ITE to improve the image of technical education. First, concerted efforts were made to reposition ITE as a post-secondary education institution, placing ITE in the same category as the local polytechnics and publicly funded universities.

With the change, students entering the ITE would have completed 10 years of formal education, comprising 6 years of primary education and 4 years of Normal (Technical) secondary education. This essentially means that the ITE would no longer be admitting primary school leavers who might not have sufficient academic grounding to pursue a technical education in the first place. Students who are admitted to ITE following the change stand a greater chance of completing the ITE course, graduating with a qualification and advancing their careers. ITE graduates would also be eligible to gain admission to the local polytechnics thereby providing an opportunity for students to further their studies at the polytechnic and even the universities.[3]

Second, ITE engaged in an extensive marketing and branding campaign to create a new image for technical education in Singapore. Newsworthy stories about the ITE and its students were shared with the media to give it every opportunity to reach out to the public. Former CEO of the ITE, Law Song Seng (2015: 174) noted that he must have given some 200 interviews and speeches. "I have no doubt that the value of the media highlighting our work helped in our efforts in rebranding ITE".[4] Presentations and road shows were organised on a regular basis for parents, potential students and the public to showcase the ITE. Secondary school students were invited to ITE campuses to learn more about the institution and its courses. Through such visits, students became more aware of ITE, the type of projects that ITE students worked on and relevance of ITE education. ITE hosted more than 1,000 overseas visitors annually, including Presidents, members of the royalty, ministers and government officials and leaders from top private firms around the world to share its experience and showcase the institution. By providing train-the-trainer programmes and expertise to countries like Nigeria, India, and Vietnam, ITE gained greater visibility at least within the vocational education sector at the regional and international level.

Third, ITE, as a statutory board, took advantage of its connection with the Singapore government to garner support and endorsement from political leaders. Goh Chok Tong, as Prime Minister of Singapore, was the guest-of-honour at the inauguration of ITE on 31 March 1992. Ministers for Education, from Teo Chee Hean to Heng Swee Keat, had put up good words about ITE education and qualification in their speeches.

Law (2015: 174) acknowledged that "the presence of the Prime Minister and Ministers at official functions, such as the launching of new ITE campuses and graduation ceremonies, had helped to showcase our progress and reinforce the important role of ITE in society". Law highlighted an especially important occasion where 43 Members of Parliament, at the invitation of Teo Chee Hean, visited ITE campuses in 2002. The endorsement from Ministers and MPs helped to boost ITE's reputation and attract positive media coverage. The media generated from the visits "not only helped to move the hearts of the public, but also changed the perception of policymakers," allowing ITE to "reach out to the various constituents and community at large" (*Ibid*: 174).

Credit has to be given to ITE team of staff and management for focusing on organisational excellence, which leads us to the fourth factor. ITE has a vision to be the global leader in technical education. ITE was bold and had a strong ambition to be a world class technical education institution. Campus facilities in the three sites at Simei, Chao Chu Kang and Ang Mo Kio are top notch, not usually seen in vocational institutions. Aerospace students are trained on an actual Boeing 737. Students in the hospitality programme are trained in a 22-room campus hotel. ITE worked hard to develop closer relationship with the industry partners, inking over 100 Memoranda of Understanding with world class companies such as Rolls-Royce, Adobe, McDonald's and others — a significant testament to the quality of its courses. ITE has also put in place the Developing a Curriculum system, a process that requires the curriculum to be endorsed and signed off by industry representatives basically to ensure that the course learning outcomes are packed with knowledge and skills required by the industry. Industry involvement extends to industry representatives gracing the graduation ceremonies, sponsoring awards and prizes, donating equipment, bursaries and scholarships, and providing opportunities for staff and students of ITE to work with companies (Varaprasad, 2016: 166). In December 2016, *The Straits Times* reported that applications to the ITE have increased by more than 10% over the last 10 years. In 2015, the ITE took in 24.5% of the Primary 1 cohort, up from 20.6% in 2010. Students were attracted to the ITE because of its practical style of teaching and learning.[5]

ITE is benchmark against the Singapore Quality Award (SQA) model of business excellence, making strong efforts to review and improve key processes and practices. ITE became the first education institution in Singapore to qualify for the Singapore Quality Class (SQC) and win the SQA for business excellence in 2005. In 2007, ITE scaled new heights by winning the Global IBM Innovations Award in Transforming Government conferred by the Ash Centre for Democratic Governance and Innovation at Harvard University's John F. Kennedy School of Government, earning the recognition as "the jewel in Singapore's crown". *The Straits Times* published a report noting that "ITE has gone from being an institution of last resort for low-achieving students to being internationally recognised…. There were high hopes the ITE could shed the negative image of vocational institute students as dropouts and low achievers".[6] In 2011, the ITE took home the SQA with Special Commendation Award.

What are the implications of ITE's experiences and success to the private education sector? The success story of the ITE is a testament to the hard work that members of the institution have put in over many years. The Council for Private Education (CPE) in particular can learn from how the ITE has managed to revamp the image of technical education to capture students', parents' and employers' hearts. The ITE case has shown that one needs to put in a strong, consistent, and deliberate effort to alter the image. The ITE realised that there was a serious lack of information about the ITE and its work. It undertook an extensive rebranding and marketing exercise to reach out to parents, students and the public, tapping on the support from the political leaders to achieve the cause. Stakeholders in the private education sector may in a similar vein take stock of the strengths of private education provision and embark on branding and marketing campaigns to achieve greater acceptance of private education in Singapore.

Notably, excellence in every aspect of the organisation is essential. ITE has relentlessly pursued organisational excellence under the SQA framework. Today, ITE education is no longer viewed as a poor alternative for academically weak students. It is perceived today as a legitimate post-secondary education path for students to develop and deepen their skills and specific strengths. PEIs should similarly strive to bring quality and excellence to their organisations and avoid the situation where commercial objectives override everything else. The CPE should strengthen the regulatory framework that emphasises academic excellence and standards.

Private education and technical education are confronted with very similar problems.[7] They are unlike other institutions of higher learning in Singapore which are catered to more academically inclined group of students. They do not compete directly with National University of Singapore (NUS), Nanyang Technological University (NTU) or Singapore Management University (SMU). ITE and PEIs are social enablers, providing their students a second opportunity to develop their potential to the fullest to improve their economic and social standing. The ITE case illustrates the importance of forward looking and strategic planning as it embarks on a journey of transformation. Private education sector in Singapore must recognise that they cannot continue to offer the same goods and services in the same way. Deliberate and targeted efforts need to be put in place on organisational excellence and to create products that are relevant to the industry. The CPE and PEIs should aim for breakthroughs so significant that they attract the attention of political leaders and excite the media to want to publicly talk about them. The CPE and the PEIs must work together to raise the profile of private education in Singapore to survive and thrive in this challenging economy.

9.3 Framework to Emphasise Academic Quality and Standards

As highlighted in Chapter 3, the CPE has put in place a regulatory framework to improve the standard of PEI governance. The current framework requires the PEIs to develop procedures and processes, and provide paper work evidence to demonstrate compliance. A procedure-focused approach, while serving its objectives to impose some accountability mechanisms, is necessary, but is not sufficient. Moving forward, as I have argued elsewhere, it is necessary for the CPE to pay more attention to the quality of the academic programmes and the learning outcomes attained by the students.[8] This would require greater scrutiny of the curriculum, delivery methods, modes of assessments and teaching hours to ensure that students are not deprived of quality education. Greater emphasis on academic excellence will result in further restructuring of the private education market, including the possibility of reducing the number of PEIs in the industry. Ultimately, what matters is to legitimise the PEIs and give greater assurance to students that the qualifications they attain are of good quality and recognised by hiring companies.

The Private Education Act 2009, through the Enhanced Registration Framework (ERF) and EduTrust, requires the PEIs to comply with pre-scribed criteria that have a strong association with procedure and process development. For example, criterion 3.1.1 of the EduTrust certification scheme (Version 2.0) requires the PEIs to have "a comprehensive moni-toring process for all engaged recruitment agents to ensure that they con-duct proper pre-course counselling and abide by the code of conduct"; "procedures to verify that agents have conducted proper pre-course coun-selling"; and "procedures to take appropriate, timely and necessary action when any agent violates the contractual agreements and/or code of con-duct" (Council for Private Education, 2009: 42). The Examination Board is responsible primarily for the *development* and implementation of the *processes* [emphasis added] that govern the conduct of formative and summative assessments, duties of invigilators and markets, appeals with regard to examination and assessment and security of the examination papers and answer scripts (Section 16, Private Education Act, 2009). There is no mention of the Board's responsibility for confirming the pro-gression and award decisions.

The regulation has shaped the industry structure as the number of PEIs shrank significantly to about 300 players today. Although financial support to comply with stricter standards was available to the PEIs in the transition period, some of the players have exited the industry for failing to meet the requirements of the newly established regulations.[9] There were possibly others who did not expect to reap a positive net benefit by undertaking the costly exercise to comply with the ERF and EduTrust criteria. The massive amount of data and reports for the CPE incurs a huge opportunity cost on the private education institutions, particularly the smaller players, with a large amount of resources devoted to the cause. Unlike higher education learning institutions such as public universities, private schools face a more serious constraint of limited resources as a consequence of their profit orientation.

The CPE current framework has set the minimum quality floor, a necessary step to legitimise the existence of the PEIs and to enable the

PEIs to operate. The CPE prescribes procedures and processes for the PEIs to deal with matters such as student contracts and the recruitment of lecturers. Auditing is largely confined to making sure that the processes and procedures are in place, and looking for evidence of compliance.

But the bar has to be raised. It may be thought that a procedure-based approach makes processes more consistent but, instead, this makes it harder for the PEIs to improve. The processes are standards that are applicable to all PEIs, and they are insensitive to the sector's large diversity. The current regulatory system is not able to accurately reflect quality differences among the PEIs that have nevertheless met the ERF requirements, offering no added benefits to PEIs that have emphasised academic excellence more than others. In addition, the framework does not indicate the duration of PEI certificate and diploma courses nor does it require the PEIs to submit student guides, session plans and assessment details prior to course commencement. It pays no attention to the module or programme content. There is no requirement to ensure that the assessments are appropriate at the certificate level or the diploma level. There is no check on whether the assessments have been carefully crafted to meet the learning outcomes.

Another contested CPE criterion concerns the review requirement of modules and programmes awarded by the PIEs. Criteria 5.2.1 and 5.1.2 of the EduTrust certification scheme stipulate the requirements for the PEIs to have a comprehensive "curriculum planning process for all the courses" (Council for Private Education, 2009: 66) and "review process to regularly review the curriculum for all courses" (*Ibid*: 64), respectively. Without the involvement of academics who are well versed in their respective fields, the reality is that it would not be easy for the CPE inspectors to tell whether the requirement is merely treated as a paper exercise with no real benefit. Some of the schools may have the tendency to review and change the course materials on a more frequent basis than before so as to show the authority that something has been done rather than doing so for the benefit of triggering positive students' learning experience. The main argument is that failure to plan carefully may result in less than desirable outcomes. For one thing, the resultant superficial changes in curriculum impose unnecessary constraints on the teachers, especially those who are teaching on a part-time basis.[10] One possible reason for the failure of the innovations (i.e. changes in the curriculum) is that they are introduced into an environment that is hostile. For an innovation to survive, it needs to be carefully conceptualised and legitimated. Doing so hurriedly, without careful deliberation with the stakeholders, will not bring significant benefits. Even if one is sympathetic to the arguments against the lack of reviews, it does not automatically follow that an extensive form of review would be better.

In this regard, the standards applied by the CPE differ from the Workforce Development Agency (WDA). WDA develops the Workforce Skills Qualifications (WSQ) framework in various industries to equip students with the necessary skills to enter and raise their productivity level in these industries. To teach WSQ modules, education providers, including the PEIs, are required to obtain course accreditation from the WDA to teach a module, multiple modules or full qualification leading to the award of WSQ Certificates and Diplomas and they must submit course lesson plans. It is mandatory for the education providers to provide course assessment plans, trainer guides and learner guides to the WDA and the materials must be developed by persons with Advanced Certificate in Training and Assessment (ACTA) and Diploma in Adult and Continuing Education (DACE) qualifications. It is worth noting that WSQ courses are recognised nationwide despite the fact that the courses are run by approved PEIs as opposed to PEI courses (which are perceived to be lower in quality).

What needs to be done? For a start, it is important for the CPE to pay more attention to the academic aspects of the private education business. This should take place in full view of the fact that the reputation of the PEIs can potentially affect the reputation of Singapore as a learning destination. Promoting academic excellence has to be the focus. The CPE should recognise the different levels of complexity and degrees of achievement of the various programmes — certificate, diploma and advanced diploma levels — and specify the desired learning attributes for each of the levels. By indicating the broad knowledge and skills for each level, CPE should revise its framework to provide for the PEIs to design the course and assessment tasks that are commensurate with the expected student outcomes. The learning outcomes of each course should be explicitly identified and mapped to the graduate attributes of the institution. Similarly, the learning outcomes of each module should be aligned with the objective of the programme. Students should demonstrate the learning outcomes through the design of the module, and the latter should be reviewed periodically to ensure that they remain relevant. The PEI should be held responsible for ensuring the provisions of the graduate attributes and learning outcomes through the module and programme review exercise, and that its students have satisfactorily met the requirements prior to awarding the qualifications. PEIs must take adequate steps to comply with the guidelines stipulated by the CPE, and flag and show cause for any non-compliance to the authority.

Currently, there is no prescribed method to determine the course contact hours. As a result, the duration of a PEI diploma course can range from 6–15 months. Academic improvement calls for the PEIs to locate the load of courses by developing a credit points system. The credit points assigned to the modules should add up to the total credit points as determined by the CPE for a particular level of study. The system would allow the CPE to provide useful guidelines to the PEIs on the allocation of hours for lab activities, tutorials and lectures. The information should be published and made available to the public to allow potential students (and eventually the hiring companies) to gauge the performance of PEI graduates in relation to student learning. In designing the credit points system, the CPE has to bear in mind that the PEI Diploma is not equivalent to a typical 3-year Diploma course offered by Singapore polytechnics. In most cases, PEI courses are positioned as equivalent by level to the first year of study of an undergraduate programme.

The CPE has the responsibility of ensuring that students have benefited from enrolling in PEI courses by ascertaining the true quality of private education and identifying areas for improvement. The CPE should facilitate the process of academic reform and make certain that the changes will bring more educational gain than loss but the PEIs must lead the movement. The CPE appoints and sends inspectors to the PEIs to gather paper evidence to check whether the procedures have been complied with and raise areas for improvement for non-compliance, and there is hardly any attempt to inspect the quality and content of the programmes. Auditors who are familiar with the subject matter should be appointed by the CPE and be responsible in inspecting the relevant documents and seeking answers from students and lectures to make sure that the provisions make sense to the stakeholders and are complied with. Focusing on the product quality would not be effective if the inspectors are not able to make sense of the technical aspects of the modules.

In summary, the establishment of the ERF and EduTrust schemes in Singapore's private education sector was reactive in the sense that the authority recognised the need to interfere more closely after unethical practices of some private schools were exposed through the media, suggesting that pre-CPE measures were inadequate in mitigating improper practices among the private education providers. When schools made the decision to cease operation, students were left stranded, imposing on them both monetary and non-monetary costs. The scandals adversely affected Singapore's reputation as a safe place for parents from abroad to send their children to pursue their education. The number of cases of misbehaviour was actually trivial relative to the size of the industry but the perceived impact of the scandalous behaviour was so great that it led to enactment of new rules and policies that effectively affected all players.

Singaporean publicly funded universities have placed a strong emphasis on reputation building as reflected in their focus on moving up the university rankings. Safeguarding the integrity of the education sector in the city–state is a priority. The government would not want any negative news or scandal originating from either the private or public education sector and, in this regard, there is tremendous pressure on the CPE to ensure that the PEIs are well run. I have presented the case for the CPE to shift its focus from process and procedures to product, to give greater assurance to students that the qualifications attained are useful and beneficial. Sub-standard academic programmes ill-prepare students for the real world. There is no shortcut to success. If the PEI offers a diploma that falls short of the standard, the discrepancy should be easily identified by students and hiring companies. Such a level of quality assurance is necessary. I have argued here that the profit motive should not be a barrier to upholding academic standards.

Chapter 10

Back to the Basics

10.1 Introduction

How to stay competitive is the big question on the minds of the private education institutions (PEIs). In this concluding chapter, we show that a balance is required between educational objectives and commercial goals to operate the PEIs successfully. The chapter also emphasises the importance of placing students at the centre of everything the PEIs do particularly in relation to students' learning experience. A useful starting point is to gain a better understanding of the nature of business the PEIs are in.

10.2 Characteristics of Education

Education is characterised as a risky form of investment. Potential students form expectations about the service and quality of the programmes, and compare with the actual experience upon enrolment and class commencement. Student–staff interaction determines the level of functional quality as perceived by the students, offering the PEI the crucial opportunity to demonstrate to students why they should choose to pursue their education with the PEI. It is also essential for the PEIs to consider the delivery of the service as a full package — the facilities, curriculum and actions and decisions of the receptionists, programme consultants, agents, operations executives, academics as well as those expected from members of the management team.

Image matters considerably. Students read and hear about the PEI and its products through promotional and marketing activities before enrolling into the programme. They may visit the PEI to attend the course previews and interact with students and staff members of the PEI to assess their behaviour, obtain advice and gain a better understanding of the PEI and its courses. Employees and overseas agents with high customer contact must have the knowledge about the PEI, programmes, module requirements, assessment methods, fees charged, application procedures, exemption policies, articulation pathway, and others. The service delivery must be planned and executed well to furnish correct information to students, and align the expectations of the students. If the expectations are not met when the service is being delivered, it may be too late to take corrective actions.

One of the challenges facing the PEIs is the inability of employees to fully comprehend the module and programme requirements, and understand the PEIs' target segment, which results in students forming and transmitting an inaccurate impression of the demands and requirements of the programme to potential students. Overcoming the challenge requires the PEI to put together training sessions for programme consultants to present the courses in respect of the curriculum and any other topics it feels are pertinent to have better equipped recruitment officers. There has to be a deliberate effort to strengthen the relationship between the academic staff and programme consultants or recruitment officers. The latter has an agenda or is subject to key performance indicators that are not necessarily in line with those from the academic division. Working in isolation creates discontentment among the students when they realise the disparity between perceived and actual learning experience after they are enrolled into the PEI course.

Education is in the service business, a performance or an effort that is largely intangible. Students buy educational services, including knowledge acquisition, academic advice and a dream to have a better future. Most service providers also produce tangible output such as food in restaurants and typed contracts in the banking and financial sector. Schools produce tangible items such as course materials; subject guides which describe the module learning outcomes, assignment tasks and submission and marking guidelines; students' handbook, which contains description of the school's academic and non-academic policies, process, rules and regulations. Certainly, clarity of the language helps to enhance the image of the school.

10.3 Student Centricity

The importance attached to customers is succinctly summarised by Sam Walton, founder of Walmart, in the following words: "There is one boss — the customer. And he can fire everybody in the company from the chairman on down, simply by spending his money somewhere else".[1] Without emphasis on student satisfaction and a good understanding of the ingredients that satisfies students, PEIs are living on borrowed time. Conversely, PEI students who have a positive learning experience are crucial sales and marketing agents for the PEI. Their actions and discussion about the PEI in a positive way help to drive business performance forward in terms of revenue, profit, and profitability. The PEIs have to consider student experience and student satisfaction as important parts of their business.

Services are rarely used in vacuum. The decision to visit a supermarket is dependent on the ease of travelling to the location and the availability of parking lots and trolleys, which affect the perceived value of going to the supermarket. In considering the learning journey of students, PEIs should look across complementary products and services offerings. One useful way to get around this issue is to consider students' learning journey before, during, and after they have completed their studies. Consider the case of international students. Making an effort to pick up the students upon arrival at the airport is an appreciated if not expected gesture from the school, following up with clear instructions to students on getting around the city and hotlines to contact in case of emergency. During the course of study, PEIs should consider organising personal development workshops to facilitate students' transition into tertiary education and fun extra curricular activities to mix the local and international students. Students worry about getting a job. Connecting international students to hiring companies through a PEI job portal would be positively received by students and parents.

Student centricity may inevitably lead to higher cost to the PEIs because of differentiated service provision. This will inevitably put pressure on the PEIs to raise course fees. What the PEIs need to do is to convince potential students how paying the course fees helps them to lower other costs. Suppose a PEI charges a higher course fee and part of the cost increase is a result of the PEI's decision to factor in the purchase price of the prescribed textbooks. Because the PEI is able to pre-order the books and buy in bulk, it enjoys superior discounts from the publisher. This translates to overall cost saving to the students. Moreover, the books are made available to students prior to course commencement therefore saving students' time to hunt for the books. Let these be made known to students. Consider another example. Some of the PEIs invest heavily on the use of technology or virtual learning system such as Moodle and Blackboard. While the investment may translate into higher course fees, it makes life easier for the students as it allows students to view contents online, download and upload documents, attempt online quizzes, and communicate with teaching staff after classroom hours. There are many ways to add value and benefits to the students. Some of the initiatives may reduce the students' other costs and lead to a whole array of positive benefits.

There is a misconception that being student-centric correlates with the use of technology in teaching and learning. Little or no use of technology in classroom can be student-centred as well. Identifying students who need academic help early in the course and providing academic support to help them cope with their studies is an example of a learner-centred activity. Smaller classes or smaller schools with fewer students offers lecturers a fantastic opportunity to know the students better, address their concerns and accord greater ownership to the students through, for example, flip teaching and presentation opportunities. Students enjoy their lessons and learn more, benefiting from smaller class size, and sharing their experience with friends and relatives. On the other hand, a fully online-based course does not automatically translate to more student centricity if students are not able to comprehend the materials put online. Student centricity is not about treating customers as bosses. It is about laying the foundation of trust that will strengthen the organisation's commitment to providing quality education through, for example, commitment to quality teaching.

10.4 Address the Language Issue

Language requirements are established to determine the eligibility of students for admittance to an academic programme. Language proficiency is an important consideration because it measures the ability of students to read, speak, and write the English language — a crucial factor in student's failure or success in academic performance. These apply to both domestic and international students. The latter deserve more attention from the PEIs probably because of their lack of exposure to the use of English in the home country.

International students will continue to be an important source of growth for the PEIs, and efforts to recruit international students will remain strong. The transition from the native speaking and learning environment to undertake courses that use English as the medium of instruction is not easy, leading to students struggling in their studies, dropping out from the programme, copying others work without proper acknowledgement, cheating in the examinations and stress.[2] It is important for the PEIs to provide good language support programmes to students to improve students' command of the English language, and for the PEIs to highlight the initiative as a key differentiating factor.

Consider students from China. In most cases, they feel nervous in using the English language when they arrive at the English-speaking environment. To be sure, Chinese student are exposed to English classes in Mainland China at the early age of 10 through secondary schools, which translates to over 5 years of English language learning. English has even been made a compulsory subject to take in *gaokao* for students to enter higher education, and success in examinations in the language is a prerequisite for many jobs. Yet, many find it difficult to cope with the language demands of the courses. Why is this so?

Notably, the nature of the Chinese language itself plays a role. There is a big linguistic difference between English and Chinese, exceeded only by the linguistic difference between English and Japanese (Grimes and Grimes, 1993). Chinese is a logographic and tonal language with grammar and vocabulary that are dissimilar with that of English. That is possibly why English is not taught in China before Grade 3, to enable students to concentrate in Grade 1 and 2, on learning the Chinese language and characters which requires considerable time and effort. Ideographic Chinese is more difficult to learn than phonetic English. If you are able to speak English, it is highly likely that you can read and write. On the contrary, being able to speak Chinese does not automatically translate to the ability to read and write. Learning by rote is common in learning the Chinese language as each stroke and dot in Chinese characters can make a difference in the meaning and pronunciation.

Public schools in China adopted the Grammar-Translation method of teaching English, which emphasised on reading and writing and rote memorisation of words and meaning (Hu, 2002), producing what has been known as 'deaf and dumb' English learner — students who were unable to engage in authentic communication beyond greetings even though they were able to pass English exams in reading and writing (Fan, 2010; Liu *et al.*, 2016). Use of English in China is also largely confined to hours when English lessons are taught in school. Students have limited chance to use the language outside the classroom where Mandarin and local dialects dominate in the day-to-day conversions.

What can be done? Debra Lee has identified five issues — listening ability, differences in cultural background, oral communication skills, vocabulary and writing — as key problem areas that lecturers must take into consideration to ease international students' "transition to an alien academic system" (Lee, 1997: 93), and suggested teaching methods for the lecturers. Writing key terms on the board, for example, is a good practice to help students who are lacking in vocabulary. To improve students' writing skills, lecturers could provide models and explain in simple but detailed terms that lecturers expect from students. Table 10.1 summarises the teaching strategies to help alleviate the problems.

Educationalist Betty Leask (2008) identified 16 characteristics of transnational teachers, and grouped them into three categories — universal characteristics (which are associated with good teaching in *all* environments), hybrid characteristics (teaching skills that are important at home and transnational classrooms) and unique characteristics (skills that are important in transnational classrooms but not relevant in a home classroom). The characteristics are presented in Table 10.2. Six characteristics are classified as universal whereas ten characteristics are classified as either hybrid or unique, suggesting that there are specific skills and

Table 10.1:   Strategies for teaching international students.

Issues	Strategies
Listening ability	• Speak slowly and clearly • Repeat key terms and write them on the board • Write homework assignments on the board or use a handout • Provide copies of notes or make clear which sections of the book are being covered each day (or both) • Recommend that international students listen to news programmes on television or the radio
Differences in cultural background	• Provide background information about companies, locations or ideas • Recommend magazines or books for library research for culturally specific assignments • Recognise that students are probably suffering from cultural shock (in this regard, it may be useful to spend more time with the students, make clear what constitutes good writing in class and have the students explain the assignment in their own words)
Oral communication skills	• Provide review questions • Provide an atmosphere conducive to questions, for example, by asking students to write on the board or make students rephrase the question • Give students time to reflect
Vocabulary	• Try to avoid idiomatic language or slang • Write key terms and vocabulary on the board
Writing	• Provide models • Explain in simple but detailed terms what the lecturers expect

Source: Lee (1999).

abilities that transnational teachers have to possess in delivering their classes. The results prompted Leask to conclude that:

> "the differences between home and transnational teaching are substantial and that they are spread across the entire range of skills and knowledge required of teaching staff. We cannot therefore assume that teachers who are experienced and effective in their home environment will necessarily be so immediately in the transnational classroom" (Leask, 2008: 122).

Table 10.2:   Essential characteristics of transnational teachers.

Characteristics by category	Type
Discipline knowledge	
Knowledge of the discipline and related professions in the local context as well as more broadly in an international context	
Cultural knowledge	
Understanding of local culture including the political, legal and economic environment	Hybrid
Understanding of how the teacher's own culture affects the way they think, feel and act	Hybrid
Understanding of how culture affects the way we interact with others	Hybrid
Understanding of social, cultural and educational backgrounds of students	Hybrid
Teaching skills	
The ability to evaluate feedback from students	Universal
The ability to include local content in the programme through examples and case studies	Hybrid
The ability and flexibility to change the teaching approach to achieve different course objectives	Universal
The ability to adapt learning activities in response to needs of offshore students	Unique
The ability to use different modes of delivery to assist student learning	Universal
The ability to provide timely and appropriate feedback on student performance	Universal
The ability to engage students from different cultural backgrounds in discussion and group work	Hybrid
The ability to reflect on and learn from teaching experiences	Universal
The ability to communicate with other staff teaching on the programme	Hybrid
Policy and procedural knowledge	
Understanding the accrediting institutions' policies and procedures	Universal
Understanding of the local provider's policies and procedures	Unique

Source: Leask (2008: 123, Table 12.1).

Chinese students or Asian students for that matter may lack familiarity with Western teaching methods. It is not helpful to bark on negative practices — rote learning, surface learning, lack of understanding of academic scholarship and extensive plagiarism — that have been associated with Asian students, and persist with the western teaching style that celebrates interaction, collaboration and student autonomy. Instead, PEIs should ensure that their teaching staff are familiar with *their* students' learning styles and adapt the course structure to suit the learning needs of students. PEIs should undertake these commitments and be prepared to justify them if challenged.

10.5 Grow the Business.......

Today's education market is characterised by an abundance of brand names. There is no shortage of PEIs. Instead, there is a shortage of qualified students, both domestic and international. The business-as-usual mentality and do-nothing strategy are doomed to fail. To stay ahead of the competitors, PEIs have to understand students' needs and consider strategic activities.

Students' needs analysis is about assessing the needs of students, measuring their extent and determining whether a profitable opportunity exists. It constitutes an important component of the planning. As Kotler (1999: 36) noted, "wherever there is need, there is an opportunity". Kotler defines an opportunity as "an area of buyer need and interest in which there is a high probability that a company can perform profitably by satisfying that need" (*ibid*). The Education Workgroup of the Economic Review Committee established in the early 2000s to review Singapore's education industry has identified three opportunities for the industry (MTI, 2002b).

- Education contributed between 0.5% and 5.5% of gross domestic product (GDP) in top international student host countries, namely Australia, United Kingdom and the United States, which indicates that education could be a significant contributor to the economy.
- Global market for higher education was around US$30 billion at that time with 1.6 million international student enrolment of which

45% of the students were from Asia with China, Korea, Japan, Malaysia, and India making the top five source countries.
- There was growing demand for quality education at various levels, especially from China where there was unmet demand from the rising number of middle class population.

The three opportunities spoke positively about favourable external environment. It is not surprising that extensive recruitment of international students soon followed and aided by government agencies like the Economic Development Board and International Enterprise. There was a large inflow of international students into public education institutions and PEIs. Despite the achievements, Singapore was confronted with several challenges. First, there was extensive reporting of poor quality PEI courses and fraudulent PEIs. Many international students were the victims, and left stranded with money and time wasted and without a paper qualification that they had hoped to obtain. Second, the massive flow of international students was a cause of concern among the local parents and students as the former squeezed out local students at public universities.

While attracting and recruiting international students remain essential in a small nation like Singapore, the PEIs must consider other avenues for expansion. In the context of the private education sector in Singapore, two opportunities can be identified.

First, there is a lot on emphasis on acquisition of relevant skills and knowledge for the future. The publication of the report by the ASPIRE committee and the establishment of SkillsFuture Singapore Agency are just some examples of initiatives that have emphasised skills to match new job requirements.[3] PEIs should seriously think about their current curriculum, and explore offering knowledge and skills-based courses that are outside of their comfort zone but are necessary to attract students. Some of the PEIs like Kaplan Singapore and Management Development Institute of Singapore (MDIS) have taken the leap forward by offering a wide range of corporate training workshops that are eligible under the SkillsFuture Credit scheme.

Second, advancements in technology provide PEIs the opportunities to facilitate teaching and students' learning. The most impactful technology advancement on the education sector has to be online courses. It started in the summer of 2011 when Standard University computer scientists Sebastian Thrun and Peter Norvig introduced the Massive Open Online Courses (MOOCs) free over the Internet. The courses consist of a series of mini-lectures and interactive quizzes, and have attracted more than 10,000 people to sign up for the courses within days of the set-up. More jumped into the bandwagon, including Coursera, a company founded by Andrew Ng and Daphne Koller, also from Stanford University, that has established collaborations with elite universities like Stanford, Princeton and the University of Michigan. Unlike the retail sector where the Internet (e.g. Amazon and Alibaba), vending machines and robots have been extensively used, affecting the brick and mortar retailers' level of competitiveness in the process, technology has yet to create the level of disruption on the education industry. As Martin Ford points out in "Rise of the Robots", a consequence is that the cost of education has "become ever more burdensome" (Ford, 2016: xvii). The resistance to change has come from the academics. They have been against the use of algorithmic grading for written essay. The most well-known was the petition "Professionals Against Machine Scoring of Student Essays in High Stakes Assessments" signed by 4,000 education professionals, including well-known intellectual Noam Chomsky. But as schools find ways to cut costs, algorithmic grading will feature more prominently. As Ford (2016: 131) argues; "In situations where a large number of essays need to be graded, the approach has obvious advantages. Aside from speed and lower cost, an algorithmic approach offers objectivity and consistency in cases where multiple human graders would otherwise be required. The technology also gives students instant feedback and is well suited to assignments that might not otherwise receive detailed scrutiny from an instructor".

These examples are meant to illustrate the potentials that technology can bring to the education sector, opportunities that PEIs can tap on to distinguish itself from the rest. PEIs have to go beyond Learning Management Systems as a depository platform. The PEIs should explore introducing micro-modules in English, supported by audio and visuals, and interactive quizzes to reinforce learning. There is also a great potential for technology to facilitate learning for adult learners. A majority of them own smart phones, and they often have to juggle between work, family, and studies. Adult leaders therefore appreciate the provision of online support through the Internet or other digital means to allow them to finish the programme. That said, PEIs should be mindful of the learning style of adult students. Generally speaking, they would prefer that the information is presented briefly, for example, a 10-minute video to illustrate a particular concept, with opportunities for them to apply and reflect on the materials covered. And ideally, there should be a platform for adult leaders to communicate with their lecturers outside of class time, and with their peers. This is especially important for adult learners who may not be able to attend classes punctually or be present in all the sessions due to work and other commitments. Giving students the ability to ask questions and talk about the assessment can make a big difference in students' happiness and satisfaction levels towards the education provider.

Understanding students' needs should lead to innovation, to introduce new courses into the market, offer better or differentiated products to better serve the market. This may entail transforming the spectrum of the supply chain — from marketing to recruitment to exam results processing and student progression. To do so effectively, the PEIs must proactively assess the portfolio of programmes currently on offer, evaluate the service delivery, and align them with students' expectations.

Two further aspects of strategies and growth can be considered.

Growth through collaboration — In her book "A Bigger Prize", Heffernan (2014: 323) wrote that "the failure to inculcate the habit of collaboration may be the biggest organizational, social, and political risk we face today". Heffernan calls for greater collaboration even among 'competitors'.

Many PEIs in Singapore offer niche programmes in logistic management, financial services and entrepreneurship. Rather than working in isolation, some sort of partnership agreements should be encouraged among the PEIs to offer joint programmes, recognising that students want a range of courses and services. The niche players may offer their expertise in curriculum development and selection of academic staff whereas the other player in the market offers the classroom facilities and connection with university partners to permit articulation of the programme to a higher level. The Singapore Association for Private Education can play an effective role to facilitate the transaction and ensure that the terms and conditions are honoured by the relevant parties. For this to work, PEIs must change their mind set from considering business as a game of tennis or F1 racing where there is a winner and a loser to treating competitors as collaborators to open up new growth opportunities and drive new demand. As the Prisoner's Dilemma as commonly applied in business tells us, collaboration instead of direct competition leads to both parties winning in the 'game'.

Growth through internationalisation — Services are immobile. Haircuts in Ho Chi Minh City cost less than in Singapore but traders are not able to import the service because the service is offered in Ho Chi Minh City not Singapore. But that does not imply that one is not able to enjoy the services that are based in another country. Singaporeans are able to enrol into courses from INSEAD or James Cook University right at home. The physical space is no longer a barrier in education. Advancements in information transmission have allowed education providers to deliver education services to every corner of the globe at a faster speed and lower average cost. PEIs may find it imperative to go where the students are or risk losing the capacity to expand and grow. Bilateral trade agreements and multilateral cooperative initiatives between members of ASEAN and in the Asia Pacific region have given hope to PEIs to expand their operations abroad. MDIS inked a deal to open its overseas campus in Malaysia at EduCity Iskandar in Nusajaya in the state of Johor (the construction of the MDIS Malaysian campus started in September 2013). Advancements in technology have allowed the PEIs to communicate with colleagues from partnering institutions. Teaching materials can be easily shared thereby allowing the PEIs to use the same set of materials in classrooms regardless of where the courses are taught.

The key to success, as always, is quality of the academic programmes. The ability of the PEIs to penetrate into the foreign market depends to a large extent on how the programme is perceived there. This essentially means that the decision to expand abroad can only be made after the programme has been tested and proven to be well received by students in the home country. There should then be efforts to replicate the delivery of the programmes in the host country. Students in the host country expect the programme to be delivered in the same manner regardless of whether the programme is offered in the home or host countries. To facilitate the transition, the PEIs should make it a priority to control the delivery of the programme. There should be constant communication between the operations managers and academics from both sides to audit and quality check the delivery of services to students in the host country.

PEIs need not have to work in the blind. They could learn from how their university partners have attempted to maintain the standards and quality of their programmes, and apply the same steps and processes, perhaps with some modifications, to manage the collaboration with the PEIs' overseas partners. Taken together, it is important for the PEIs to think through thoroughly what has happened, what is happening and what might happen as part of the planning and operations. Goals must be set and communicated, and plans thought out. Being honest to oneself about the challenges and taking corrective actions when goals are not achieved are good practices.

10.6 ......Responsibly

The sustainability of the PEIs rests on two pillars — business and education. As a business entity, the leaders are responsible to the business owners and therefore required their attention to grow and expand the business. PEIs are judged by their ability to meet commercial goals and objectives.

As an education provider, the leaders are also responsible in ensuring that students gain from attending the courses and acquire the capacity to be an effective member of the workforce in the business community. The paradox is to be part of the right-versus-wrong paradox such as truth-telling versus loyalty and short-term versus long-term, which is defined by Rushworth Kidder (2005: 86) as: "when one of our values raises powerful moral arguments for one course of action, while another value raises equally powerful arguments for an opposite course, we find we can't do both. Yet we must act".

In today's environment more people are prepared to criticise behaviour which is considered as unethical even if it legal. Paying bonuses to Chief Executive Officers of companies that have failed to deliver the benefits is an example. The education business is similarly mired with grey areas, providing a challenge to PEIs to consider the appropriate decisions to make. Mere compliance of rules and regulations as formulated by the education regulatory agency is not adequate. PEI leaders have to be mindful of the reputation risk and the ability to demonstrate.

PEIs must avoid the awkward situation where commercial interest overrides every other consideration. Quality of the PEI courses and programmes has to be ensured and protected. Academic judgment has to be applied in determining the entry requirements (not setting them too low) and crafting of the assessment tasks (not setting them too easy nor too difficult). Academic policies relating to examinations, appeals against academic results, and plagiarism cases have to be clearly stated and strictly enforced. Responsible leaders recognise that these decisions are academic in nature, and ensure that the decisions rest with the academics.

Minimum entry requirement for a course is another issue that requires academic judgement unclouded by commercial goals. Ill-informed leaders judge inability of the students to cope with the demands of the programme as a non-issue that can be easily resolved (by the academics), not fully understanding the implications of permitting students who lack the relevant cognitive skills into the programme on both the students and the institution. Money-making clouds their mind. Irresponsible leaders may also succumb to improper practices in the form of rubbery academic standards by easing the progression of students from one level to another.

Private education is not an ordinary business. As a service entity, space and time spent by the lecturer cannot be stored. Unlike a meal, students are more likely to spend considerable amount of time shopping for the right course and institution. A student who chooses to enrol into a rival Diploma programme is a loss to business particularly when the student is lured to progress to the next level of study through various incentives. As such, managing a PEI is challenging and difficult.

Neither extreme effective nor ethical leadership would work in the PEIs. The former tends to focus almost exclusively on the business aspect of the education. The latter is also undesirable because of his/her tendency to rigidly protect the academic delivery and other aspects of the courses. PEIs require *'responsible leaders'* from the Chief Executive

Officer, Academic Dean down to the Academics, Programme Consultants and others.

Who is a responsible leader? To be sure, a responsible leader does not have to be one who has to possess "higher moral standard" than the rest as Joanne Ciulla (2001) has convincingly argued. But a responsible leader is expected to consider the stakeholders' interest as opposed to merely the interest of the shareholders or business owners. Thomas Maak and Nicola Pless (Maak and Pless, 2006; Pless and Maak, 2011) who were possibly the first few who have attempted to broaden the traditional leader–subordinate relationship to leader–stakeholder relationship have defined responsible leadership as "a relational and ethical phenomenon, which occurs in social processes of interaction and have a stake in the purpose and vision of the leadership relationships" (Maak and Pless, 2006: 103). A responsible leader to Maak and Pless is one who possesses high relationship intelligence, a product of the ethical dimension (make decisions that are drawn on moral norms) and emotional intelligence, which highlights the importance of understanding and managing emotions to enhance personal growth and social relations and using emotions to facilitate thought.

Against this backdrop, what are the roles of a responsible PEI leader? A responsible leader emphasises growth through *relationship* building. A responsible leader in the PEIs places the organisation as part of the larger community. They do not see business as the only function of the organisation. They view their firms as enterprises where sustaining employee morale, establishing long-term relationship with suppliers and the creditors, and having a good relationship with the government as essential obligations and foundations of their success.

A responsible leader in the PEI strives to balance the commercial and educational demands, giving neither extreme emphasis over the other, and demonstrates his/her capability to lead with integrity. While each of the leaders within the PEI has specific responsibilities and targets, he/she has to consider the relational aspect of leadership in the organisation. This requires a leader who is able to assume the *stewardship* position to safeguard personal and professional values and resources (Maak and Pless, 2006). A responsible leader navigates in a world of "complexity, uncertainty, change and conflict interests" and "protect personal and professional integrity, and steering a business responsibly and respectfully, even though troubled (global) waters, thus protecting and preserving what one is entrusted with" (Maak and Pless, 2006: 108). The leaders' role is to translate their values into actions, using the values to define the boundaries and act as guidelines when the organisation is under pressure. An organisation that values the stakeholders' interest builds on ethically sound vision and core values, and it is the duty of the leader to ensure that these are followed through.

Being a responsible and effective leader is associated with the leader's determination to demarcate the business and academic units so that the latter is not held responsible for making decisions that are tied to the financial goals. Failure to guard against academic integrity is the surest way to getting the PEI into trouble. A responsible organisation therefore has the discipline and skills to know when particular students cannot be admitted to the PEIs because of lower than required prior academic and language qualifications, and can be better served by another education provider.

The values and assumptions shared by responsible leaders help to legitimise ways of thinking by ruling-in certain ways of talking about issues and ruling-out other approaches. Newly recruited employees have to be taught and educated about the organisational values. Rather than letting them gain more in-depth understanding of the business over time, deliberate effort has to be put in to align the employees' thought process with the business.[4] As leaders, they are the role models for others for the type of behaviour they want to encourage. If they are not effective leaders or role models from the start, others will not believe what they say. A responsible leader therefore has the duty to inculcate the values to the followers and serve as a role model and be seen as someone others could trust to deal with conflicting interests. Responsible leader must possess good communication and architectural skills to "create and cultivate a work environment where diverse individuals find meaning, feel respected, recognised and included. … to contribute to their highest potential, both in a business and a moral sense" (Maak and Pless, 2006: 111).

In conclusion, where the PEI wants to be, and how its students benefited from enrolment into the courses will gain greater prominence. Equipping students with 21st century skills and competencies is an important consideration. Some of the skills such as critical thinking, problem solving, communication, flexibility, and adaptability were needed in the past century as well, but they are even more relevant today. There are other skills such as information literacy (the ability to access information efficiently and effectively and use the information competently and critically) and media literacy (the ability to use media tools to communicate) that were given less emphasis in schools but are extremely important for students to have as we move from a primarily nuts-and-bolts manufacturing economy to an economy that is largely based on data, information and knowledge. PEIs that are able to prepare students for 21st century work will stand out among the crowd.

Having joined the sector, the PEIs cannot ignore the competition. Corporate scandals like those affecting Brookes Business School in early 2000s generate significant cost to the PEIs — inability to attract students; companies are less willing to recruit students from the PEIs, among others. The bright side of competition is that it helps the PEIs and relevant stakeholders, such as the Council for Private Education (CPE) and the Singapore Association for Private Education (SAPE) to identify areas for improvement with regard to the facilities, faculty, and academic and non-academic programmes.

Epilogue

I wrote this book to help us better understand the private education sector in Singapore, and the key challenges facing the private education institutions (PEIs). I believe that education institutions, including the PEIs, have a special role to play. They are responsible for developing students' character, educating students about the nation and the society and equipping them with skills and knowledge that are relevant to the industry. An educated workforce contributes to the international competitiveness of the nation by emphasising technical innovations and the use of knowledge. Education brings unprecedented benefits to the individuals and the society.

The education sector, as economists put it, exhibits strong spillovers. Jeffrey Sachs has said "I want you to be well educated so that you do not easily fall under the sway of a demagogue who would be harmful for me as well as you" (Sachs, 2005: 253). But some individuals may forgo the opportunity to gain a higher level of education because they are unable to factor in the full benefits of education. For these reasons, the father of Economics, Adam Smith, has called for the provision of *public* education especially for the common people "who have little time to spare for education for the benefits of the whole society" (Smith, 1776/2000: 842). The public can "facilitate", "encourage" and even "impose almost the whole body of the people" to acquire the essential parts of education (*Ibid*: 843).

Education in Singapore has always been seen as a key source of socio-economic growth and development. Singapore has provided a strong base of primary education, and emphasised secondary and post-secondary education to surge ahead and remain competitive in the global economy. Higher education institutions — from the Institute of Technical Education (ITE), local polytechnics, and public universities to the PEIs — have produced engineers, IT professionals and people with strong managerial skills needed to support Singapore's industrialisation and growth strategy.

In the first 20 years following independence, the labour force in Singapore was largely made up of individuals who were less educated. The tasks required from the workers were generally straightforward. The workers' key priorities were survival and skills building. Over the years, we observe a dramatic increase in the number of years of schooling. More are entering the labour force with post-secondary education qualifications. Education attainment is considered as the passport for good life. Career anxiety, peer pressure and competition for good jobs and higher positions have led to a strong increase in the demand for education.

As demand for education rises, the shortage in places especially in public universities became more profound despite the government's effort to increase the number of places in public universities. Private education sector rides on the trend to meet the excess demand by providing diploma courses and the opportunity for students to acquire an external degree without the need to leave the country. The proliferation of the PEIs has created a highly competitive environment. The commercial aspect of the business complicates matter. Some of the PEIs have resorted to unethical practices to increase student population.

To be sure, academic frauds are not confined to Singapore.[1] In the United States, the federal government won a major court case against Corinthian Colleges, Inc. in late 2015. The latter was alleged to have advertised false placement rates by hiring its own graduates as a means to recruit students and swindled students to take out private loans at a higher interest rate. The now defunct for-profit school, which oversaw 100 schools in states such as California, Oregon and Arizona, was asked to pay back US$531 million in damages to students in October 2015.[2] In the United Kingdom, the West London Vocational Training Centre, a for-profit college in Wales, was suspended in November 2015. It was alleged that the college has accepted fake certificates from students and used them to apply for Welsh government funded students finance loans and grants. Students were effectively told that they could receive cash without having to attend classes regularly. The Welsh government suspended payments to the College and its students. The misconduct was exposed by a reporter posing as a potential student.[3]

Corruption is rife in many counties where bribery of public officers is necessary to get things done. Corporate scandals have affected small and medium enterprises as well as large private corporations both in Singapore and elsewhere. But it is particularly sad to read and hear about academic frauds because they involve youths and persons who have paid thousands of dollars to obtain a qualification, which goes to waste when the qualification turns out to be unrecognised by the employers. There are persons who are determined to 'buy' qualifications from sellers of bogus degrees or diploma mills but they represent the minority. Students who are genuinely interested to obtain good education should be protected.

The intervention of the Council for Private Education (CPE) in Singapore through its policies and frameworks has exerted pressure on the PEIs to focus on organisational excellence. New ways to do things have been proposed. The PEIs and the regulatory agency are working together towards raising the reputation of the industry. I believe that Singapore is on track to realise this objective within the private education sector.

Three Takeaways

In this book, I have made three key points about the private education sector. First, I have pointed out that the private education sector has contributed significantly to advance the Singapore economy. PEIs provide the opportunity and the platform for Singaporeans to upgrade their skills and fulfil their aspirations of acquiring a diploma and degree, after missing the opportunity to enrol into the local polytechnics and especially the public universities earlier in their life. The role of education needs to be looked at from the perspective of its contribution to the economy and the individuals themselves. Economists talk about education as human capital, which contributes to production and income, like machinery. It is worth remembering that besides yielding a return in the economic sense, education equips students with transferable or soft skills like problem solving, meeting deadlines, negotiation, team work, research skills and communication skills.

The demand for education is reinforced by meritocracy where success is based on one's competency and motivation, and not on race or religion. If this is true, graduates who have attained the PEI academic qualification, and developed the capability and attained a high motivation level through PEI education should have the same opportunity in job interviews as anyone else. The starting salary of PEI graduates should not deviate too significantly from those who have acquired a diploma or degree with the local polytechnics and universities, all other things remaining the same. Unfortunately, this has yet to be realised. The truth is, graduates from the PEIs have been subject to job discrimination by both the public and private sector organisations. PEI degree graduates have received lower starting salary as compared to their counterparts who graduated from one of the local universities. The danger of this, if it persists, is that it would lead to social exclusion where graduates from publicly funded education institutions tend to see themselves as socially more superior than others.

Second, there is a concern that too many graduates with certain skills are produced in relation to the number of jobs requiring those skills. Graduate unemployment is a serious issue in many countries.[4] The root cause is that the prospects of those who hold a non-degree qualification are being decimated by technology, prompting many to pursue a degree as a means to advance their job prospects and earn a higher income. Observing a strong incentive to pursue a college degree in the United States, Martin Ford argues that "the unfortunate reality is that this is the case not so much because opportunities for college graduates are expanding dramatically but because prospects for those with only a high school diploma are collapsing" (Ford, 2016: 263). But not many students are opting to study Science, Technology, Engineering, and Mathematics (STEM) subjects. Instead, they pursue degrees in Business Administration, Marketing, Management and the like.

As part of its effort review students' aspiration for a degree, the government convened the ASPIRE committee in November 2013 to strengthen the education pathways for ITE and polytechnic graduates. The recommendations put forward by the committee and subsequent initiatives like SkillsFuture related schemes, job training programmes, and career guidance and counselling at these institutions essentially aim to divert students' attention to deepening and mastery of skills and knowledge through internship, mentorship, specialised training, and skills acquisition rather than an unabated chase for a paper qualification especially in non-STEM fields. They aim to educate the students about the job market so that they can make wiser choices by focusing on jobs that are or will be in short supply. While it may take some years for the initiatives to significantly change the society's mindset to go beyond qualification, the initiatives will inevitably have some effect on the thinking process of some of the ITE and polytechnic graduates.

Third, I have argued that the reputation and image of private education in Singapore remains poor. Hiring companies continue to discriminate against PEI graduates. In certain countries like China, PEI graduates stand a low chance of getting a job in the public sector in their home country because PEI certificates are not recognised by the government. International students from the PEIs are also treated differently as compared to international students from the local polytechnics and local universities in the sense that the latter is allowed to work during vacation and is exempted from applying for a work permit. No such privilege exists for international students who are pursuing an education qualification with the PEIs. PEIs continue to perform poorly in the Customer Satisfaction Index compiled by the Institute of Service Excellence at Singapore Management University.

One of the sources of the discontentment is (perceived) lower quality of PEI academic qualification. The concern is not without merit. Over the years, PEIs have competed not by raising the quality of the courses. Rather, they have tried to win business by offering courses with shorter duration, and generously granting module exemptions to potential students thereby allowing the students to complete the programme in the shortest time possible, and at the lower cost. The demand side plays a part in the development. Students are increasingly more price sensitive and decreasingly loyal to the supplier. They want shorter courses and more convenience, leading to an increase in the demand for shorter and easy-to-graduate courses. Such a behaviour involved on a mass scale inevitably led to an increase in supply of courses that would meet the needs of the consumers by the PEIs as they reacted to the market movement — courses that were of questionable quality.

To address the issue on the quality of the PEIs, the Private Education Act was enacted in 2009, giving the provision for the establishment of the CPE in the same year. The CPE imposes rules and guidelines to improve corporate governance and productivity of the PEIs. The number of PEIs has significantly reduced from about 1,200 (a commonly cited figure) to about 300 today. More universities (e.g. Singapore Institute of Technology) are set up and UniSIM is offered a facelift reputation-wise at least to divert student enrolment of graduates from the polytechnics from less reputable universities in partnership with the PEIs to the two institutions. Currently, the CPE operates on a scheme that looks into consumer protection issues such as fee policies, governance and business structure, means of student redress, and an insurance scheme in case of operator failure. More needs to be done to raise academic standards and quality to garner greater recognition and respect for PEIs and their courses.

In January 2016, the government announced its plan to establish a new statutory board, the SkillsFuture Singapore Agency (SSG) to drive the implementation of SkillsFuture — a scheme devised by the government to promote Singapore as a nation of learners who would have a strong passion to upgrade their skills, apply the skills constructively and excel in what they do. The agency integrates the work done by the Workforce Development Agency (WDA) and CPE, serving as the accreditation body to formulate frameworks, regulate the PEIs and improve the quality of private education in Singapore.[5]

In parliament where the SkillsFuture Singapore Agency bill was tabled, Acting Education Minister Ong Ye Kung, explained that the SkillsFuture initiative was not about identifying skills for the future. Rather, it was about building "a foundation of skills, of depth"[6] and producing graduates with skills and abilities needed by the industries, new and old. The Minister emphasised the importance of measuring the employment outcomes of graduates of PEIs. "If you train people, you educate them to have a degree. Are you just fuelling their desire to have a degree or are you trying to answer and address an industry need? This is best measured by employment outcomes". I am in total agreement with the Minister's view. The PEIs have to change their mindset by genuinely accepting the fact that maintaining academic quality standards is compatible with holding a profit motive. The PEIs have to seriously think in terms of what and how well students have learned in their schools. As much as how the PEIs ought to change to reflect and emphasise competency, educational qualifications remain an important first-cut indicator in the screening and shortlisting process, and therefore a change in the mindset of hiring companies with regard to PEI qualifications is equally essential.

Endnotes

Preface

1. Extracted from https://www.moe.gov.sg/education/private-education on 26 November 2016.
2. "Private school grads find it harder to land jobs", *The Straits Times*, 24 September 2016.

Chapter 1   Governance, Meritocracy, and Growth Centricity

1. Book XVI: Ke She, Chapter IX. See Legge (2008).
2. See Levy (2006) and *The Economist* (2006).
3. See Low (2001). Singapore gained independence from British rule on 9 August 1965. The real Gross Domestic Product (GDP) has grown at an average of 8.1% (1965–2008), with the real per capita GDP rising from S$4,668 in 1965 to S$46,255 in 2008.
4. See Quah (2008).
5. "What drives the Singapore economy," *The Business Times*, 18 March 2015.
6. See Chia (2015), Gopinathan (2013), Gwee and Neo (2012), Ho and Gopinathan (1999), Sharpe and Gopinathan (2002) and Tan and Gopinathan (2000) for a comprehensive discussion on Singapore's education sector since independence. Excellent edited texts on related issues could be found in Tan (2012), Tan, Gopinathan, and Ho (1997) and Yip and Sim (1990).
7. The well-known Lionel Robbins Report on the Higher Education in the United Kingdom devoted a full chapter on academic freedom (Robbins, 1963), which was deemed as "the most important and the most difficult of all the problems we have had to consider". The report recommended that a "system that aims at the maximum of

independence compatible with the necessary degree of public control is good in itself, as reflecting the ultimate values of a free society". The role of the government, the report noted, was to ensure that the higher education institutions are there to serve the national needs, and the government could do so through the appointment of a Council consisting of government appointed persons who are independent from the government but with "intimate knowledge of university life and its convention".

8. Academic freedom was tested during the colonial days as seen in the arrests of members of the University Socialist Club in the 1950s because of articles published in *Fajar*, the society's magazine, which were deemed as anticolonial. See Poh (2016) for details (especially Chapters 2 and 3).

9. To read the full PAP's letter to the press which attacked Professor Enright, see Baker (2014: 84–85).

10. It did not take too long following the Enright's affair to witness another test on the university's autonomy, this time on student recruitment. The year was 1963. The PAP government allowed Chinese language stream students from Nanyang University, Singapore Polytechnic and Ngee Ann College to pursue their studies at the institutions of higher learning. The university had in the past accepted only students from schools using English as the medium of instruction. With self-governance, the PAP government opened the university to students from Chinese-medium schools. However, students from Chinese-medium schools were allowed for admission to the university only after they had been certified as suitable by the Ministry of Education. The government, as Maurice Baker noted, "feared that since the Chinese language stream schools had been penetrated by the communists, who had established cells in them and in Nanyang University, communist students would influence and disrupt the English stream undergraduates," (Baker, 2014: 86–87). The Vice-Chancellor of the University, Dr. B.B. Sreenivasan, a respected doctor, was a firm believer of admitting students regardless of their religion, class or nationality, and student recruitment and admission was the sole decision of the university. Dr. Sreenivasan refused to accept the imposition of suitability certificate produced by the Ministry of Education as a criterion for admission. Dr. Sreenivasan eventually resigned in November 1963, two years after he had assumed office, and replaced by Professor Lim Tay Boh, an economist. Under Lim, the university admitted 41 Chinese-school students in the 1964/1965 session. Candidates, regardless of their race, religion or prior academic performance, deemed to be politically impure (alleged to be tainted by communisms, for example) would be denied entry to the local higher learning institutions.

11. Koh, who was one of Enright's students, reported that Enright soon "discovered that in the new countries everything from the beginning has been political" and "in a multiracial society like Singapore, which had recently gone through a period of great instability, with two more major racial riots to come during Enright's stay, culture is a political matter; and among the most political of matters after culture, is language" (*Ibid*: 23).

12. Christopher Lingle, an American economist, wrote an article in the *International Herald Tribune* (IHT) on 7 October 1994, rebutting an article written by Kishore Mahbubani in the same newspaper. A Senior Fellow in the European Studies Programme of the National University of Singapore at the time the article was published, Lingle had suggested in the article that some Asian leaders had relied on the judiciary to bankrupt opposition politicians. The article did not mention Singapore. Political leaders in Singapore sued IHT and Lingle for defamation. Lingle fled the country and resigned from the University before charges were filed against him. Lingle was found guilty in absentia and fined. In his book 'Singapore's Authoritarian Capitalism' published two years later in 1996, Lingle launched an attack on Singapore's lack of academic freedom. He wrote that "despite its reputation as one of the premier institutions of higher education in East Asia, it appears that there is little room for academic freedom at the NUS. It is a humorless place run by rule-bound administrators that treat professors as though they are bureaucrats rather than scholars. The administration displays an insistence upon following rules paired with zero tolerance for those who would question the rationality of those dictums" (Lingle, 1996: 25).

13. In two articles published in *The Straits Times* in 1994, Catherine Lim, a Singaporean novelist, observed among other things that the government was gradually losing the affection of Singaporeans due mainly to the style of governance — alleged as arrogant, impatient and dictatorial. In particular, her comments appeared to be directed at Prime Minister Goh Chok Tong, who had taken over the baton from Lee Kuan Yew in 1990 as Prime Minister of Singapore, for continuing with the powerful control exerted by the government instead of the more open political system as Goh had promised. Lim was rebuked severely by the then Prime Minister who not only condemned her views as malicious but challenged her to enter the political arena to espouse her political views. See Tan (2009).

14. On the role of intellectuals in Singapore, see also Koh (2000). Clammer (2001: 205) argued that the community of intellectuals in Singapore's public universities — those in historical, literary and social science disciplines — has low status in the ranking of disciplines and "under constant pressure to perform the useful functional roles," giving the example of Sociology which teaches students "tools rather than substance, for integrating people into (the existing) society, rather than as critique of that society". "Criticism, whether voiced directly or embodied in the research of an independent spirit and which may call into question the current political or social verities, is seen from 'above' as at best carping and at worst as disloyalty".

15. *Transparency International* (2013: ix) reported that bribes to secure a seat at a prestigious primary school in Vietnam could run as high as twice that the country's GDP per capita.

16. The scores are reported in percentiles. A score of 99 means that the country has beaten 99% of all other countries measured for that category.

17. In 1978, Goh was asked by Lee Kuan Yew to review Singapore's education system, leading to the publication of the now classic Goh's report on education.
18. In Taiwan and Hong Kong, there were "no meritocratic procedures for selecting politicians" (Vogel, 1989: 1052).
19. Goh's (1979) report culminated into the establishment of the independent schools in 1987. Independent schools have greater autonomy in staff deployment and salaries, determining the enrolment figures, finance and setting of school fees. Receiving a per capita grant for each student from the government, the independent schools are governed by the MOE approved Boards of Governors with the power to appoint and promote staff. Explaining the rational for the introduction of independent schools, then Minister of State for Education Lui Tuck Yew commented that there was a need to "augment the education with schools that were better able to foster creativity, individual talent and the spirit of enquiry in their students". The independent schools "would be in the position to innovate and tailor their programmes to better meet the envisaged needs of their students, to prepare them for future challenges and to spearhead excellence and quality in education". As at end 2014, there were eight independent schools in Singapore, including Anglo Chinese School, Methodist Girls' School, Singapore Chinese Girls' School and St Joseph's Institution. See speech by Lui Tuck Yew, Minister of State for Education at the Independent Schools Conference on 12 March 2007, at the Anglo Chinese (Independent).
20. The government faced intense public criticism over the elitist nature of the independent schools and the high fees charged by the schools and in the wake of reduced electoral support during the 1991 general elections the government took steps to address the concerns. In 1994, for example, the government broadened the spectrum of schools in Singapore by introducing autonomous schools. Autonomous schools receive more funds from the government thereby allowing the schools to charge lower fees than independent school. They follow the national education policies guidelines but with greater autonomy in introducing programmes to stretch the capabilities of their students. Autonomous status is granted to schools with a track record of outstanding academic results, well-rounded education programmes and strong community ties, and it remains a well sought after status to acquire. In 2014, there were 28 autonomous schools, including Anderson Secondary School, Anglican High School, Yishun Town Secondary School, Victoria School and Tanjong Katong Girls' School. See Tan (2008) for a discussion on the marketisation strategies in the Singapore public education sector.
21. Lower school fees for international students through the tuition grant scheme and lucrative scholarships have attracted talented young people from abroad to study in Singapore. Each year, public universities receives 20,000 to 25,000 applications from international students for about 3,000 positions, reported the then Minister for Education Heng Swee Keat in Parliament. See "Foreign students enrolled in local universities," a speech delivered by the Minister for Education Heng Swee Keat in parliament in Singapore on 21 October 2011.

22. Paul Krugman tells us that in a depressed situation where the economy is far off the full employment target, people suffer from "loss of income" and "diminished sense of self-worth" (Krugman, 2012: 5–6). Jagdish Bhagwati has also warned that "education by itself, especially higher education, is unlikely to help. Unemployed educated youth will likely burn tram cars rather than lead to greater growth (Bhagwati, 2004: 64).

23. *The Straits Times*, 9 July 1991 (quoted in Birch, 1994: 2).

24. See Clarke and Monk (2010).

25. See Chan and Ng (2008), Mok (2008), Ng and Tan (2010), Sidhu, Ho, and Yeoh (2011) and Ng (2013).

26. See Pak and Tan (2010), Ng and Tan (2010), Ng (2013), Daquila (2013) and Waring (2013). Other countries that have experimented with attracting foreign universities have similarly experienced some problems, including Royal Melbourne Institute of Technology's (Australia) closure of its campus in Malaysia due to its financial partner going bankrupt, George Mason University from the United States closing its campus in the United Arab Emirates due to disagreement with the local partners and Sylvan from the United Kingdom closing its campus in India because of its failure to obtain accreditation from the Indian government (see Lane, 2011: 370).

27. "Resolution on Yale-NUS College passes despite objection," in https://sg. news.yahoo.com/yale-nus-resolution-passes-despite-objection.html (extracted on 1 April 2015).

28. Speech delivered by Minister for Trade and Industry George Yeo at Singapore — The Global Schoolhouse Conference on 16 August 2003. Available on the web http://www.nas.gov.sg/archivesonline/speeches/view-html?filename=2003081602. htm (extracted on 1 April 2015).

Chapter 2   Private Education Sector in Singapore

1. Joanna Seow (2014), "More taking private route to a degree", *The Straits Times*, 4 September 2014; Sandra Davie (2014), "Get private schools into push to build deep skills", *The Straits Times*, 20 November 2014.

2. Specifically, PEIs offering the following programmes must register with CPE under the Enhanced Registration Framework (ERF):

    - Degree, diploma or full-time certification programmes at the post-secondary level;
    - Full-time primary or secondary education wholly or substantially, in accordance with an international curriculum;
    - PEIs offering full-time preparatory courses for entrance/placement tests for joining Ministry of Education (MOE) mainstream schools, or for external examinations;
    - Full-time special education for students with physical or intellectual disabilities, where the private-funded education institution conducting the programme has not been extended a subvention by the Government.

(Extracted from https://www.cpe.gov.sg/for-peis/enhanced-registration-framework-erf/who-needs-to-register on 26 September 2015).

3. "About 320 private schools left in the fray after new rules kick in," *Today,* 7 July 2011.

4. See http://www.wda.gov.sg/content/wdawebsite/L101-ForIndividuals/L220A-004CETFullList.html (extracted on 21 September 2016).

5. "NSW Universities taking students with ATARs as low as 30," *The Sydney Morning Herald,* 9 February 2016.

6. A commonly cited figure is 1,200 PEIs, which is not reflective of the actual number of active PEIs in Singapore. Brandon Lee, then Deputy CEO of CPE noted that the true number of PEIs in 2009 were in the region of 500 as the rest was either defunct, merged with existing players or tuition and enrichment centres which did not fall under the Private Education Act. See "Raising the bar for private education," *The Business Times,* 1 May 2012.

7. *Ibid.*

8. For a detailed discussion on SQA, see Calingo (1995). ITE was the first educational institution to win the Singapore Quality Award in 2005.

9. For an excellent review of the quality framework, see Ong (2011).

10. "Ex-head of private school charged," *The Straits Times,* 3 July 2004.

11. "Watchdog to probe schools with low standards," *The Straits Times,* 26 February 2008.

12. "Make dodgy degrees illegal: crackdown needed to maintain Singapore's status as education hub," *The Straits Times,* 5 December 2009. The six institutions listed in ODA were Cranston University, Templeton University, Trident University of Technology, Vancouver University Worldwide, Westmore University and Lee Community College.

13. The government plans to attract 15,000 foreign students to Singapore by 2015, a level that would generate 22,000 jobs and boost the education sector's contribution to the country's GDP from 3% now to 5%.

14. Ministry of Education (2009) *Second Reading Speech on the Private Education Bill,* Parliamentary Sitting on 14 September 2009.

15. Speech by Dr. Ng Eng Hen, MOE and Second Minister for Defense at the official opening of the CPE SSC on 22 April 2010.

16. Extracted from http://www.sim.edu.sg/about-sim/pages/vision-mission-values.aspx on 11 February 2015.

17. "Excel with an international edge," *The Straits Times,* 6 June 2016.

18. The JobsCentral Learning Survey was launched in 2009. It stopped ranking top private education institutes in 2014.

19. Extracted from http://www.kaplan.com.sg/about/mission-vision-and-values/ on 11 February 2015.

20. Extracted from http://www.psb-academy.edu.sg/about/vision-mission-and-values/ on 11 February 2015.

Chapter 3   CPE, ERF, and EduTrust Certification Scheme

1. Speech by Senior Minister of State, Indranee Rajah at Private Education Conference 2013, 9 April 2013.
2. "Academic checks not out job: Case," *The Straits Times*, 28 July 2009.
3. Extracted from http://www.cpe.gov.sg/cos/o.x?c=/cpe/pagetree&func=view&rid=213 (accessed on 9 March 2010).
4. "Brookes Business School," Media Release on 7 July 2011 (available online: http://www.cpe.gov.sg; extracted on 2 February 2015).
5. "Man jailed for $2.2 million fake degree scam", *The Straits Times*, 15 October 2015.
6. See "CPE filed charges against former manager of School of Applied Studies", Media Release, 1 June 2012; "Former manager of School of Applied Studies pleads guilty to contravening Private Education Act," Media Release, 17 January 2013 (available online: http://www.cpe.gov.sg; extracted on 2 February 2015).
7. "Prosecution against ALG Education Centre Manager," Media Release, 29 November 2011 (available online: http://www.cpe.gov.sg; extracted on 2 February 2015).
8. "Prosecution against Cambridge Business School," Media Release, 1 July 2011 (available online: http://www.cpe.gov.sg; extracted on 2 February 2015); "Ex-managers of Cambridge Business School admit contravening Private Education Act," Media Release, 26 March 2012 (available online: http://www.cpe.gov.sg; extracted on 2 February 2015).
9. "CPE filed charges against manager of Process College," Media Release, 20 July 2012 (available online: http://www.cpe.gov.sg; extracted on 2 February 2015); "Manager of Process College pleads guilty to contravening Private Education Act," Media Release 27 November 2012, (available online: http://www.cpe.gov.sg; extracted on 2 February 2015); "Manager of Process College Sentenced to jail and fined for contravening Private Education Act," Media Release, 27 December 2012, (available online: http://www.cpe.gov.sg; extracted on 2 February 2015); "Private school's manager jailed for not refunding fees", *The Straits Times*, 28 December 2012.
10. "Council for Private Education to cancel registration of errant private education institution", Media Release, 20 April 2015 (available online: http://www.cpe.gov.sg; extracted on 22 April 2015).
11. "Charges filed against former managers of Kings International Business School," Media Release, 1 June 2016 (available online: http://www.cpe.gov.sg; extracted on 1 June 2016; "Ex-private school directors charged," *The Straits Times,* 2 June 2016.
12. In a recent commentary, NUS Professor Goh Beng Lan noted that the desire of her university to participate in global university and publication rankings has "subjected scholars to the publish or perish culture". In Goh's words, "there is tremendous pressure at my university for faculty to publish in international rather than regional publishing houses for promotion and tenure as well as for annual reviews. At my university, regional publications are deemed to be of a lower order (perhaps due to a

perception that they are not international enough) than those in western locations —
namely, by a hierarchy whereby North American (university) presses are ranked on
top, followed by European, Australian, and then subsequently those from 'other'
locations, including those in Southeast Asia" (Dominquiz, 2015: 381–382).

13. Data extracted from "Complaints statistics related to private schools" (https://www.
cpe.gov.sg/student-services/student-resources/complaint-statistics-related-to-private-
schools) on 18 May 2016.

14. Council for Private Education (2016: 22).

15. Sandra Davie (2015), Aussie campus gets star ranking, *The Straits Times*, 15 April
2015.

16. Amelia Teng (2015), Lasalle awarded EduTrust Star, *The Straits Times*, 9 October
2015.

17. The discussion below refers to Version 2 of the EduTrust Certification Scheme, published in November 2009, which remains valid as on December 2016.

18. See Bernasconi (2013) and Kinser (2013).

19. http://www.cpe.gov.sg (accessed on 7 December 2016).

20. Extracted from https://www.cpe.gov.sg/cpe/slot/u100/News%20and%20Events/
Press%20release/2016/Media%20release%20for%20new%20measures%20
cleared%20Final%20website.pdf (accessed on 26 November 2016).

Chapter 4   Aspirations and ASPIRE

1. See Cham (2014) for an interesting account of the NTU story.

2. NUS and NTU were established by Acts of Parliament. They were statutory boards
that reported to the Ministry of Education (MOE). SMU was different. It was a private university that received funding from the Singapore government. SMU was
incorporated as a company limited by guarantee under the Companies Act. The
Singapore Management University Act was passed by Parliament on 1 April 2000,
allowing SMU to confer and award degrees, diplomas and certificates and receive
funding from the government from time-to-time as might be provided by the
Parliament. MOE would work out the funding for SMU with "very broad guidelines,"
as Tony Tan said in an interview. "As far as staffing was concerned," Tan said, "the
only two appointments which the Minister for Education would need to give approval
to, or would have his agreement for, would be the Chairman of the Council (Board of
Trustees) and the President of the University. All other decisions would be left to the
SMU Council and the SMU management to work out". See Tan, K.Y. (2011)
Conceptualising SMU: the people and ideas behind the SMU Study, Oral History
Interview with Tony Tan Keng Yam (excerpt with video), *Oral History Collection*,
Paper 3 (http://ink.library.smu.edu.sg/smu_oh/13). On SMU, see Tan (2015).

3. In 1998, the Committee on Singapore's Competitiveness (CSC) called for an increase
in foreign talent, arguing that an inflow of foreign talents would not result in "a loss

of jobs for locals, but will instead increase the economic pie for all to benefit". Led by Lee Yock Suan, the Committee recommended "setting aside more places for foreign students in our education system from primary to tertiary levels and by offering more scholarships to foreign students to study in Singapore" (Ministry of Trade and Industry, 1998: 91).

4. For an analysis of the 2011 General Election results, see Ortmann (2011) and Chiang (2015).

5. Suppose the CPR is 25%. This means that one in four students from each Primary One cohort obtains a place in one of Singapore's publicly-funded universities. In 2012, the CPR in Singapore stood at 27%, which was higher than that of South Korea and Hong Kong, but significantly lower than welfare centric European countries. See Sam (2016a).

6. GE2015 registered a national swing in the votes in favour of the People's Action Party (PAP). The party secured 70% of the popular votes, registering higher percentage of votes won across all constituencies and winning 83 of the 89 seats contested. While the foreigner issue remained hotly debated in the run-up to the election and as expectedly in the GEs to come, the GE2015 results suggest that the PAP has managed to reaffirm the voters that the government had taken steps to control the inflow of immigrants and convinced voters of the necessity to view the immigration issue on a wider perspective. See Leong (2016).

7. *JobsCentral Leaning Survey Report* (2014: 2, 3).

8. "Singapore parents spend $21K a year to send kids to uni," *The Straits Times*, 10 June 2016.

9. On measures of social mobility in Singapore, see Ng (2007, 2015). While absolute social mobility has increased in Singapore, Ng's measure of intergenerational mobility shows that Singapore's intergenerational mobility has been 'moderately low' as compared to other developed countries. Another concern relates to the potential decline in relative social mobility where students with parents who possessed the social capitals tend to do relatively better. Using a larger set of data, an economist at the Ministry of Finance, Yip Chun Seng, showed that higher absolute intergenerational mobility in Singapore as compared to Ng's estimates (Yip, 2012), but as sociologist Tan Ern Ser (2015a: 45) pointed out, a table in Yip's report showed that proportion of children attaining university education was 0.72 for children with fathers with university education whereas the comparative figure for households with fathers possessing only primary education was 0.2, prompting Tan (2015a: 45) to conclude that "such measures indicate that while mobility is present scores classes, the probability of getting to the higher rungs of the social ladder decreases as we move down the ladder". It is worth noting that unlike the early decades following independence, Singaporeans are experiencing greater economic uncertainty and job security. Economic fluctuations caused by the 1997 Asian financial crisis, Sept 11 terrorists attacks in the United States and 2007/2008 global financial meltdown had led to contraction of the Singaporean economy and more people, particularly

professionals, managers, executives and technicians (PMETs), losing their jobs in significant numbers. With inflation, low birth date and ageing population to worry about, Singaporeans face the concern of downward mobility. The situation is worsened when educational attainment after years of hard work does not automatically translate to more income security, possibly resulted from mismatch between qualifications acquired and actual skills required by industries, a concern raised by Applied Study in Polytechnic and Institute for Technical Education Review (ASPIRE) (see Tan, 2015b).

10. See Mincer (1974, 1993).

11. Ministry of Manpower (2014: T31, Table 21) *Labor Force in Singapore 2014*, Singapore.

12. On demand-related causes of education–job mismatch, see Autor and Dorn (2013), Croce and Ghignoni (2012), Goos *et al.* (2014) and Kupets (2016).

13. For detailed description of Singapore's early attempts in manpower and training development, see Chan (2002), Chiang (1998), Low *et al.* (1993), Pang (1982), Schein (1996), and Varaprasad (2016).

14. The book tells the success stories of the vocational education in Singapore, preparing students for gainful employment upon graduation and showing that to be successful in Singapore does not equate to being a degree holder.

15. Ong Ye Kung (2016), "What SkillsFuture is about", *The Straits Times*, 21 April 2016.

16. "From 'study book' or *du shu* to learning with joy for life". Speech delivered by the Minister for Education on 6 March 2015. Also published in *The Straits Times* on 7 March 2015.

17. Davie, S. (2014) "More training and career pathways for ITE, poly grads," *The Straits Times*, 27 August 2014.

18. "Singapore must value engineers they way Silicon Valley does," *Today*, 18 February 2016.

19. "PM's call to rethink engineering lauded," *The Straits Times*, 20 February 2016.

20. The government took the lead in raising the prospect of engineers in Singapore by announcing its plan to recruit 1,000 engineers in the public sector, review the salaries of public sector engineers and groom them for higher positions within the public sector. "Government to hire 1,000 engineers this year," *The Straits Times*, 17 February 2016.

21. "Why engineering grads move on to other jobs", The Straits Times, 25 November 2014.

22. Quoted in Varaprasad (2016: 151).

23. Huo (1993: 22) writes that "ever since Confucius, the Chinese have divided all work into two categories — intellectual and manual. According to this ancient idea, intellectual work — that is to say, the work of the mandarins — is glorious and honourable, whereas manual work — work carried out by doctors, actors, craftsmen, agricultural labourers and others — is inferior and lowly because the mandarins led the country. Later, intellectual work was no longer limited to mandarins but included

offices was always despised by 'cultivated' people. This concept still has a certain influence on students and prevents them from studying applied disciplines and from devoting themselves to social work".

24. Despite being Chinese and speaking Mandarin, Singaporean Chinese do not necessarily respond positively to the inflow of Chinese from China. In his interesting article, Liu (2014) argued that the conflict between the two groups has promoted interracial solidarity (among the Chinese, Malay, and Indian Singaporeans) in Singapore.

25. The scores can be obtained from The Hofstede Centre (http://geert-hofstede.com/; extracted on 11 January 2016).

26. The maintenance of the traditions and cultures of different ethnic groups in Singapore is seen favourably by Indians from India as well. In one of the education fairs, an Indian father revealed his decision to send his son to study in Singapore rather than the United States because of Singapore's perceived attachment to "traditional Asian values", which provides "a far safer place where Indian children will not get not spoilt by Western values". See "Indians throng Singapore education fair," *The Straits Times*, 13 September 2004.

Chapter 5   External Degree Programme

1. Jason Lane (2011) has alluded to the demand creation effect of transnational education — the ability of such programmes to spark interest among local and international students to acquire higher education qualification. Transnational education programmes help reduce emigration of Singaporean international students because they allow Singaporeans to acquire essentially a similar qualification at a much lower cost (Ziguras and Gribble, 2015).

2. SMU State of the University Address (2014). Available online at http://www.smu.edu.sg/smu/about/university-information/state-university-address-2014 (accessed on 29 December 2014).

3. "SUTD admits record 386 students," *The Straits Times*, 18 May 2015.

4. "SUTD taking in record 467 students," *The Straits Times*, 12 May 2016.

5. "Private schools seeing dip in local student numbers," *The Straits Times*, 16 March 2015.

6. See, for example, "UniSIM a popular pick among working adults", *The Straits Times*, 20 October 2016.

7. Gaining greater recognition of the PEI courses by the hiring companies remains a challenge as will be discussed in Chapter 7.

8. However, lower entry requirements and shorter programme duration can be a marked disadvantage in getting a job. Often, hiring companies use difficulty in getting into a university and programme duration as proxies for the quality of graduates. Applicants

who do not the meet the hiring companies' requirements fail to pass even the resume screening stage. Hiring companies that follow the requirements strictly are the losing party, passing over candidates who studies part-time while holding a full-time job, obtained good grades through hard work, perseverance and many sacrifices.

9. Extracted from Kaplan Singapore's website http://www.kaplan.com.sg/university/full-time-courses/university-college-dublin/ on 13 March 2015.

10. Extracted from SIMGE's website http://www.simge.edu.sg/gePortalWeb/app manager/web/default?_nfpb=true&_st=&_pageLabel=pgPartnerUniversitiesDetail &fid=Discover_Universities&contentID=SIM000676&countryName=UK#UK on 13 March 2015.

11. Extracted from SIMGE's website http://www.simge.edu.sg/gePortalWeb/appman-ager/web/default?_nfpb=true&_st=&_pageLabel=pgPartnerUniversitiesDetail& fid=Discover_Universities&contentID=SIM000674&countryName=UK#UK on 13 March 2015.

12. As noted on SIMGE's website "The ranking exercise known as the "Research Excellence Framework (REF)" is run by the UK's higher education funding bodies, to assess the quality of UK research and to inform the distribution of public funds for research until the next ranking exercise in 2020." Extracted from SIMGE's website http://www.simge.edu.sg/gePortalWeb/appmanager/web/default?_nfpb=true&_ st=&_pageLabel=pgPartnerUniversitiesDetail&fid=Discover_Universities&contentI D=SIM001158&countryName=UK#UK on 13 March 2015.

13. *Ibid.*

14. http://www.smu.edu.sg/about/financial/tuition-fees (accessed 22 June 2015).

15. http://admissions.ntu.edu.sg/UndergraduateAdmissions/Pages/FeesTuitionGrant. aspx (accessed on 22 June 2015).

16. That said, there are externally driven factors that could affect the cost of education. For international students, one such factor is exchange rate. In early 2014, for example, Malaysian ringgit was trading at around RM2.50 the Singapore dollar. In early 2016, it was around RM3.00 to the Singapore dollar. Suppose an undergraduate programme is priced at S$40,000, at the current exchange rate, Malaysians pay an average of RM20,000 more for a course in Singapore.

17. Based on an annual fee of A$25,440 per year and the exchange of A$1 = S$1.07 (as at 29 November 2016).

18. See McBurnie (2008).

19. For details, see Edwards, Crosling, and Edwards (2010).

20. "M2 Academy to close down after just a year," *The Straits Times,* 10 October 2015.

21. Council for Private Education (2010: 24).

22. The Private Education Act 2009 stipulates that an advertisement relating to the PEI shall be presumed to be false and misleading if it (i) falsely describes the PEI; (ii) contains any false or misleading information concerning the PEI or any course offered or provided by the PEI; or (iii) does not contain such information, or is not in accordance with such requirements, as may be prescribed. PEI that contravenes shall

be guilty of an offence and liable to a fine not exceeding $5,000 or to imprisonment for a term not exceeding 6 months or to both. See Section 46 of the Private Education Act 2009.

23. The Private Education Act 2009 requires every registered PEI to ensure that the student contract does not contain any provision that would allow the PEI to make unilateral changes to any condition of the contract or collect any fee for the remainder of the course from any students who have withdrawn from a course before its end date. The measures are meant to protect the students from improper practices from the PEIs. See Section 25, Para 6 of the Private Education Act 2009.

24. Edwards, Crosling and Edwards (2010: 305) consider such as arrangement as "alienating" because the teaching staff have "little sense of ownership" and "commitment to the programme." The result "may be anything but a quality teaching and learning experience for both the students and the teachers."

25. Similar concerns have been raised elsewhere. See Ghenghesh (2015), Holmes (2004), Ramburuth (2001) Snow (2009), and Stoynoff (1997) and Trice (2003).

26. Typically, to enable learning, students need to acquire contextual language skills which can be attained within 2 years (Kerr and Desforges, 1988: 41).

27. Research has no conclusive evidence to suggest that the lack of proficiency would adversely affect academic performance (Berman and Cheng, 2001; Stoynoff, 1997).

Chapter 6   Business Schools

1. See Clarke (2008), Mintzberg (1996), Muller *et al.* (1988), and Pfeffer and Fong (2002).

2. Michael Patry (2010: 9) suggested that much of the innovations in firm pricing and financial products have actually led to a better world from a broad perspective but they lack rigorous empirical testing of the theories. They have been "developed by private commercial organisations, and had business school professors been able to access the data and replicate the valuation and pricing decisions of these organisations, the market for these products would have been more robust and efficient …… many of the innovations, once polished and properly reassessed, will prove to be valuable tools to manage risks in the long run".

3. See, for example, Bloom, Sadun, and Van Reenen (2012).

4. Tan, (2015: 36).

5. In the late 1968, Singapore Polytechnic abandoned the plan to turn into a University of Technology as the projected number of tertiary students then did not justify establishing a third university (see Chiang, 1998: 83).

6. SAB was renamed the Nanyang Business School (NBS) in 1995.

7. At the polytechnics, business related courses are equally popular among the students. It ranked as the second most popular course among the male students, with 17% of the students opting to read courses related to business, after engineering sciences,

which attracted 43% of the total male student enrolment. Among the females, business and administration is the most popular course, attracting 31% of the total female student enrolment in 2014. At the second place was Health Sciences with 13%.

Enrolment in polytechnic diploma courses (2014) — male students

Course	Number of students	% of total male students
Engineering Sciences	19,405	43
Business and Administration	7,414	17
Information Technology	7,085	16

Source: *Yearbook of Statistics*, Singapore 2015.

Enrolment in polytechnic diploma courses (2014) — female students

Course	Number of students	% of total female students
Business and Administration	12,267	31
Health Sciences	5,219	13
Engineering Sciences	4,920	12

Source: *Yearbook of Statistics*, Singapore 2015.

8. The certificate programme serves as a bridge to admit students who do not meet the entry requirements of the diploma programme (progression from a certificate course to a diploma programme is common in PEIs, and this practice is not confined to business programmes).

9. An exception is SIMGE diploma programmes, which take approximately 18 months to complete. SIMGE diploma programmes consist of 15 modules as compared to eight to nine months in other PEIs.

10. The author would like to express his gratitude to Brian San for permission to use the table.

Chapter 7   Competitive Analysis

1. The new ruling kicked in from October 2016 for all new PEIs. Existing PEIs need to meet the minimum credit rating by June 2017. See "Shake-up to raise quality of private education," *The Straits Times*, 22 October 2016.

2. The study reported the results of 13 higher education institutions in the United States. For the full report, see http://news.vanderbilt.edu/files/Regulatory-Compliance-Report-Final.pdf (extracted on 19 December 2015).
3. "Compliance costs a new, growing worry: poll", *The Straits Times,* 29 December 2016.
4. There is very little that The Association of Private Schools and Colleges and The Singapore Association for Private Education can do in this regard. As representatives of the private education sector, a more pertinent role of the associations is to engage with government agencies and other stakeholders and promote acceptance of the private education programmes. The associations have not showed much progress in this regard, especially in reversing the mindset of the public and private sectors as they remain skeptical about the programmes. Endorsement from the industry remains sparse, and financial support from the government for students embarking on an undergraduate programme with the PEIs remain non-existence.

Chapter 8   Academic Quality, Course Recognition

1. In 2016, SIT received a total of 13,000 applications from 'A' level and polytechnic diploma holders for 2,400 places in 42 degree courses, up by 35% from the previous year. See "New degrees add to SIT's draw," *The Straits Times,* 3 May 2016.
2. "Poly grads' starting pay rises after flat two years", *The Straits Times,* 9 January 2016.
3. Keynote Address by Council for Private Education Chief Executive, Brandon Lee, at the Singapore Association for Private Education (SAPE) "Education for the New Economy" Conference 2015 on 30 October 2015 (extracted from http://www.cpe.gov.sg on 28 December 2015).
4. Trend analysis is limited because of the change in data collection method. In 2014, responses from the PEI students were obtained via an online survey as compared to face-to-face interviews in previous years, possibly affecting its comparability.
5. Sandra Davie (2015), "Aussie campus gets star ranking," *The Straits Times*, 15 April 2015.
6. Sandra Davie (2016), "James Cook to get coveted branch campus status", *The Straits Times*, 11 May 2016.
7. The JobsCentral Learning Rankings and Survey Report 2013, December 2013, p. 3. "School's Reputation" and "Course Fees" were noted as the second and third most important factors, respectively.
8. The JobsCentral Learning Rankings and Survey Report 2015, January 2016, p. 4. School's reputation took second place with 89%. Course syllabus, course fees and course lecturers made up the remaining three spots with 86%, 84% and 83% of the voters indicating them as very important factors.

9. The paper proceeded to ascertain if the expectations have been met or otherwise. It is remarkable that the gap between the expectation and actual level of service was negative — actual being lower than expectation — for all dimensions, attributed possibly to the setting of high expectations that were difficult to realise or the inadequacy in service provision by the PEI to manage and meet students' expectations or both. The study focuses on the experience of MDIS, one of the bigger players in the market. In a related article, Min and Khoon (2013) concluded that different nationality and gender have explanatory power in determining the motives and perception of services, suggesting that it might be useful for the PEIs to customise their service provision to enable them to provide better education services.

10. As CPE notes on its website: "Registration with CPE is not an endorsement or accreditation of the school or the quality of courses offered. Recognition and acceptance of private school qualifications for employment, further studies or other purposes are at the discretion of the individual prospective employer, education institutions or organisations". Extracted from http://www.cpe.gov.sg on 11 March 2016.

11. Extracted from "FAQs on Minimum Entry and Examination Requirements", (extracted from http://www.mas.gov.sg/Regulations-and-Financial-Stability/ Regulations-Guidance-and-Licensing/Financial-Advisers/FAQs/2014/FAQs-on- Min-Entry-and-Exam-Rqmts.aspx on 28 December 2015).

12. Quoted from Laura Philomin (2014) "Fast track private degrees gaining popularity here," *Today*, 20 August 2014.

13. Laura Philomin (2014), "Fast track private degrees gaining popularity here," *Today*, 20 August 2014.

14. The nine participating PEIs are Curtin Education Centre, ITC School of Laws, James Cook Australia Institute of Higher Learning, Kaplan Higher Education Institute, Management Development Institute of Singapore, Ngee Ann-Adelaide Education Centre, Singapore Institute of Management, SMF Institute of Higher Learning and Trent Global College of Technology and Management.

15. "Private school grads find it harder to land jobs," *The Straits Times,* 24 September 2016.

16. *Ibid.*

17. Rachel Au-Yong (2014), "Seeking private degree? Do your homework," *The Straits Times,* 5 September 2014.

18. Quoted from Laura Philomin (2014), "Fast track private degrees gaining popularity here," *Today,* 20 August 2014. http://m.todayonline.com/singapore/fast-track- private-degrees-gaining-popularity-here.

19. "Higher education that helps young land jobs," *The Straits Times,* 30 May 2016.

20. To apply to the WDA, the PEI must be registered in Singapore with the relevant authorities (e.g. Accounting and Corporate Regulatory Authority). The applicant is required to provide, among other things, the list of courses that the organisation conducts in the year of application, and sample copies of attendance register. WDA requires the funding recipients to clock at least 75% attendance for the course, attempt all prescribed examinations and complete the course within the stipulated time frame.

Chapter 9   Transforming the Private Education Sector: What Needs to be Done?

1. Law Song Seng was the founding Director and CEO of ITE (1992–2007).
2. Quoted in Law (2015: 167).
3. Progressing to a degree is still a rarity in Singapore. Ho Kwon Ping (2016: 52) reminded us that "the rarity of an ITE graduate making in to university justifies a news headline; this should become normal in future". In Germany and Switzerland, on the other hand, "both the technical education (meaning polytechnic courses) and university tracks are equally rigorous in their different ways and technical education in these countries is an attractive option, not a fallback for failing to enter university" (*Ibid*: 52).
4. Years later, Law recalled being open to the media was a bold and unusual step to take. Law said "ITE was very transparent with the media about the plans it had. This openness to the media was quite unheard of in those days, as the Public Service was generally more conservative then". See http://www.challenge.gov.sg/print/letters-to-a-young-public-officer/a-mission-made-possible (extracted on 5 July 2016).
5. "Vocational learning the vogue for more students," *The Straits Times,* 14 December 2016.
6. Quoted in Law (2015: 136).
7. Like the case of qualifications attained through the PEIs, the starting salary of ITE graduates remains lower as compared to graduates from the local universities. Ho Kwon Ping (2016: 52) wrote "The starting salary of a Singapore university graduate is about 30%–35% higher than a poly graduate, whilst in Europe the gap is only about 10–15%. *The gap is much higher for an ITE graduate*" (emphasis added).
8. See Sam (2016b).
9. The CPE has worked in collaboration with SRING Singapore and the Association for Private Schools and Colleges offers to offer financial assistance to the PEIs in preparing and meeting the EduTrust requirements. Known as the EduTrust Support Scheme (ESS), the initiative would provide private education institutions up to S$26,500 in grants to review and upgrade their capabilities. The grants are given in two phases. The first phase allows private schools to obtain up to S$4,000 to engage consultants to review their systems and processes in accordance with the EduTrust regulations. In the second phase, private schools are to embark on improving the problem areas (such as curriculum development, human resource and financial management) as identified in the first phase. The schools are eligible for up to S$7,500 for each problem area, up to maximum of three areas. See *The Straits Times,* 31 March 2010: "Private schools get help to upgrade".
10. Hunkins and Ornstein (1989) remind us that curriculum projects may fail to take root if the innovators focus most of their energies on changing the programme while paying scant attention to the needs of the teachers. "The status quo tends to be maintained if those suggesting change have not presented precise goals of the new program being suggested — that is, have not planned adequately what the new

program will look like or indicated in ways in which the new program will be superior to the existing one" (1989: 111). O'Donoghue and Clarke (2010: 54) further add that the sustainable development of education institutions involve teacher collaboration, to develop the "capacity for fresh perspectives on existing knowledge and experience' and generate 'learning among teachers and students".

Chapter 10   Back to the Basics

1. From "Sam Walton: Bargain Basement Billionaire". See http://www.entrepreneur.com/article/197560 (extracted on 24 March 2016).
2. See Woodbine (2007), Zhang (2001) and Nasarudeen *et al.* (2014).
3. The government launched the SkillsFuture scheme in January 2016 to encourage Singaporeans to pick up skills (Singaporeans aged 25 years old and above are offered an initial S$500 credit to pay for skill courses). By August 2016, more than 80,000 Singaporeans have signed up for courses, and S$22.5 million in SkillsFuture credit had been tapped. "$22.5m in SkillsFuture credit tapped", *The Sunday Times*, 16 October 2016.
4. Maak and Pless (2006) use the term 'coach' to describe this role of a responsible leader.

Epilogue

1. Academic frauds come in various forms, including fabrication of documents from legitimate education institutions, purchase of degrees and diplomas from bogus institutions with zero or minimal attendance and assessments required from the students.
2. The United States Department of Education has earlier fined the college US$30 million for overstating the job placement rates. See "Obama to cancel debts owned by defrauded for-profit college students," *The Huffington Post*, 3 December 2015; "Will Corinthian Colleges be able to pay back students?," *The Atlantic*, 30 October 2015.
3. "College payments halted amid fraud allegations," *BBC News*, 27 November 2015; "Police talking to Welch government over college fraud," *BBC News*, 2 December 2015.
4. Singapore is no exception. Human Resource experts have reported a significant drop in job vacancies for fresh graduates in June 2016 as compared to the previous year whilst data from the Ministry of Manpower Singapore showed a decline in the number of job vacancies for four consecutive quarters to 53,700 in December 2015. "With jobs scarce, graduates grab whatever is on offer," *Today*, 11 June 2016.
5. The SSG bill was passed in parliament on 16 August 2016. The bill stipulates the functions of the agency, which include planning and developing policies,

programmes and services to support the provision of adult education and further education in Singapore, developing models of provision of adult education and further education in consultation with employers and industry representatives, accrediting courses in adult education and further education, including courses offered by institutions outside of Singapore, facilitating the improvement of quality of courses provided in Singapore, including the standard of teachers and providing meaningful and accurate information relating to the quality of courses in adult education and further education in the city–state. The CPE was renamed the Committee for Private Education in October 2016, and came under SGG. The SGG would administer the Private Education Act 2009, which was previously overseen by the CPE. In July 2016, the Chief Executive Officer for SSG was announced. Ng Cher Pong who was CEO of the WDA assumed the post. Ng was concurrently appointed as deputy secretary (SkillsFuture) at Ministry of Education (MOE). He was previously deputy secretary (Services) and deputy secretary (policy) at MOE. The agency consists of between 9 to 15 members, and is led by a Chairperson. The day-to-day administration and management of the agency is undertaken by the Chief Executive Officer. "CEOs for stat boards to boost lifelong learning announced", *The Straits Times*, 16 July 2016.

6. "SkillsFuture Singapore Agency Bill, Second Reading Bill" on 16 August 2016, Singapore Parliament. Obtained from https://sprs.parl.gov.sg/search/topic.jsp?currentTopicID=00009787-WA¤tPubID=00009800-WA&topicKey=00009800-WA.00009787-WA_2%2Bid-506c9513-07bf-4dd9-b112-02e92cad26b7%2B# (accessed on 22 September 2016).

References

Abin, R. (1991) Developments in Indonesia-Singapore bilateral relations: Politics. In Teik Lau and Bilveer Singh (Eds.) *Singapore-Indonesia Relations: Problems and Prospects*. Singapore: Singapore Institute of International Affairs.

Autor, D. and Dorn, D. (2013) The growth of low-skill service jobs and the polarization of the US labor market. *American Economic Review*, **103**(5): 1553–1597.

Baker, M. (2014) *The Accidental Diplomat: The Autobiography of Maurice Baker*. Singapore: World Scientific.

Bernasconi, A. (2013) The profit motive in higher education. *International Higher Education*, **71**: 8–10.

Berry, L.L. (1980) Service Marketing is Different. *Business (March–June, 1980)*.

Bhagwati, J. (2004) *In Defence of Globalization*. New York: Oxford University Press.

Bhati, A. and Anderson, R. (2012) Factors influencing Indian student's choice of overseas study destination. *Procedia — Social and Behavioural Sciences*, **46**: 1706–1713.

Bhati, A., Lee, D. and Kairon, H.S. (2014) Underlining factors in deciding to pursue Australian Higher Education in Singapore — an international students' perspective. *Procedia — Social and Behavioural Sciences*, **116**: 1064–1067.

Birch, D. (1994) Cultural studies in the Asia Pacific. *Southeast Asian Journal of Social Science*, **22**(1): 1–12.

Bloom, N., Sadun, R. and Van Reenen, J. (2012) Does management really work? *Harvard Business Review*, **November**: 1–7.

Bryman, A. (2007) Effective leadership in higher education: Literature review. *Studies in Higher Education*, **32**(6): 693–710.

Calingo, L.M.R. (1995) *The Corporate Guide to the Singapore Quality Award*. Singapore: EPB Publishers Pte Ltd.

Cham, T.S. (2014) *The Making of NTU*: *My Story*. Singapore: Straits Times Press.

Chan, C.B. (2002) *Heart Work*. Singapore: Singapore Economic Development Board and EDB Society.

Chan, K.W. and Mauborgne, R. (2005) *Blue Ocean Strategy*: *How to Create Uncontested Market Space and Mark the Competition Irrelevant*. Boston: Harvard Business School Press.

Chan, D. and Ng, P.T. (2008) Similar agendas, diverse strategies: the quest for a regional hub of higher education in Hong Kong and Singapore. *Higher Education Policy*, **21**: 487–503.

Chan, H.C. (2000) The role of intellectuals in Singapore politics: an essay. In Grover, V. (Ed.) *Singapore*: *Government and Politics*. New Delhi: Deep and Deep Publications Pvt Ltd.

Cheit, E.F. (1985) Business Schools and their Critics. *California Management Review*, XXVII (3): 43–62.

Chia, Y.T. (2015) *Education, Culture and the Singapore Developmental State*: *'World-Soul' Lost and Regained?* New York: Palgrave MacMillan.

Chiang, H.D. (2015) *Elections in Singapore*. Singapore: Straits Times Press.

Chiang, M. (1998) *From Economic Debacle to Economic Miracle*: *The History and Development of Technical Education in Singapore*. Singapore: Ministry of Education/Times Edition.

Cho, H.J. (2015) The spec generation who can't say no: overeducated and under-employed youth in contemporary South Korea. *Positions*: *East Asia Cultures Critique*, **23**(3): 437–462.

Chua, B.H. (1995) *Communitarian Ideology and Democracy in Singapore*. London: Routledge.

Ciulla, J.B. (2001) Carving leaders from the warped wood of humanity. *Canadian Journal of Administrative Sciences*, **18**(4): 313–319.

Clammer, J. (2001) The dilemmas of the over-socialized intellectual: the universities and the political and institutional dynamics of knowledge in postcolonial Singapore. *Inter-Asia Cultural Studies*, **2**(2): 199–220.

Clarke, G. and Monk, A. (2010) Government of Singapore Investment Corporation (GIC): insurer of last resort and bulwark of nation-state legitimacy. *The Pacific Review*, **23**(4): 429–451.

Clarke, T. (2008) The business schools: 50 years on. *Education and Training*, **50**(1): 52–54.

Cohn, E. and Ng, Y.C. (2000) Incidence and wage effects of overschooling and underschooling in Hong Kong. *Economics of Education Review*, **19**: 159–168.

Council for Private Education (2010) *Handbook*: *Enhanced Registration Framework*. Singapore: Council for Private Education.

Council for Private Education (2012) *Annual Report 2009/2011*. Singapore: Council for Private Education.

Council for Private Education (2013) *Annual Report 2012/2013*. Singapore: Council for Private Education.

Council for Private Education (2014) *Annual Report 2013/2014*. Singapore: Council for Private Education.

Council for Private Education (2015) *Annual Report 2014/2015*. Singapore: Council for Private Education.

Council for Private Education (2016) *Annual Report 2015/2016*. Singapore: Council for Private Education.

Croce, G. and Ghignoni, E. (2012) Demand and supply of skilled labour and overeducation in Europe: a country-level analysis. *Comparative Economic Studies*, **54**: 413–439.

Daquila, T.C. (2013) Internationalizing higher education in Singapore: government policies and the NUS experience. *Journal of Studies in International Education*, **17**(5): 629–647.

Deaton, A. (2013) *The Great Escape*: *Health, Wealth, and the Origins of Inequality*. Oxford: Princeton University Press.

De Boer, H. and Goedegebuure, L. (2009) The changing nature of the academic deanship. *Leadership*, **5**(3): 347–364.

Department of Statistics (2011) *Singapore Census of Population 2010*. Singapore: Department of Statistics.

Deming, D.J., Yuchtman, N., Abulafi, A., Goldin, C. and Katz, L.F. (2016) The value of postsecondary credentials in the labor market: an experimental study. *American Economic Review*, **106**(3): 778–806.

De Onzono, S.I. (2010) Management Education: the Best if Yet to be. Paper in "From Challenge to Change: Business Schools in the Wake of Financial Crisis" published by Global Foundation Management Education (GFME).

Dixit, A.K. and Nalebuff, B.J. (2008) *The Art of Strategy*: *A Game Theorist's Guide to Success in Business and Life*. New York: W.W. Norton and Company.

Dominquez, V.R. (2015) A perspective on anthropology from Southeast Asia: an interview of Dr. Goh Beng Lan of National University of Singapore. *American Anthropologist*, **117**(2): 379–383.

Dunn, L. and Wallace, M. (2008) *Teaching in Transnational Higher Education*. New York: Routledge.

Edwards, J., Crosling, G. and Edwards, R. (2010) Outsourcing university degrees: implications for quality control. *Journal of Higher Education Policy and Management*, **32**(3): 303–315.

Enders, J., De Boer, H. and Weyer, E. (2013) Regulatory autonomy and performance: The reform of higher education re-visited. *Higher Education*, **65**: 5–23.

Ennew, C.T. and Yang, F.J. (2009) Foreign universities in China: a case study. *European Journal of Education*, **44**(1): 21–36.

Fan, F. (2010) A discussion on developing student's communicative competence in college English teaching in China. *Journal of Language, Teaching and Research*, **1**(2): 111–116.

Ford, M. (2016) *Rise of the Robots*: *Technology and the Threat of a Jobless Future*. New York: Basic Books.

Gellner, E. (1983) *Nations and nationalism*. New York: Cornell University Press.

Girdzijauskaite, E. and Radzeviciene, A. (2014) International branch campus — framework and strategy. *Procedia — Social and Behavioural Sciences*, **110**: 301–308.

Goh, C.B. and Tan, W.H. (2008) The development of university education in Singapore. In Lee, S.K., Goh, C.B., Fredriksen, B. and Tan, J.P. (Eds.) *Toward a Better Future*: *Education and Training for Economic Development in Singapore Since 1965*. Washington D.C.: The World Bank.

Goh, K.S., *et al.* (1979) *Report on the Ministry of Education*. Singapore: Ministry of Education.

Goos, M., Manning, A. and Salomons, A. (2014) Explaining job polarization: routine-based technological change and offshoring. *American Economic Review*, **104**(8): 2509–2526.

Gopinathan, S. (1997) Education and development in Singapore. In J. Tan, S. Gopinathan and W.K. Ho (Eds.) *Education in Singapore*: *A Book of Readings*. Singapore: Prentice-Hall.

Gopinathan, S. (2013) *Education and the Nation State*: *The Selected Works of S. Gopinathan*. Oxon: Routledge.

Gopinathan, S. (2015) *Education*. Singapore: Straits Times Press and Institute of Policy Studies.

Grimes, J.E. and Grimes, B.F. (1993) *Ethnologue*: *Languages of the World* (13th Ed.). Dallas: Summer Institute of Linguistics.

Gwee, J. and Neo, B.S. (2012) Leading change in the Ministry of Education. In Gwee, J. (Ed.) *Case Studies in Public Governance*: *Building Institutions in Singapore*. Oxon: Routledge.

Hamilton-Hart, N. (2000) The Singapore state revisited. *The Pacific Review*, **13**(2): 195–216.

Han, F.K., Fernandez, W. and Sumiko Tan (1998) *Lee Kuan Yew: The Man and His Ideas*. Singapore: Times Edition.

Harman, G. (2003) Australian academics and prospective academics: Adjustment to a more commercial environment. *Higher Education Management and Policy*, **15**: 105–122.

Heffernan, M. (2014) *A Bigger Prize: How We Can do Better than the Competition*. New York: PublicAffairs.

Hensen, M., de Vries, R. and Corvers, F. (2009) The role of geographic mobility in reducing education-job mismatches in the Netherlands. *Papers in Regional Science*, **88**(3): 667–682.

Ho, K.P. (2016) *The Ocean in a Drop: Singapore, The Next Fifty Years*. Singapore: World Scientific.

Ho, W.K. and Gopinathan, S. (1999) Recent developments in education in Singapore. *School Effectiveness and School Improvement*, **10**(1): 99–117.

Hofstede, G. (1980) *Culture's Consequences: International Differences in Work Related Values*. CA: Sage.

Hofstede, G. (1984) The cultural relativity of the quality of life concept. *Academy of Management Review*, **9**(3): 389–398.

HSBC (2015) *The Value of Education: Learning for Life*. London: HSBC Holdings, plc.

Hu, G. (2002) English language teaching in the PRC. In Silver, R.E., Hu, G. and Iino, M. (Eds.) *English Language Education in China, Japan and Singapore*. Singapore: National Institute of Education.

Hunkins, F.P. and Ornstein, A.C. (1989) Curriculum innovation and implementation. *Education and Urban Society,* **22**(1): 105–114.

Huo, Y. (1993) Higher education in China: problems and current reform. *Higher Education Policy*, **6**(4): 20–24.

Independent Commission Against Corruption (2015) *Learning the Hard Way: Managing Corruption Risks Associated with International Students at Universities in NSW*. New South Wales: Independent Commission Against Corruption.

Jauhiainen, S. (2011) Over-education in the Finnish regional labour markers. *Papers in Regional Science*, **90**(3): 573–588.

Jayakumar, S. (2015) *Be at the Table or Be on the Menu: A Singapore Memoir*. Singapore: Straits Times Press.

Kahneman, D. (2011) *Thinking, Fast and Slow*. London: Allen Lane.

Kanter, R.M. (1995) *World Class: Thriving Locally in the Global Economy*. New York: Touchstone.

Khan, S. (2012) *The One World School House: Education Reimagined*. New York: Twelve.

Kidder, R. (2005) *Moral Courage*. New York: Harper.

Kierszlyn, A. (2013) Stuck in a mismatch? The persistence of over-education during twenty years of the post-communist transition in Poland. *Economics of Education Review*, **32**: 78–91.

Kinser, K. (2013) The quality-profit assumption. *International Higher Education*, **71**: 12–13.

Koh, T.A. (1990) The Mendicant Professor: a self-confessed liberal in Singapore, 1960–1970. In Simms, J. (Ed.) *Life by other means*: *essays on D.J. Enright*. Oxford: Oxford University Press.

Koh, T.A. (2000) The role of intellectuals in civil society: going against the grain? In Gillian Koh and Ooi, G.L. (Eds.) *State-Society Relations in Singapore*. Singapore: The Institute of Policy Studies and Oxford University Press.

Kotler, P. (1999) *Kotler on Marketing*: *How to Create, Win, and Dominate Markets*. New York: The Free Press.

Kritz, M. (2016) Tertiary education and development: strategies of global south countries meet growing tertiary demand. In G. Hooks (Ed.) *The Sociology of Development Handbook*. California: University of California Press.

Krugman, P. (2012) *End this Depression Now!* New York: W.W. Norton and Company.

Kupets, O. (2016) Education-job mismatch in Ukraine: too many people with tertiary education or too many jobs for low-skilled? *Journal of Comparative Economics*, **44**: 125–147.

Lane, J.E. (2011) Importing private higher education: international branch campuses. *Journal of Comparative Policy Analysis*: *Research and Practice*, **13**(4): 367–381.

Law, S.S. (2015) *A Breakthrough in Vocational and Technical Education*: *The Singapore Story*. Singapore: World Scientific.

Leask, B. (2008) Teaching for learning in the transnational classroom. In Dunn, L. and Wallace, M. (Eds.). *Teaching in Transnational Higher Education*: *Enhancing Learning for Offshore International Students*. New York: Routledge.

Lechuga, V.M. (2008) Assessment, knowledge, and customer service: Contextualizing faculty work at for-profit colleges and universities. *The Review of Higher Education*, **31**(3): 287–307.

Lee, D.S. (1997) What teachers can do to relieve problems identified by international students. *New Directions for Teaching and Learning*, **70**: 93–100.

Lee, E. (2008) *Singapore*: *the Unexpected Nation*. Singapore: Institute of Southeast Asian Studies.

Lee, E. and Tan, T.Y. (1996) *Beyond Degrees*: *The Making of the National University of Singapore*. Singapore: Singapore University Press.

Lee, H.A. and Muhammed Abdul Khalid (2016) Discrimination of high degrees: race and graduate hiring in Malaysia. *Journal of the Asia Pacific Economy*, **21**(1): 53–76.

Lee, K.Y. (2000) *From Third World to First*: *The Singapore Story* (*1965–2000*). Singapore: Straits Times Press.

Lee, K.Y. (2012) *My lifelong Challenge*: *Singapore's Bilingual Journey*. Singapore: Straits Times Press.

Lee, K.Y. (2013) *One Man's View of the World*. Singapore: Straits Times Press.

Legge, J. (2008) *The Analects of Confucius*. East Bridgewater: World Publications Group, Inc. Singapore: iT21 (Singapore) Pte Ltd.

Leong, Y. (2016) The foreigner issue and dilution: from GE2011 to GE2015. In Terence Lee and Kevin YL Tan (Eds.) *Change in Voting*: *Singapore's GE2015 General Election*. Singapore: Ethos Books.

Levy, D.C. (2006) The unanticipated explosion: private higher education's global surge. *Comparative Education Review*, **50**(2): 217–240.

Li, M. and Bray, M. (2007) Cross-border flows of students for higher education: push-pull factors and motivations of mainland Chinese students in Hong Kong and Macau. *Higher Education*, **53**: 791–818.

Lim, L. (2016) Fifty years of development in the Singapore economy: an introductory review. In Lim, L. (Ed.) *Singapore's Economic Development*: *Retrospection and Reflections*. Singapore: World Scientific.

Lim, R. (2014) *Strait Talk*: *Reflections on Singapore Politics, Economy and Society*. Singapore: Straits Times Press.

Lingle, C. (1996) *Singapore's Authoritarian Capitalism*: *Asian Values, Free Market Illusions, and Political Dependency*. Barcelona: Edicions Sirocco, S.L.

Liu, H. (2014) Beyond co-ethnicity: the politics of differentiating and integrating new immigrants in Singapore. *Ethnic and Racial Studies*, **37**(7): 1225–1238.

Liu, N., Lin, C.K. and Wiley, T.G. (2016) Learner views on English and English language teaching in China. *International Multilingual Research Journal*, **10**(2): 137–157.

Loh, Y.H. and El Farran, C. (2015) *A Nation of Skilled Talents*. Singapore: Script Consultants.

Longden, B. and Belanger, C. (2013) Universities: public good or private profit. *Journal of Higher Education Policy and Management*, **35**(5): 501–522.

Low. A., Quliaris, S., Robinsonn, E. and Wong, Y. (2004) *Education for Growth*: *the Premium on Education and Work in Singapore*. Monetary Authority of Singapore Staff Paper No. 26.

Low, D. and Vadaketh, S.T. (with contributions from Lim, L. and Jtin, T.P.) (2014) *Hard Choices*: *Challenging the Singapore Consensus*. Singapore: NUS Press.

Low, L. (2001) The Singapore Developmental State in the New Economy and Polity. *The Pacific Review,* **14**(3): 411–441.

Low, L., Toh, M.H., Soon, T.W., Tan, K.Y. and Hughes, H. (1993) *Challenge and Response*: *Thirty Years of the Economic Development Board*. Singapore: Times Academic Press.

Lu, D. (1998) Do Values Matter to Development? Reflections on the Role of Confucianism in Singapore's Public Policies. In Lim, H. and Singh, R. (Eds.) *Values and Development*: *A Multidisciplinary Approach with Some Comparative Studies*. Singapore: Centre of Advanced Studies.

Maak, T. and Pless, N.M. (2006) Responsible leadership in a stakeholder society: a relational perspective. *Journal of Business Ethics*, **66**: 99–115.

Mahathir, M. (2006) *Islam, Knowledge and Other Affairs*. Selangor: MPH Group Publishing Sdn Bhd.

Mahbubani, K. (2015) *Can Singapore Survive?* Singapore: Straits Times Press.

Marks, D. (2007) The unsettled meaning of undergraduate education in a competitive higher education environment. *Higher Education in Europe*, **32**: 173–183.

Mauzy, D.K. and Milne, R.S. (2002) *Singapore Politics Under the People's Action Party*. New York: Routledge.

McBurnie, G. (2008) Quality assurance for transnational education: international, national and institutional approaches. In Dunn, L. and Wallace, M. (Eds.) *Teaching in Transnational Higher Education*: *Enhancing Learning for Offshore International Students*. New York: Routledge.

Min, S., Khoon, C.C. and Tan, B.L. (2012) Motives, expectations, perceptions and satisfaction of international students pursuing private higher education in Singapore. *International Journal of Marketing Studies*, **4**(6): 122–138.

Min, S. and Khoon, C.C. (2013) Demographic factors in the evaluation of service quality in higher education: international students' perspective. *International Review of Management and Business Research*, **2**(4): 994–1010.

Mincer, J. (1974) Schooling, experience and earnings. New York: National Bureau of Economic Research, Columbia University Press.

Mincer, J. (1993) *Investment in U.S. Education and Training*. Paper presented at the International Conference on Human Capital Investments and Economic Performance at Santa Barbara, 17–19 November 1993.

Ministry of Education, Singapore (2012) *Report of the Committee on University Education Pathways Beyond 2015 (CUEP)*. Singapore: Ministry of Education.

Ministry of Education, Singapore (2014) *Applied Study in Polytechnics and ITE Review (ASPIRE) Report*. Singapore: Ministry of Education.

Ministry of Manpower (2014) *Labor Force in Singapore 2014*. Singapore: Ministry of Manpower.

Ministry of Trade and Industry (1998) *Committee of Singapore's Competitiveness*. Singapore: Ministry of Trade and Industry.

Ministry of Trade and Industry (MTI) (2002a) *Developing Singapore's Education Industry*. Singapore: Ministry of Trade and Industry.

Ministry of Trade and Industry (MTI) (2002b) Panel recommends Global Schoolhouse concept for Singapore to capture bigger slice of US$2.2 trillion world education market. https://www.mti.gov.sg/ResearchRoom/Documents/app.mti.gov.sg/data/pages/507/doc/DSE_recommend.pdf (extracted on 17 March 2015).

Mintzberg, H. (1996) Musings on management. *Harvard Business Review* (July-August): 61–67.

Mok, K.H. (2008) Singapore's global education hub ambitions: university governance change and transnational higher education. *International Journal of Educational Management*, **22**: 527–546.

Mok, K.H. (2010) When state centralism meets neo-liberalism: managing university governance change in Singapore and Malaysia, *Higher Education*, **60**: 419–440.

Montez, J. M., Wolverton, M. and Gmelch, W. (2002) The roles and challenges of deans. *The Review of Higher Education*, **26**(2): 241–266.

Mukherjee, H. and Wong, P.K. (2011) The National University of Singapore and the University of Malaya: Common Roots and Different Paths. In P.G. Altbach and Jamil Salmi (Eds.) *The Road to Academic Excellence*: *The Making of World-Class Research Universities*. Washington D.C.: The World Bank.

Muller, H.J., Porter J.L. and Rehder, R.R. (1988) Have the business schools let down US corporations? *Management Review*, **77**(10): 24–31.

Nasir, K.M. and Turner, B.S. (2014) *The Future of Singapore: Population, Society and the Nation*. New York: Routledge.

Nasirudeen, A.M.A, Koh, W.N., Lau, L.C., Lim, L.S. and How, A.L. (2014) Acculturative stress among Asian international students in Singapore. *Journal of International Students*, **4**(4): 363–373.

Neubaum, D.O., Pagell, M., Drexler, J.A., McKee-Ryan, F.M. and Larson, E. (2009) Business education and its relationship to student personal moral philosophies and attitudes toward profits: an empirical response to critics. *Academy of Management Learning and Education*, **8**(1): 9–24.

Ng, I. (2007) Intergenerational income mobility in Singapore. *The B.E. Journal of Economic Analysis and Policy*, **7**(2): 1–33.

Ng, I. (2015) Education and Intergenerational Mobility. In Faizal Bin Yahya (Ed.) *Inequality in Singapore*. Singapore: World Scientific.

Ng, P.T. (2013) The global war for talent: responses and challenges in the Singapore higher education system. *Journal of Higher Education Policy and Management*, **35**(3): 280–292.

Ng, P.T. and Tan, C. (2010) The Singapore Global Schoolhouse: An analysis of the development of the tertiary education landscape in Singapore. *International Journal of Educational Management*, **24**: 178–188.

Oakes, J. (1985) *Keeping Track: How Schools Structure Inequality*. New Haven, CT: Yale University Press.

O'Donoghue, T. and Clarke, S. (2010) *Leading Learning: Process, Themes and Issues in International Contexts*. London, UK: Routledge.

OECD (2013) *Education at a Glance 2013*. Paris: OECD Publishing.

OCED (2015) *Education at a Glance 2015*. Paris: OECD Publishing.

Ong, C.H. (2011) School improvement and the Singapore School Excellence Model (SEM): musings of a practitioner. In William Choy and Charlene Tan (Eds.) *Education Reform in Singapore: Critical Perspectives*. Singapore: Pearson.

Ortmann, S. (2011) *The 2011 Elections in Singapore: The Emergence of a Competitive Authoritarian Regime*. Working Paper No. 112, City University of Hong Kong, November 2011.

Pak, T.N. and Tan, C. (2010) The Singapore global schoolhouse: an analysis of the development of the tertiary education landscape in Singapore. *Journal of Educational Development*, **24**: 178–188.

Pan, J.Y., Wong D.F.K., Joubert, J. and Chan, C.L.W. (2007) Acculturative stressor and meaning of life as predictors of negative affect in acculturation: a cross-cultural comparative study between Chinese international students in Australia and Hong Kong. *Australian and New Zealand Journal of Psychiatry*, **41**: 740–750.

Pang, E.F. (1982) *Education, Manpower and Development in Singapore*. Singapore: Singapore University Press.

Patry, M. (2010) Business education and the current economic crisis: an institutional perspective. Paper in "From Challenge to Change: Business Schools in the Wake of Financial Crisis" published by Global Foundation Management Education (GFME).

Pfeffer, J. and Fong, C.T. (2002) The end of business schools? Less success than meets the eye. *Academy of Management Learning and Education*, **1**(1): 78–95.

Pitcher, G.S. (2013) Managing the tensions between maintaining academic standards and the commercial imperative in a UK private sector higher education institution. *Higher Education Policy and Management*, **35**(4): 421–431.

Pless, N.M. and Maak, T. (2011) Responsible leadership: pathways to the future. *Journal of Business Ethics*, **98**: 3–13.

Poh, S.K. (2016) *Living in a Time of Deception*. Singapore: Function 8 Ltd.

Porter, M. (1980) *Competitive Strategy*: *Techniques for Analyzing Industries and Competitors*. New York: The Free Press.

Porter, M. (2008) *On Competition*. Boston: A Harvard Business Review Book.

Pritchett, L. (2001) Where has all the education gone? *World Bank Economic Review*, **15**(3): 367–391.

Quah, J. (2008) "Good governance, accountability and administrative reform in Singapore" *American Journal of Chinese Studies*, **15**(1): 17–34.

Rajaram, K. and Bordia, S. (2011) Culture clash: teaching western-based management education to mainland Chinese students in Singapore. *Journal of International Education in Business*, **4**(1): 63–83.

Ramos, O. and Sanroma, E. (2011) Over-education and local labour markets in Spain. Discussion Paper No. 6028. Bonn: IZA.

Robbins, L. (1963) *The Robbins Report on Higher Education*. United Kingdom.

Sachs, J. (2005) *The End of Poverty*: *How We can Make It Happen in Our Lifetime*. New York: The Penguin Press.

Sakellariou, C. (2003) Rates of return to investments in formal and technical/vocational education in Singapore. *Education Economics*, **11**(1): 73–87.

Sam, C.Y. (2016a) Governing higher education institutions in Singapore: an agency framework. *Serbian Journal of Management*, **11**(1): 55–68.

Sam, C.Y. (2016b) How does Singapore govern the private education institutions? *Pacific-Asian Education*, **28**: 19–30.

Saxena, N.C. (2011) *Virtuous Cycles*: *The Singapore Public Service and National Development*. New York: United Nations Development Programme.

Schlossman, S.M., Sedlak, H. and Wechsler, H. (1987) The 'new look': the Ford Foundation and the revolution in business education. *Selections* (Winter): 8–28.

Schein, E. (1996) *Strategic Pragmatism*: *the Culture of Singapore's Economic Development Board*. London: The MIT Press.

Sen, A. (1999) *Development as Freedom*. New York: Alfred A. Knopf, Inc.

Sharpe, L. and Gopinathan, S. (2002) After effectiveness: new directions in the Singapore school system? *Journal of Education Policy*, **17**(2): 151–166.

Sidhu, R., Ho, K.C. and Yeoh, B. (2011) Emerging education hubs: the case of Singapore. *Higher Education*, **61**: 23–40.

Smith, A. (1776/2000) *The Wealth of Nations*. New York: The Modern Library.

Spender, J.C. (2014) The Business School Model: a flawed organizational design? *Journal of Management Development*, **33**(5): 429–442.

Tan, K.P. (2009) Who's afraid of Catherine Lim? The state of patriarchal Singapore. *Asian Studies Review*, **33**: 43–62.

Tan, C. (2012) "Our shared values" in Singapore: a Confucian perspective. *Educational Theory*, **62**(4): 449–463.

Tan, C. (2013) For group, (f)or self": communitarianism, Confucianism and values education in Singapore. *The Curriculum Journal*, **24**(4): 478–493.

Tan, B. and Teh, M.K. (2013) Singapore. In C.J. Russo (ed.) *Handbook of Comparative Higher Education Law*. Lanham: Rowman and Littlefield Education.

Tan, E.S. (2015a) Discussant: education and intergenerational mobility. In Faizal Bin Yahya (Ed.) *Inequality in Singapore*. Singapore: World Scientific.

Tan, E.S. (2015b) Social mobility in Singapore. In David Chan (Ed.) *50 Years of Social Issues in Singapore*. Singapore: World Scientific.

Tan, J. (Ed.) (2012) *Education in Singapore*: *Taking Stock, Looking Forward*. Singapore: Pearson.

Tan, J. and Gopinathan, S. (2000) Education reform in Singapore: towards greater creativity and innovation? *National Institute for Research Advancement (NIRA) Review*, **7**(3): 5–10.

Tan, J., Gopinathan, S. and Ho, W.K. (Eds.) (1997) *Education in Singapore*: *A Book of Readings*. Singapore: Prentice Hall.

Tan, K.Y.L. (2015) *Daringly Different*: *The Making of the Singapore Management University*. Singapore: Singapore Management University.

Tepperman, J. (2016) *The Fix*: *How Nations Survive and Thrive in a World in Decline*. London: Bloomsbury Publishing.

The Economist (2016) *Class Apart*, March 19th 2016.

Thian, L.B., Alam, G.M. and Idris, A.R. (2016) Balancing managerial and academic values: Mid-level academic management at a private university in Malaysia. *International Journal of Educational Management*, **30**(2): 308–322.

Toh, M.H. and Wong, C.S. (1999) Rates of return to education in Singapore. *Education Economics*, **7**(3): 235–252.

Transparency International (2013) *Global Corruption Report*: *Education*. Oxon: Routledge.

Tsang, E.W.K. (2001) Adjustment of mainland Chinese academics and students to Singapore. *International Journal of Intercultural Relations*, **25**: 347–372.

Tsui, K.C. (2015) Shaping graduates: head, heart and habit. In Euston Quah (Ed.) *Singapore 2065*: *Leading Insights on Economy and Environment from 50 Singapore Icons and Beyond*. Singapore: World Scientific.

UNESCO and OECD (2005) *Guidelines for Quality Provision in Cross-Border Higher Education*. Paris: United Nations Educational, Scientific and Cultural Organization and the Organization for Economic Co-operation and Development.

Varaprasad, N. (2016) *50 Years of Technical Education in Singapore*: *How to Build a World Class TVET System*. Singapore: World Scientific.

Vogel, E.F. (1989) A little dragon tamed. In Sandhu, K.S. and Wheatley, P. (Eds.) *Management of Success*: *The Moulding of Modern Singapore*. Singapore: Institute of Southeast Asian Studies.

Ward, D. (2007) Academic values, institutional management and public policies. *Higher Education Management and Policy*, **19**: 1–12.

Waring, P. (2014) Singapore's global schoolhouse strategy: retreat or recalibration? *Studies in Higher Education*, **39**(5): 874–884.

Wilkins, S. and Huisman, J. (2012) The international branch campus as transnational strategy in higher education. *Higher Education*, **64**(5): 627–645.

Woodbine, G.F. (2007) Accounting education in modern China: an analysis of conditions and observations. *Asian Review of Accounting*, **15**(1): 62–71.

Yeo, K.Y., Toh, M.H., Thangavelu, S.M. and Wong, J. (2007) *Premium on Fields of Study*: *The Returns to Higher Education in Singapore*. Singapore: Singapore Centre for Applied and Policy Economics.

Yip, C.S. (2012) *Intergenerational Income Mobility in Singapore*. Singapore: Ministry of Finance.

Yip, J. and Sim, W.K. (Eds.) (1994) *Evolution of Educational Excellence*: *25 Years of Education in the Republic of Singapore*. Singapore: Longman Singapore Publishers.

Zhang, J.L. (2001) Exploring variability in language anxiety: two groups of PRC students learning ESL in Singapore. *RELC Journal*, **32**(1): 73–88.

Zhao, L.T. (2016) Growing educational exchanges between Singapore and China. In Zheng, Y.N. and Lye, L.F. (Eds.) *Singapore-China Relations*: *50 Years*. Singapore: World Scientific.

Ziguras, C. and Gribble, C. (2015) Policy response to address student 'brain drain': an assessment of measures intended to reduce the emigration of Singaporean international students. *Journal of Studies in International Education*, **19**(3): 246–264.

Zimmerman, J.L. (2001) Can American business schools survive? Working Paper No FR 01–06, University of Rochester.

Index